Contents

Minding Your Own Business

Survival Strategies for
Starting Up on Your Own

Cherry Chappell

A & C Black • London

First published 2004
A & C Black Publishers Limited
37 Soho Square, London W1D 3QZ
www.acblack.com

© 2004 Cherry Chappell

ISBN 0–7136–6881–4

A & C Black uses paper produced with elemental chlorine-free
pulp, harvested from managed sustainable forests.

Typeset in 9.75pt on 13 pt Utopia
Printed and bound in Great Britain by
Creative Print and Design (Wales), Ebbw Vale

Preface: The Mindful Author

When I first had the idea of writing a book for people starting up on their own, I hugged it to my chest for a while to see if it would fade or grow. I asked myself what qualifications I had to write it, then realised that longevity in independence was a qualification in itself. As I complete this book I have just celebrated 20 years as an independent writer and public relations practitioner, working mainly in the fields of medicine and education, often in the not-for-profit sector.

Because independence offers flexibility, I have branched out over the years into special events organising, as well as continuing in straight newspaper or magazine journalism whenever an interesting story arose. At one time, I became diverted and starting working in an area where I was not a specialist. It was a mistake and I banged my knees badly. The experience, though painfully expensive, served me well in that I learned not only to appreciate my own particular talents and strengths but also to listen more closely to that little inner voice which is usually the best guide of all.

When I tested the notion of this book on a few friends in other independent areas, my problem was not to coax them into giving their views but rather to stem the flow. Every one of them, dear reader, wanted to offer you help and advice. What was also clear was the vast range of experience and know-how they could all offer, and equally fascinating were the adventures they had had along the way.

The independent route is about more than earning a crust; it's about creating a different lifestyle, one that is uniquely yours. I would like each and every reader to succeed in making a richer, more exciting life. That may mean adding value to the career you already have – setting up alone doesn't suit everyone – or it may mean climbing on to the high wire of independence for thrills, spills and a terrific view!

Cherry Chappell, Chelsea, London
www.mindingyourownbusiness.biz

Dedication

For my parents, Mansel & Joan Chappell

Acknowledgements

Thanks go to all those people who spared me time to interview them, allowing me to turn them into case studies or advisers in various chapters. Additional heartfelt thanks go to Nick Gundry, counselling psychologist, who gave me valuable insight for the sections on isolation, motivation and rejection; Michael Austin of Bluedot Consulting who made sure that the financial and taxation advice is correct, and Céline and John Nicholls, dear friends who read the book from end to end.

I would also like to express my personal gratitude to Thomas Augustin, my first client as an independent, and to Andreas Augustin who partly inspired me to tackle this book; to all the other clients who over the years have provided me with a fascinating working life; and to friends, the Reverend Canon Celia Thomson, Julia Levy, Christabel Hargraves, Andy Williamson, and Andie Airfix of Satori, who encouraged me during the writing time. Lastly, blessings to my agent, Laura Morris. What a journey this has been!

Introduction: Mind Over Matter

There have always been the wildly entrepreneurial, the mavericks, and the craftsmen and artists who have functioned best in a loose structure of their own making. In recent years, however, all kinds of practitioners who previously would have operated from within a company or organisation have emerged as independents. Only in retail has there been a continued move towards large chains, in everything from coffee shops to hardware stores.

Many of the new wave of independents are refugees from multi-national corporations or professional institutions. In the past, large implied safety, a belonging, a global brand and logo that provided personal as well as commercial badges from recognition or, in the higher reaches of the professions, the umbrella of prestige. Now, clearly, the culture of hierarchy and rigid job descriptions is being re-examined. Companies and organisations have realised that the challenge of recruitment and retention can only be met by a more genuine investment in the lives of their workforces by way of individual training programmes, shorter hours and a more humane approach overall to the vicissitudes of human existence.

Added to this is an overall awareness that few jobs are for life. There is little career security. The pressures of materialism and 21st century living continue to spiral.

It's hardly surprising, then, that more and more people are taking their fate into their own hands; the trend today is increasingly towards individualism, local solutions, independent working and down-sizing. These last two are not necessarily interlinked: some people on becoming their own boss aim for growth and high turnover, while others seek a different way to live. The best 'tools' for the current work pattern are flexibility, an ability to adapt and change, and the willingness to retrain where necessary.

Recently, the move to independent practice has been acknowledged by several major professional representative organisations, notably in law and accountancy, where members setting up on their own are offered designated helplines and support groups. Yet many educational institutions providing courses where students are likely to work on their own or in small groups still only pay lip-service to the need for business skills training. This leaves their alumni not only with student loans to repay, but also unprepared and vulnerable in the important initial stages of their careers. Several of the people whose stories appear later in this book – the osteopath, the interior designer and the photographer – made particular mention of the omission of any form of business training in their college courses.

Take a further example. Richard Clark-Monks has recently set up his own fashion label, producing quirky but elegant women's clothes. He ran away from home at 17 and came to London to join the rock music scene. For many years he was a singer with a band and enjoyed not only performing but also presenting himself on stage. The girlfriend of the bass player worked as a freelance pattern-cutter for John Galliano and it was after spending time in her studio that Richard began to take his interest in fashion seriously. He took a course in dressmaking at Chelsea College, then a foundation course which led him successfully on, at 36, to a degree course in fashion at Middlesex University.

Richard says: 'In all that time, although most design students were aiming to go out on their own, there was not one minute of business studies. All my fellow students complained but it just didn't happen. We wanted lectures from people who were running their own enterprises, and to learn not just the fashion industry side but also how to do the books, pitch for a loan and market our businesses.

'I'm lucky. My partner and many of my friends are independent or running small businesses so at least I have people to ask. But even so, I've learned more in the last few months than in five years of formal education. Some of the other ex-students are wondering if it is better to learn in a design studio than in college.'

The independent practitioners featured in the following chapters fall into two groups. Some people knew extremely early in life what they wanted to do and followed a path to ensure that it happened. The second group didn't know, but were determined to roust around, and push and shove, until they found what they were happiest doing. In both cases, there was little compromise.

The words 'free' (as in freelance) and 'independent' are immensely attractive. If you have no particular plan but would simply like to move out of the place you are currently in, you may need to do some very honest soul-searching to avoid the old from-the-fat-into-the-fire syndrome, and then start researching to see what truly appeals to you. You will spend far too long planning, working at and servicing your new business not to be entranced by it.

Minding Your Own Business starts with the premise that you are seeking not just your fortune but also a different kind of working life. It also makes the assumption that you are truly enthusiastic about what you wish to do; that you are fascinated by your subject, have a vision of your contribution, and so are fully fired up about your plans.

If you have your idea ready-to-go, this book will help you decide if it is likely to be profitable and rewarding. Its aim is to help you promote and build your business – but it also points out that there is a downside. Not everyone is cut out to work for themselves. Not everyone wants the commitment it requires, the drain on time, effort and energy. Some people find the journey a very lonely one; others find it difficult to kick-start themselves in the morning. I believe that these are the areas where many people starting off on their own experience their greatest difficulties. Even with really fabulous ideas, great creativity, superbly honed skills, terrific and clever products, many people return to the safe harbour of direct employment because they had not realised that the challenges lay elsewhere. The right mindset is the key to successful independence, and developing strategies for defusing the problem areas is crucial.

If you proceed, I suggest that you read the book right through once, marking up the areas that are pertinent to you. It's a good idea then to make a special study of the areas you are least familiar with, because these are the ones you are most likely to worry about. If you decide to go ahead, these will be the things you should knock on the head (or find the right person to do it for you) right at the beginning, and the rest becomes easier.

It is well worth putting all the systems in place before you start, with as much as possible of the research and the practical, mechanical bits completed in advance. Then, when you launch yourself, you are ready to start working and earning from Day One.

You may also like to consider the advice of a friend's mother who is a gifted needlewoman. Her advice on sewing – and life – is that it is never a waste of time to tack.

The Board Decision

Do you have the right mindset? – the downsides – the upsides – talk it over with your dependents – take a walk – decide!

There are all kinds of reasons why someone might decide to take the path of independence. Some people never work for anyone else. From the outset, they choose to create their own careers in their own very individual way. Others come to independence after some or even many years of working in other people's businesses or large organisations. For them the transition may sound wonderful and exciting but may also prove to be challenging. Whatever the motivation, the decision to go out on your own is not one to be taken quickly or lightly.

I believe that there are three main reasons why people consider this way of life:

The career choice (those who are born great)
These are mainly people who aspire to being their own boss and to organising their lives to suit themselves. They wish to avoid the nine-to-five routine or to step off the corporate or organisational ladder. They are usually entrepreneurial and have identified a market gap or a need that is not being met, or they have a mission, or they have some new and innovative products.

In many ways this is the easiest journey. If you fall into this category, you will probably have time to save for your initial expenses and build up a financial cushion until you start to earn. It is likely that you have some plans about which you are excited, and you may be able to do at least part of the research and development of those plans while you are still at school or college, or directly employed. You may even be able to negotiate your first clients or customers – although I must add a caution here to anyone considering poaching work from an existing employer. There could be legal restrictions about doing so – and anyway, being unethical is a poor way to start on a new path in life!

Circumstances (whose who have greatness thrust upon them)

Some people are almost forced into independence by adverse circumstances such as repeated redundancy, encountering ageism, or experiencing personality clashes in the existing workplace. This is a more difficult route into solo working because you are not making the choice yourself for entrepreneurial reasons, but out of bleak necessity. You may therefore be making a cold start, without inspiring ideas and all the excitement of making a long-held ambition come to life. There may also be financial pressures which tempt you to cut short the very necessary stage of research and development, and to compromise on promoting the launch of your enterprise.

Do not feel discouraged, however. One friend, now very successful in his independence, maintains that he is always at his most creative when he is hungry!

Part-time as a way into or out of full-time employment (those who become great)

Many parents and carers wish to give proper attention to the upbringing of their growing families or to care for older relatives, and will therefore opt for part-time work on a freelance basis. Sometimes this takes the form of work outsourced from their former employers. Part-time is also a way back into full-time employment for women whose children are growing up, but who are still restricted by school hours.

People facing retirement may choose to take a similar path. Understandably, many are daunted by the prospect of losing the full-on pressures, demands and sense of usefulness that is employment, virtually overnight 'falling off a cliff', as one commentator put it. It is indeed a sad waste of all that talent and experience, particularly if the person concerned can offer up-to-date skills, is still young in outlook and is fully committed.

And there is another important and growing group of older part-timers. Our government is telling us that the majority of people do not have adequate pension provision, so there will be an increasing number who will see part-time working on an independent basis possibly not as desirable, but as financially necessary.

Do you have the right mindset?

Whatever your reason for considering going solo, please understand that the independent path does not suit everyone. Putting practical and financial considerations aside, the first major decision is whether you will truly enjoy working on your own. Not everyone does. This is not a negative or shameful thing, just a feature of your personality and possibly your circumstances too. People who live on their own may not wish to work alone as well. Many people are happiest working in a team, enjoying the creativity and comradeship that this can engender. They may prefer fixed hours so they can give attention and energy to other interests, or be specialists who do not want to take the full weight of responsibility for every aspect of the business they are in.

One of the main changes you will encounter as an independent is that you will no longer be doing just one thing. Let's imagine that you are a brilliant designer or mechanic and you know that the small company you work for only survives because of the excellence of your designs or engineering. Clients and customers adore your work and always ask for you. They bring you bottles of wine at Christmas in gratitude. Despite the value of the talents you expend for the company's well-being, you are on a fixed salary. Unsurprisingly, your ambition is to run the whole show in your own way and to benefit properly by receiving all the profits of your very hard work.

However, if you make the big break and go solo, the reality is that you are no longer 'just' a designer or mechanic: you become a jack of all trades. Previously you have benefited from someone else finding the premises, putting in the equipment, paying the bills, making contacts, finding the work, doing the marketing, advertising or publicity necessary to bringing in more, calculating the expenses, writing out invoices and the accounts books, chasing payments and answering the phone. Perhaps you had a receptionist to meet and greet clients or someone to do the administration, and a boss to make sure that all these people were doing their jobs. Now that you are independent, who will do all these tasks and supervise the work of anyone else involved? That's right. You must.

Not only do you accomplish all this yourself – plus the actual work, of course – but you buy the coffee, make it and order the stationery while you are drinking it. Are you really prepared to do everything (and some of it is very boring) that is now required of you?

If so, bear in mind that your design work, or time spent working as a mechanic, is likely to be much less as a result. It is received wisdom that the average time spent on paid work is only about 60%; the rest is spent on servicing the existing business and looking for new clients. I believe that you should aim to work for at least 75–80% of your time, streamlining the chores and keeping them – along with the business networking – to around 20% of your time.

The second major change you need to consider is being totally on your own. Will you cope with and even relish the solitariness?

The downsides of going independent

Let's have the bad news first! The three major drawbacks of working solo are isolation, rejection and motivation. These are themes we return to throughout this book. If they are just words at this stage, then consider the following:

- *You will no longer be part of a team.* Even if you once were a member of an organisation and now sell your services back to it (i.e. outsourcing) you are no longer part of the 'inner group'. You therefore cannot rely on having help from other team members, unless you are bringing in other freelance associates. If you are sick, overstretched or against a deadline, you cannot call upon your client to fill in for you.
- *There is no 'coasting'.* You are only ever as good as your last job. You may exhaust yourself working late into the night for one client but if, the next day, you are working for someone else, they will rightly expect you to be firing on all cylinders, and bright-eyed to boot.
- *You can't 'brainstorm'.* If you work alone there are no colleagues to bounce your ideas off or to ignite the fires of creativity. Discussion sessions and focus groups are no longer available to spark off or test your ideas.
- *There is no Christmas lunch.* This may sound flippant but the lack of a work-linked social life is another element that many people going solo miss enormously. Often these semi-social

affairs help us to cement our working relationships and add texture and change to our working lives. Even in the smallest company there are drinks to celebrate someone's birthday or wedding, and some sort of 'do' at Christmas. In larger companies, there are sports clubs, out-of-hours yoga classes, charity events and corporate days out. People make friends through their work. As an independent, you have none of this.

- *You are expected to know.* You are now the authority the client is paying for. Whether you are building a wall or putting together a legal brief, you will be expected to have all the relevant knowledge at your fingertips and be required, sometimes with little warning, to deliver the correct solution or answer. That is what your client is buying: your expertise and experience.

- *You have a different culture.* In most workplaces, there is a culture or way of working accepted by everyone. For instance, it may be deemed perfectly acceptable for everyone to leave early on Fridays or to have an occasional long lunch hour if the time is made up elsewhere. You can adopt the same practice in the privacy of your own workspace but it is *never* wise to do other than fully-paid-up time if you are working directly for a client in their premises – no matter what their staff may do.

- *You could become boring.* It's unlikely that anyone else, including your family and friends, will be as interested in your activities as you are. Your family will obviously want to know that you are making good progress, particularly if they are financially dependent upon your efforts, but don't expect them to be absorbed by the details. Beware of boring your friends too!

- *You have no official title.* If you have been used to working in a position of authority, with a smart title, your underlings will have deferred to your decisions and will have used their talents to make your projects or ideas a reality and a success. People in other organisations will at least have given you a hearing because of your job title. In an independent world, you will lack the status of a well-known company or organisation until you have made a reputation and 'title' of your own.

- *There's no boss.* No-one will tell you when to ease up, go home, check a fact, learn a new skill or go for broke. And there's no-one to spur you into being at work on time or prod you to get cracking on some of the chores.

- *Sometimes you don't get the job.* You plan for it, price it at the right level, give a brilliant interview or presentation, like the client, feel that you achieve much for them, and persuade yourself that it's in the bag. But, in the end, it goes to someone you feel is completely undeserving. This kind of rejection can feel very personal, although in reality the decision may have been made based on factors that have nothing to do with you.
- *You may not like some of the work.* There will be elements for which you don't have an aptitude or that you actively dislike doing, such as cold calling, invoicing, chasing late payers or doing the VAT returns. They still have to be done and will frequently take time that you would much rather spend on other things.
- *You cannot expect praise or applause.* It's quite possible that only you will know when you have pulled off something particularly clever or innovative. By and large, clients will assume that this level of achievement is quite normal – it's what they are paying for – and only the rarest and most wonderful clients say thank you, well done, you have done a great job.
- *Some people may not be supportive.* Your friends and, if you have worked for a company before going independent, your former colleagues will still be in their secure jobs. You will no longer be part of that group and they may view your independence in many different ways. Hopefully some will be very supportive, but be prepared for others to start to regard you as a rival and even be jealous that you made the break.
- *It is hard work.* You must be prepared to put in extra time; most independents work extremely hard.

There is no Christmas lunch. This may sound flippant but the lack of a work-linked social life is another element that many people going solo miss enormously.

If you feel that you can cope with all these disadvantages, and more, then you need to proceed to the next set of considerations. There are five; the first three are covered in more detail in later chapters and it is important that you read these to ensure that you have all the resources that you need.

Financial backing

It cannot be stressed strongly enough that, if you enjoy sleeping properly at nights, it is well worth having a substantial 'stake' behind you. This should cover not only your set-up expenses but also your mortgage or rent and living costs for at least three to six months. Even if you have clients or customers lined up waiting for you to start your new business, it takes time for the money to flow in and you will probably have set-up and launch costs to pay.

Working area and equipment

From now on, you will be responsible for everything that you require for your business: your office space, workshop or retail premises, your vehicle (if you need one), stationery, special clothing, telephones, faxes, computers, desk, chair, reference books and tools. Most beginners are shocked to find how long the list is.

Bookkeeping, accountancy and legal services

In making your initial budgets, you will need to allow for professional services. Some people enjoy doing their own book-keeping; others undertake it as a chore until they can afford help. Whatever route you take, it is likely that you will require at the very least some advice from an accountant and, if you are issuing contracts, from your professional organisation or a legal service.

No corporate support

You will only be paid for the time you spend working. If you are sick, there is no company sick pay. Holidays are very expensive from now on: you will pay for the holiday itself *and* for the time you spend away, not earning. You cannot expect a redundancy payment either. If your services are no longer required, at most it will be a bleak one month's notice.

Stamina and determination

This is the big one. You need robust health, a strong spirit and a big portion of self-discipline. This is the leap over the chasm; you simply can't do it in several tentative steps.

When considering the downsides of going solo, be very truthful. The only person you have to convince is yourself and, if you are not entirely honest, the only person you are fooling is you. Are you still willing to proceed? If so, good! I believe that the advantages far outweigh the irritating bits – which is why so many of us are happy in the independent lifestyle – but not everyone is comfortable so far out on a limb.

The upsides of going independent

By far the major plus point of going solo is that you are on a different journey – one that, by and large, you can direct yourself. You can take *all* the credit for its success, and be beholden only to the tax man. You now make the rules, take the responsibility, and enjoy all the profit and the kudos. You can opt to be top of your particular tree or in a very specialist niche or somewhere comfortable further down the scale that allows you time for things other than work. It's your choice. And there are many more advantages:

- *You can create your own job title.* In fact, it's a very good idea to do so. Position yourself as you see yourself in your new role.
- *You can be flexible.* You don't have to stick to your former job specification. Something may come along that is outside your normal remit; if it appeals to you and you believe you can do it competently, you are free to tackle it. It could expand your experience and your career history, and might lead to more work in a new and exciting area.
- *You are free to train or retrain.* You can choose to train in a complementary – or entirely different – subject which will widen your skills-base and make you more attractive to potential employers, while absorbing you at the same time.
- *You are truly independent.* Unless it is specifically your job to do so, you do not have to train staff, subscribe to the company ethos, dress in the same style as the managing director, join in peculiar team-building activities or run the Flora London Marathon (unless you really and truly like that kind of thing). You can and should avoid your clients' company politics. You can watch in fascination from the sidelines as any internal issues are fought out.

- *You bring your own status with you.* You do not fit into any organisational structure and so can speak on equal terms with anyone you meet. On one occasion a friend of mine was introduced to a very grand lady who prodded him in the chest and demanded: 'And who and what are you?' 'I am the chairman and managing director of my own company,' he replied gravely. As an eminent freelance journalist, indeed he was.
- *You can set your own schedule.* To a certain extent, and depending on the nature of your business, you can make your own timetable, choose your own holiday periods, work through the night and take time off during the day. If a piece of work isn't flowing as it should and you are not against a deadline, you can put it aside for the next day when it may go much easier. Only you will know.
- *You can respond quickly to changes in the market place.* You are able to adapt prices, goods and services, offload what is stale and dated and present the right 'product' to match the current mood of your buyers or clients. Unlike bigger concerns, you have no need to go through planning meetings, consult focus groups or wait for board decisions. If you know that you can get ahead of the game, no-one will stop you. This flexibility may well prove to be a lifeline in a fast-changing world.

Even if you do not become fabulously rich and famous, you can expect a much richer, more interesting and varied working life than any employee. And, if you don't, it's in your hands to change it.

- *There's also the question of integrity.* You can refuse to do a piece of work if it is against your principles or outside your comfort zone. You can – and should – refuse to work for a client who may be untrustworthy, unscrupulous or who has a bad reputation.
- *You are your own 'quality control'.* You can – and should – turn down work when you are asked to fulfil the task within an unrealistic timeframe or without the necessary resources, so the quality of the work will be affected. On the other hand, you can spend whatever time you decide is appropriate to perfect a

project, or 'double up' timewise if a project comes together quickly. You set the standards of quality.

* *You can set your own fees. You* decide when the time is right for increasing your fees. You don't have any staff assessment processes. If your client or customers are happy and you are offering high-quality work, you may ask for the going rate – and maybe even a little bit more!

Even if you do not become fabulously rich and famous, you can expect a much richer, more interesting and varied working life than any employee. And, if you don't, it's in *your* hands to change it.

Making your decision

Talk it over with your dependents

If there are people who are dependent on you financially, obviously you must share your ideas and discuss your plans very thoroughly with them. Even if they are not wholly dependent on your income they will need to understand and be prepared for major changes in the way you approach life. You may not achieve a stable income right away. You will probably work intensively for long hours. You are likely to become totally absorbed in your new venture to the exclusion of all else.

Will your nearest and dearest accept that you may become anti-social, bone-weary and financially insecure for a while? Will they find it difficult to tolerate the peaks and troughs of your business, in terms of either money or the demands of your work? Will they be willing to use part of your joint savings to help you set yourself up or to even out the lumpy cash flow for a while? Will they understand that there may be recurring periods of lumpiness? What would be the impact of any failure?

Are they willing to accept a lower standard of living for a time?

Counselling psychologist Nick Gundry specialises in several areas, one of which is problems in the workplace. He advises: 'If you have a partner, it is very important to spend time discussing your ambitions and plans – and theirs. Your partner will have hopes, aspirations and dreams of their own and these may no longer match yours.

'Your partner may find it hard to have you working at home, for example. Or, if he or she is used to one kind of lifestyle and suddenly you are expecting them to live another, perhaps on a reduced income, there may be real unhappiness.

'A strong partnership might tolerate these differences for a time but, by talking, you can be aware of any stresses and strains and compensate for them. In some instances, where there is a real division of interests, you may have to consider the viability of your plans.'

Take a walk

Take a long hard look at yourself, your plans, your enthusiasm and your motivation. Set aside the stage fright – those nerves that kick in at the idea of something so different – and forget logic for a moment. What is the little inner voice really saying, the one they call a hunch in men and intuition in women? Can you do this? Even if there are scary bits and areas that you don't know how to tackle yet? Under it all, do you believe that you are made of the right stuff for this kind of lifestyle?

Be explicit, ask yourself those uncomfortable searching questions. Has something happened in your career to make you insecure? Is there something you should address, something that is wrong, such as poor work relationships, that is underpinning your decision? Some people try to go it alone on the back of a bad experience rather than because they are entrepreneurial, and so fail, compounding a lack of self-esteem. Some skills only survive in a corporate setting but do not translate to a country village or a Welsh hillside. Be sure that you are not running away; there is no safety in being on your own.

Suppose that someone suddenly offers you a fascinating job at an amazing salary and with lots of perks. Are you tempted to take it and, if so, why? Would you be relieved that you didn't have to embark on the independent journey – or somehow disappointed? Few people have a broad beam of light pierce the clouds to show them the way forward, but most of us know on some deep level whether a particular course of action is right for us.

So what qualities do you need to become an independent? Passion, adaptability, creativity, a sense of direction, perseverance to the point of stubbornness, resilience, imagination, charisma, a capacity for very hard work, a wry sense of humour – and a great big dollop of luck!

> **Things to do**
>
> - Consider your circumstances, and your mindset.
> - Weigh up the downsides and the upsides of going solo.
> - Talk the decision over with your dependents.
> - Go for a walk and take a long hard look at your plans –
>   from every conceivable angle. Ask yourself the
>   uncomfortable questions, and be very honest about the
>   answers.
> - Make your decision. If it's to go ahead. . . then read on!

Monica Jönsson

*'I could probably extend my practice, run two clinics and take
on staff, but that would take me away from what I love best,
which is treating people.'*

**Monica Jönsson is a practitioner in Traditional Chinese
Medicine, a member of both the Register of Chinese Herbal
Medicine and British Acupuncture Council, with a practice in
Wandsworth, London.**

I came from Östersund, a small town in Sweden, not far from
the Lapland border. When I left school I was set on being a
graphic designer and I loved signwriting. I came to England as
an *au pair* to improve my English. That was in the 1960s when
London was swinging, and everything was new and exciting. I
went for interviews in graphics studios, but the field was
dominated by men. For a time I worked in Kensington Market
for the designers, Stirling Cooper: they just had a small stall
and it was great fun. I went travelling and when I came back, I
found them again – but by then they were in Bond Street with
a large staff!

While I was travelling in America I became aware that I may
have been anorexic. We didn't even know the word then; it was

called malnutrition. I had lost most of my hair, had no periods and my weight was way below normal. I had been living on an Indian reservation in New Mexico and had eaten poorly. There was no-one to help me so I bought all the books I could find on nutrition and health and started to cure myself.

I was my first patient. When I realised that I could help myself, I knew what I wanted to do. Had there been a college of nutrition in England, I would have gone to it but at that time the only alternative therapies were osteopathy, homeopathy and acupuncture.

Nowadays, everyone who studies acupuncture has had the treatment and been inspired by it. I had never had acupuncture but I found the first school of Traditional Chinese Medicine in Leamington Spa, and took a course that lasted three and a half years. It taught Five Element Acupuncture which means that you treat the person, not the disease, so in a way you become a psychologist. I followed this with a further two-year advanced course in Traditional Chinese Medicine at the Institute of Complementary Medicine in London. I loved what I was doing. I went to bed reading books on any aspect of Chinese medicine – gynaecology, food, psychology, anything.

You don't have to chase something you really want. If it is meant to happen, it will. I desperately wanted to join a study group going to China, but I didn't have the money. At the last moment I received a small, totally unexpected inheritance from my aunt in Sweden which was just the amount I needed. I went to work in a hospital in Chengdu in Sichuan where I became particularly interested in skin diseases and realised that Chinese herbs had remarkable results in dermatology treatments. When I returned to the UK there was no training for herbalists, but in 1991 I was able to take a two-year course at Imperial College.

Even when I was qualified, I didn't earn much but it was always enough to subsidise my learning. I set up my own practice but I did not advertise; I would have felt vulnerable inviting strangers into my home. I decided that word of mouth was the best method and it has worked. Over the years, I have seen thousands of patients and they have all come through recommendation. My patients are my PR.

I could probably extend my practice, run two clinics and take on staff, but that would take me away from what I love best, which is treating people. I see patients on four days of the week. On the fifth day, I work on patients' notes and research. Diagnosis takes time: the reasons behind the illness, the triggers, the underlying weaknesses in the organs and constitution. If I want to give herbs, I must work out the formula for that individual patient. And then there's the normal business administration!

I'm thrilled that Chinese herbal medicine is becoming properly regulated. My dream is to see hospitals in which Eastern and Western medicine work together. I would like to see a physician send a patient to me for herbal medicine, and I would like to send a patient for blood tests or a scan or, if necessary, to a surgeon.

Monica's advice

There's a saying: 'Never listen to anyone in any field who hasn't achieved what you desire.' I couldn't advise someone if I didn't subscribe to health myself, and live the way of life I'm recommending. If you wanted to lose weight, you wouldn't take any notice of a fat doctor; you don't ask financial advice from a beggar. You must set an example. Then everyone will ask what you are doing and will want some of that for themselves.

It's a law of this world: cause and effect. Every action has a reaction and you reap what you sow. I have studied for seven and a half years; I love helping people. Often patients come to me when they have tried many other ways and so are desperate. The reward is when a patient phones up and says: 'I am well!'

2

The Research & Development Department

The likely demand – the competition – your 'added value' – location: home or away – pricing – do you have a business? – taking advice – professional advisers – protecting your property

Some incredibly lucky people just plough straight in and make their way on their own without a hitch. Most of us start with a good idea, one or two potential leads, and crossed fingers. Learning from mistakes – and most of us make whoppers in the first year or so – is a time-honoured educational method, but it can also be a very painful and expensive one. Better then to invest some time in identifying the obvious minefields so they can be avoided or at least accommodated.

Accurate research should confirm that your business idea is viable. Inspiration is a key factor in success, and your motivation is another; but the third 'driver' is the need for your talents, products or services. Therefore, the starting point is to test the market.

Despite the diverse range of activities which can be done on an independent basis – from writing to bricklaying, graphic designing to market trading, management consulting to television producing – the basic premise is the same. Who really requires the goods or services you propose to offer? Can you make a living from your idea?

Consider the following areas for investigation. Some, if not most, will apply to your new business:

- likely demand
- competition
- your 'added value'

- location
- pricing

If you have the safety net of an extensive set-up budget, the wisest route is to find a good market research company. But if, like the majority of us, you are starting up on a restricted budget, you must undertake the research yourself – with a little help from the Internet or your family and friends if you need it.

The likely demand

Be very realistic about this. Who will be attracted by what you are proposing to offer? How many such clients or customers are there? If you are a consultant in a highly specialist area, two to three major clients may be all you require in any one year. If you are a solicitor, chiropodist, hairdresser or trader, you will rely on having a constant flow of new clients or customers.

Are there lots of other bright, motivated people already offering the same product or service? Is there growth in the market? Are you positive that there is room for another practitioner?

If you are not sure about the answers to these questions, start finding out. One way to do this is to pretend to be a client or customer yourself and think about how you would find out about your product or service. Obvious sources are the Internet, adverts in local newspapers, the library, telephone directories, chambers of commerce, and people you know – ask them for recommendations. You can use the same routes to search out the competition.

Inspiration is a key factor in success, and your motivation is another; but the third 'driver' is the need for your talents, products or services. Therefore, the starting point is to test the market.

Competition

Who are the competition? Do you know precisely what they offer and what they charge?

If you don't know and wish to remain anonymous, ask distant cousins on your mother's side of the family (that is, with a different surname) or friends, or former colleagues to find out for you. Ask them to send for or collect brochures, price lists and any other details that might be useful to you.

In taking a long hard look at competitors' businesses, you may wish to assess their outlay in terms of premises, equipment and additional help. You might estimate how much they spend on advertising and promotion and what their current workload is. If you are able to establish their charges as well, this should give you some idea of their income and – as important – their profit. This will help you to decide whether there is a living to be made for you.

Consider your competitors' strengths and weaknesses. Where are they located? Is this convenient for their customers? What added extras do they offer and are these appropriate to the kinds of customer you hope to attract? Do they change their products and services regularly? Do they stay up-to-date? Do the owners have a local profile? Are they well known in their business community and amongst their customer base?

How long have each of your competitors been established? Do they subscribe to a Code of Practice or display professional or trade qualifications? How do they promote their quality or value for money? What kinds of promotion do they use and how do you estimate the effectiveness of their marketing?

Beware of making a case for what you want to hear – that is, just picking up on competitors' faults. The chances are that if they have been in business for some time, they are getting something right.

Your 'added value'

This is a good time to start considering what you propose to offer that is different from and better than your competiors' products or services. This need not necessarily mean cheaper: if you are offering a superior service, it is very possible that you can and should be charging more. You may find it useful to start a list of the areas where you have an obvious advantage over the opposition. Include intangibles such as 'originality', or 'many years' specialist experience', or 'holistic treatment' or 'caring, ethical approach', or whatever is appropriate and genuine. These may be the very things that ultimately bring you success. (*See* also Chapter 3, *The Marketing Department.*)

Location

In some kinds of business, where your clients and customers are unlikely to come and see you, success does not rely on where the workspace is based. The decision will then be whether it is possible – and desirable – to work from home (*see* also 'Home or away', pp. 19–22). Other kinds of business people – such as therapists, solicitors and retailers – are totally dependent on their location being accessible. Choosing the right site is an art form, and your knowledge of your locality will be a vital ingredient. I therefore only offer the following for your consideration:

- If you are planning to set up a retail outlet or market stall, how many others are there in the immediate locality? Sometimes it can be an advantage to be in the same area as similar (but not exactly the same) businesses. People go to certain areas because there is a wide choice of certain kinds of goods: London's Charing Cross Road for bookshops, Harley Street for private medical practitioners, the Fulham end of the Kings Road for antiques, and so on. Other places flourish because they are centres for DIY, interior design shops, galleries, restaurants, craft stalls or organic food shops. Would you benefit from being in an area where there are already established businesses of a similar nature?
- Obviously, if you are opening a hairdressing salon, laundry, solicitor's practice, chiropody surgery or similar community-based service, you may wish to find a location with as little competition as possible.
- If you are dependent on people reaching you easily, you will need to consider what the local transport is like. If you are relying on customers walking past, you may have to pay a little more for a prime site. Ensure that the people walking past are the sort of people likely to buy from you.
- If members of the public are coming to your premises, you may be required to provide disability access and facilities. Check with your local authority.

When you come to make a final decision about your location, there may be other considerations:

- If you have to commute long distances, your actual working time will be cut down or your working day lengthened. Is this acceptable?
- If you need to buy materials, are there good local suppliers who can respond quickly to your requirements? Are there late Royal Mail collections or motorcycle messengers or any other services you use regularly close at hand?
- Can you find local help (secretarial, administrative) if you require it?
- Finally, when you are checking out rental costs, look not only at the cost per square metre but also at the hidden extras such as heating, lighting, security, insurance and reception services. See if there are any penalty clauses should you have to end the lease before its due term for any reason. This is one area where the advice of a good solicitor may be invaluable, and save you money in the longer term.

Build a file of background research. Put in it everything that is relevant and a few things which might be applicable or useful in the future. Keep competitors' literature, estate agents' rental sheets and so on – you may find them useful later on. Even if you never look at your research again, the exercise will not have been wasted: it will have started the process of you planning and thinking about your business in real 'out-there' terms, as opposed to as a fuzzy notion in your head.

If you have done your research carefully, by now you should have some idea of who you are competing against, what you can offer that is different and better, where your business should be located and possibly an idea of what you can charge.

Home or away

The nature of some independents' business means that they have the option either to work from home or to take office space elsewhere. Each person's situation will be different but here are some considerations when making that important decision:

The upsides of working from home

- There is no rental; however, you may incur business rates on a contained working area (study, garden shed, etc.). Your local council will advise you.
- Heating, lights, lavatory and catering facilities are already on site.
- There's no commuting.
- You can check answering machines and email at any time of the day or night without going out.
- You can ensure that your work schedule fits around family commitments, such as the school run or GP appointments, and there's cover for the school holidays.

The downsides of working from home

- Some people find that it is easy to be distracted by domestic chores or neighbourhood matters (that is, a gossip with some-one next door!).
- If you have always worked outside the home, and your partner has been home-based, you will be invading his or her work-time space. You will be thrown together for much more of the time, and you may have to adjust and find ways to give one another privacy.
- There are no meeting rooms. However, you can always agree to meet clients in the lounge or coffee shop of a smart local hotel.
- You may have to go out to take the post or for photocopying. You will need to make arrangements with neighbours when you're not at home and a messenger or parcel is expected.
- You never leave work. This can present an immense problem, particularly for those of us who tend towards workaholism. It's all too easy to carry on 'for a few more minutes' rather than taking a very necessary walk or going to the gym or simply talking to other people. The office beckons as you get up in the morning and is still waving to you last thing at night.
- It is very isolating. This is another problem many independent people face, especially those whose work requires long periods of quiet concentration. One friend who was a researcher would work for several days at a time without talking to another human being between the hours of 9.00 a.m. and 6.00 p.m.

  If this way of working is necessary, you will need to create an active family and social life to balance it. One chum has lunch out every day, either with a friend or with a business contact. Another goes to the pool or the gym every lunchtime. Yet a third has bought a little dog who must be taken on regular walks and is a great stress-buster. There are more ideas for tackling the problem of isolation in Chapter 12, *The Human Resources Department.*

The upsides of working from an office

- If you choose a workspace where there are lots of other small businesses and freelancers, you should find a special culture. There will be people to celebrate with when you land a new piece of work, and people who understand when you need to moan because your client has forgotten to pay you.
- There's often help with the chores (which you should reciprocate): taking in parcels, pooling resources to bulk-buy stationery, sharing expertise when the computer goes on a wobble, and so on.
- Sometimes you can find new work within the community of small businesses, or you can sub-contract services from them.
- Some workspace complexes have communal resources such as meeting rooms, reception services and photocopiers. There will often be a central system for collecting post too.
- You close the door, mentally as well as physically, on your work at the end of the day.

The downsides of working from an office

- It's an expense that you may not initially wish to bear. In addition to the rental for the space, there may be separate charges for rates, lighting, heating, reception, photocopying and so on. You will also need to take out office insurance.
- There may be travelling time.
- It's just one more thing to 'administer'.

Julia Smith is a freelance charitable trust fundraiser from Cambridge. She has found that a home-based office, away from the family parts of the house, gives her the privacy she needs to concentrate on her work, but also enables her to be close at hand if suddenly needed by her young family. She started her career as a PA at the Royal College of General Practitioners, enjoying the association with the medical work. For a time she was diverted, working for a director of a large City insurance company, but decided that ultimately she wanted to work in the voluntary sector. She became assistant fundraiser at what is now CancerBacup and subsequently moved to the British Lung Foundation where she trained in charitable trust fundraising. She loved working for 'this vibrant, young charity' but when her sons were born it was necessary for her to go part-time.

'Even then, it was quite draining timewise, particularly when Jude, then Ollie, needed taking to nursery school. There was a lot of juggling. I was also very torn, for instance, when one of them had a temperature. I decided to take some time out but soon realised that I needed to do something,' she explains.

The solution came when Julia was approached to put together a fundraising strategy for a medical research charity. This was to become her first freelance client and she still works for them.

'Going freelance has worked very well for me. My husband works long hours in a very stressful job. I have the flexibility to work two to three days a week but arrange my hours around the children. I can go to their carol concert or be there to collect Jude from his sports sessions. Luckily the charity sector goes quiet in the summer months so I have coped around school holidays.

'We moved to Cambridge but that hasn't been a problem either; I can easily reach Central London for important meetings. I have my own office in the attic of the house, and this has proved important: in charity work there's always the potential to do more but this way, I can close the door on it and run!'

Julia admits that isolation is sometimes a problem, although she needs a element of quiet in order to concentrate and so finds home-working very productive.

'What I miss most is having someone to bounce ideas off. But sometimes I run things past my husband. I also stay in touch with someone I worked with at the British Lung Foundation, now freelance herself, and occasionally I go to meetings at the Institute of Charity Fundraising to top up my skills.'

Pricing

There is no set formula for this, and no known guideline – in fact, there is very little to help you at all. The setting of fees and prices is yours and yours alone to decide, and it takes wisdom, experience and steel-like nerves. This is where a sense of humour often helps, otherwise it all becomes too intense. By and large, there are three major factors in deciding your prices or fee structures:

Clients' expectations

Some research should help you to decide what is acceptable to your clients or customers and realistic for you.

Consider the area you would like to operate in, whether it be a geographic area or a specific industry area. Investigate what potential clients might expect to pay for a service such as yours. One way is to ask them what they are currently paying.

Be prepared for wide variations. For example, if you are offering a service to charities or not-for-profit organisations, they will expect to pay less than commercial companies, even though they anticipate the same quality of work.

Another example is that customers in a wealthy area will expect to pay more to local suppliers (from catering to interior decorating) and will feel they are not getting the best unless they do so!

The competition

Look at the rates charged by competitors in your chosen area. You might also find it useful to compare rates in other parts of the country, maybe in areas with a similar overall property/income level, or in similar industries.

Consider the quality of competitors' work. If your work is of a higher quality, it should be reflected in your pricing.

Many of us drop our prices out of insecurity, particularly when we are just starting out. We are anxious for the work and so we wish to appear very reasonable and competitive. Sometimes, under-cutting the opposition is indeed the way to land the business. However, in other fields, a lower fee tells the prospective client that you are unable to command a higher rate.

your costs

By now you should also be starting to have some idea of what your costs – overheads, marketing and publicity, equipment and supplies – will amount to (look at the list on page 26 as a guide). Then add in what you need to earn (as opposed to what you would *like* to earn – this comes later when the business is established).

The other considerations are not related to costs but to the value your potential customers will place on your goods and services. There are certain elements which will influence that value: people are willing to pay a premium for convenience, fashion or if the product is a limited edition. They will expect to pay less for the end of a line, a launch price or a special offer. The state of the nation's finances may also play a part in your decision on fee levels or your pricing of goods, depending on whether there is spare cash around or a recession.

Rupert Hanbury Tenison, a lifestyle photographer, lives in a beautiful stone farmhouse on the wildest part of Bodmin Moor. It looks idyllic but oddly enough it causes complications when setting his fees. 'I've lost out on jobs in London because I haven't given a high enough fee estimate. If I had had the courage to charge two or three times the amount I normally charge, I would have probably won the work. In London they assume that if you charge a lot you must be good – yet my usual fee is much too high for work here in Cornwall. It's a matter of finding a regional balance.

If you charge fees

Many independents will wish to charge fees, based on the length of time they spend on a piece of work. If, for example, you are a painter and decorator, a healthcare practitioner or a legal beaver, you will probably want to devise a fee structure which is quite simply a fixed amount per hour or per day, over and above the costs of any materials you use. It's up to you if you wish to base your time structure on other time periods: beauticians and therapists, for example, often have quarterly or half-hour appointments and will need to decide a suitable fee to accommodate this. Other people, such as interior designers, may charge by the project.

You may wish to introduce a different – probably higher – rate for *ad hoc* work or for a sudden rush job, while you may reward regular customers with a slightly lower rate. It is up to you; you are the boss.

Some kinds of consultants and advisers – in public relations, accountancy and law, for example – can ask for a retainer payment. This is a regular sum, usually received on a monthly basis and payable *in advance* to ensure that the time the client requires is available to them.

If the consultant starts working additional time to that which is covered by the retainer payment, they usually notify their clients. In this way the clients are aware of, and can give approval (or not) to that extra time and budget. The consultant can then invoice the extra time, in the normal way, which is usually in arrears. In this instance you will find that keeping accurate time sheets is essential (*see* the section on time sheets under 'Good practice' in Chapter 7, *The Production Department*).

Estimating the time you will spend on a project or on ongoing work may prove to be a new challenge. Experience is a great teacher: if you get it wrong initially, you will just have to bite the bullet – and do better next time. You really can only ask for more money if the brief has changed.

You may then decide – and negotiate – the expenses you will incur in undertaking your clients' work. This is discussed further under 'Contracts' in Chapter 9, *The Finance & Legal Department* but you should consider what costs you intend to recharge. The most usual expenses are travel (you may wish to decide a mileage cost for car travel), hotel costs and subsistence, phone and fax charges, email, photocopying, and unusual amounts of stationery and postage. These expenses are most usually invoiced in arrears. If they are likely to be substantial, you can either arrange for a 'float' to be paid up front or you can consider marking up the final amount by a small percentage to cover loss of interest or the charges incurred.

Do you have a business?

List all your running costs and consider the ghastly total against the revenue you believe that you can generate if you are working fully at normal hours. If you haven't finally decided your charges yet, try this exercise at several different rates. If you are taking on premises, count the rent, and make a judgement on all the running costs (electricity, heating, insurance, etc.). Add in – or 'guesstimate' – all your other costs. These may include:

- accountancy/bookkeeping
- other professional services such as legal advice
- any outside administration or secretarial services
- personal income tax and national insurance contributions
- health insurance
- income protection or mortgage protection
- pension payments
- bank charges
- materials/tools
- specialist equipment
- protective clothing
- any reference books
- stationery
- computers
- up-to-date software
- storage space for products or materials
- insurances (risk, office and equipment, professional indemnity)
- vehicle (if it is necessary)
- telephone rental, Internet and mobile phone charges
- subscriptions to professional organisations
- annual subscriptions (networking organisations, publications)

You may also need to invest in a good suit or outfit for when you go after new business. I am very serious about this: from now on you should dress for success (*see* also Chapter 4, *The Public Affairs Department*). For the same reason, you may require handsome portfolios, and a computer or slide presentation.

Some of these will be one-off costs; others will be ongoing or annual. Even so, making a list – frightening though it may be – will enable you clearly to see the realities of running your own business. At the end of the day, you would like to make a good living in a reasonable time span. You may have to live thin at the outset but what you must decide at this point is whether there is a livelihood to be made from your idea in the longer term.

Unless you have a number of guaranteed customers or clients, it is very important to set aside an adequate budget for launching and continuing to promote your new business. This is discussed at some length in the next chapters but please err on the generous side rather than skimp on this budget.

After taking all these factors into account, you may decide that you don't yet have sufficient resources to go it alone. This is where you must make a decision about whether to delay your plans until you have saved additional funds or whether you will need to seek a set-up loan. This will also require research. You will obviously want to take on board all the available advice about how to apply for and set up such a loan, and the best way to repay it. We look in some detail at this aspect in Chapter 9, *The Finance & Legal Department*, but it's never too soon to start taking advice.

Taking advice

If you believe that your business idea holds water, test it out on others. Add into your research the advice of people you know and respect. Choose carefully: your close friend may be marvellous when there is a family or local crisis, but may not be best equipped to help you make a decision about your new business. Former colleagues or workmates may have other axes to grind, and one or two of them may even be jealous of your new enterprise. You need to identify those people around you who will be impartial but at the same time have your best interests at heart.

When you explain your plan to your chosen advisers, give them time to think it through. You want a considered response, not an instant one. If they then come up with views which don't fit into your master plan, try not to reject them out of hand. In the same spirit, consider them carefully and then test them out further.

A friend who had a small but secure business decided to branch out quite dramatically and poured all his resources into a project which sounded exciting but was way, way out of his league. No one was able to tell him that he might be overstretching himself; he simply refused to listen. He was totally convinced that all his friends and the people whose advice he would normally have heeded were being conservative to the point of obstruction. When the crash came, it was an ear-splitting affair. He was made bankrupt and was forced to continue his mainstream business from abroad. He has paid back all his debts now (although it has taken more than five years) and says that he really wishes he had listened to the friends of his father who were experienced businessmen. 'I undervalued their judgment because they weren't saying what I wanted them to!' he explains ruefully.

Keep *asking!*

Ask anyone else you think might be able to help you, even if you don't know them. Seek guidance on any aspect of your business from people who have experience in the field relevant to you. Obviously it would be unwise to ask a potential competitor, but you can always seek out someone who works in a similar, but slightly different, area.

Again, it is courteous and considerate to make contact, explaining that you would be most grateful for their guidance and specifying the amount of time you are asking them for (say, a phone conversation of 10–15 minutes or a meeting of 20–25 minutes). Don't be shy about this: people can only say no, and they may well agree to see you and dispense invaluable assistance.

People are usually very flattered to be asked for their advice. When I was interviewing the people whose stories are in this book, they were more than willing to give you their advice. In fact, it was as if most of them had been waiting for this opportunity for *years*.

Professional advisers

There is a lot of free professional advice out there, some of which will apply to you and may prove very valuable. Don't feel intimidated or hesitant about seeking the support of the increasing number of organisations out there whose job it is to help small businesses, including independents, to flourish. Full contact details are at the end of this book but, for now, consider:

- *Business Link* (Small Business Gateways in Scotland; Business Connects in Wales and Northern Ireland). This Government-backed network is formed by partnerships between local enterprise agencies, chambers of commerce, local authorities and some major corporates. There is access to yet more business support organisations, plus information and advice from public and not-for-profit sectors. The main services are information and advice on setting up, training services (including marketing and finance), specialist services such as IT and e-commerce, and networking on a brokerage basis for specific initiatives and local or regional projects. There are Personal Business Advisers and an excellent website.

- *Chambers of Commerce.* There is a national network of about 100 Chambers of Commerce with around 135,000 subscribing members. They are non-profit-making and non-party-political. On offer is a ready-made management support team, business training, information resources, networking opportunities and savings on products and services. They are part of the global network of chambers so can helping existing or potential exporters too.
- *Enterprise Agencies (Local Enterprise Trusts in Scotland).* These are local, independent, not-for-profit organisations that offer free confidential help and advice to intended and existing small businesses. Based on counties and metropolitan areas, they each offer start-up advice, counselling, mentoring, and help with business plans and cash flow forecasts.
- *Federation of Small Businesses (FSB).* This is a membership organisation with principal branches in London, Glasgow, Blackpool, Cardiff and Belfast. FSB aims to be 'the voice of small business' and has a strong lobbying arm. At the same time, it offers discounted services on such things as legal, tax, financial and Internet services and even has networking events.
- *Home Business Alliance (HBA).* This is positioned as the only trade association for independents. It is a not-for-profit organisation and its patron is Sir Irvine Patnick, former MP and Lord Commissioner for HM Treasury. Subscribing members receive free business advice, including accounting, legal, tax and Internet advice, discounts from other members and free publicity both on the website and via HBA's journal, *The Boss.* They also offer a Code of Ethical Business and use of their logo for business stationery.
- *Jobcentre Plus.* Part of the Department for Work and Pensions, this has special personal advisers for people who are starting up on their own. They will provide moral support during the first few months, help you put together a business plan and secure funding to cover some of your start-up costs. There are leaflets

(Work for Yourself) available from the Jobcentres, and a website. Jobcentre Plus can also tell you what childcare is available in your area.

- *Banks.* Many of the major banks have been targeting small-business customers in recent years. They usually have start-up packs, special offers on new business accounts, and some have highly imaginative and informative websites. My own bank's website even has pages where small businesses can advertise their goods and services free of charge.

  Banks can offer valuable advice – but be aware that they are in business too, and will be keen to sell you all kinds of products and insurances. Resist signing up for any of these on the day. Some of them may be just what you need, but you should take time to see what else is on offer. Also bear in mind that some banks' advisers have only ever been employees of large companies; they have no experience of the journey you are undertaking. Listen by all means, but you may need to take other advice too.

- *Trade and professional organisations.* If you belong to any kind of trade organisation or professional body, this is the time to contact them to see if they have any support or facilities on offer for independents. The Institute of Public Relations runs a match-maker scheme to match potential clients with PR consultants, with a special register for freelances. Many other organisations will do the same. For example, the Law Society and the Institute of Chartered Accountants also have special groups and advice lines for solo practitioners.

- *Your accountant.* Some accountants specialise in small businesses; often, they are small businessmen themselves. They are usually mines of information and good advice. It is worth the investment to pay for a consultation to go through your plans and the methods in which you can trade. They will also help you write a business plan for your bank or any other organisation you are approaching for a loan (*see* also Chapter 9, *The Finance & Legal Department*).

Protecting your property

If you have a wonderful fresh idea or product, or have created an exciting brand name, you may wish to investigate how you can protect these properties from being hijacked by rivals. This is a complex area, so you will need to do some relevant research. This may include:

Inventions

You may need to patent your invention, giving it legal protection against 'poachers'. Before a patent can be issued, your product must meet specific requirements: contact the UK Patent Office for details. If your invention has a potentially wide market you may also require a European Patent – the UK office can advise you about this too.

Trade marks

If you are developing a brand and have devised your own – unique – trade mark or logo, you can register it with the Trade Mark Registry. This is another branch of the Patent Office.

Copyright

This is a highly complicated area of law, particularly relevant to designers, photographers and other creative people. If you are working in a creative field, it would be wise to be fully conversant with the ownership of copyright as it affects your work and your obligations to your clients. For example, copyright may be an issue that should be covered in your contract, and you should know when and where it is appropriate to waive your rights. There are different ramifications for different kinds of properties. Many trade and professional organisations – the Photographers' Association being just one example – have specialist lawyers who will help guide their members through the maze.

Things to do

- Put in the spadework in your locality or business arena to assess the demand – realistically.
- Research your competitors, and identify what it is you offer that is different and better.
- If location is important, get out your walking shoes. Look at local transport facilities, and check if there's passing trade. See estate agents, compare prices and check that there are the local suppliers you may need to operate effectively.
- If location is not important, decide between working at home or in an office.
- Take into account your clients' expectations as well as your costs when setting your prices.
- When you know what your costs are, and what you can charge, see if you have a business.
- Seek advice to test your theories.
- If necessary, protect your idea or invention.

Richard Harry

'I've never decided to go into any particular product, but I've responded to the requests that have come along. Then I've picked out the ones that made money and concentrated on those.'

Richard Harry is a blacksmith and farrier from St Nicholas, Glamorgan.

My father, grandfather and great-grandfather were blacksmiths in this village, although they sometimes had other business interests as well. I had vague dreams about becoming a racehorse trainer or an auctioneer, but it never seriously occurred to me not to follow on. I loved horses and farm life. I was apprenticed to my father after school and attended Hereford Technical College. I left with a City & Guilds in blacksmithing and a RSS (Registered Shoeing Smith) certificate, and became an Associate of the Worshipful Company of Farriers, one of the oldest guilds in the country.

By the time I had completed my training, my father was ill, and he died when I was 23. I was just married when I inherited the blacksmith's shop – the forge – in St Nicholas. Fortunately I had been brought up with the business so the management side was second nature. Some of it had to be tidied up; in my father's day, the bills only went out once a quarter! If someone ordered gates from me, I would ask for a third up front and the balance on delivery.

Most of my business then was working for the farms and estates in this area. My client base was about 400 horses, some of which were racehorses which had to be shod every month. The horses that people rode for pleasure were shod less often, about every six weeks or two months. Frequently, on a Saturday, the yard would be full of children and their ponies. The blacksmith side was mainly making gates and repairing agricultural machinery. It has always been very busy and I've never been short of work. I have had apprentices but, restricted by the size of the forge, I haven't expanded otherwise. I suppose that I could have gone into a factory site in Barry or Cardiff but that's not the sort of life I've ever wanted. My mother lives next door to the shop, and my family and I live next door to her.

The business had to change when I damaged my back because I couldn't manage shoeing any more. I've missed that side. I knew everyone who came in and they would chat while I worked. My customers ranged from the lord of the manor to the local gypsy. If I had two or three horses in from the racing stables, it became quite a social event. I would hear all the gossip. It's been lonelier since. Customers just come in to buy.

The work has mutated over the years. Because there's no production line and everything I do is handcrafted, I can adapt to the fashions. In the 1980s, for instance, when lots of houses around here were being done up, people opened up the chimneys and therefore wanted fire baskets and fire irons.

Then there was a fad for metal curtain poles. Nowadays, it's all garden furniture, obelisks and arches. I've never decided to go into any particular product, but I've responded to the requests that have come along. Then I've picked out the ones that made money and concentrated on those.

I'm about to retire now. My son does something completely different. That's sad, but I wasn't forced into this business and I certainly wouldn't force him. There's a good living to be made as a farrier, although young people find it hard to gain an apprenticeship. There's less money in blacksmithing and, with premises and the equipment, it costs a lot to set up. People are not so interested in the old crafts now, they prefer to buy cheaper imports. That's how crafts die out. I'm offering to rent out the blacksmith's shop and equipment but we haven't had any takers so far. There's no other blacksmith in the area, so I don't know where to send my old customers.

Richard's advice:

Think hard before you move from a city to the country. However pretty it looks, country life is not idyllic. Villages have changed. When I was young, there were always people about, lots of local characters, the farm labourers and the stable lads. And it seemed like there was always time to talk. Now there's no community. There are fewer farms with fewer people working on them. It's all streamlined. Other people commute from the village to offices in the nearest town. Be aware that, if you dream of working in the country, it could be isolated and extremely lonely.

There are two routes when you go out on your own. You can opt for a good quality of life, doing work you enjoy to your own standard. Or, you can choose to become a millionaire. If you are going to do that, you will probably end up managing a workforce rather than doing what you started out to do. Only you will know which makes you happier.

Jill Lee

'Wherever I am and whatever I am doing, I am constantly picking up the trends in colour, fashion, music, style. I try to stay ahead and it's usually at least six months before anyone else catches on.'

Jill Lee is a picture framer and runs a framing, poster and card shop in Fulham.

I won an art competition when I was 11 and from then on knew I wanted to do something linked to art. I completed a Foundation Course at the London School of Printing, covering graphic design, photography, print-making and 3D work, and then I took a BA course in graphic design. My grant was small, so I supplemented it by making silver jewellery. Sometimes I even had a commission to work in gold.

I loved college and panic set in when I had to start thinking about a job. When I left, they were few and far between. I designed letterheads for friends. I did a summer job painting pictures on glass which were exported to Italy and Germany and then a couple of stints looking after antiques shops in the Kings Road, Chelsea. There was another short period with a contemporary print shop, where I catalogued all the work that had been stuffed into plan chests. It proved to be a useful contact later on.

Then I went to work for the man who later became my husband. Mark and his business partner, Mike, were making mouldings for picture frames. After a time, a shop became vacant on the Kings Road and I pushed them into taking it. I helped them to establish the business, which was surrounded by antique shops, and to decide a style to fit in with the kind of customers drawn to that area.

By the early 1980s I felt increasingly that I wanted to do something more up-to-date. The first art posters were coming in from the USA and Europe; people were using them to create an interior rather than just fill up the walls, and there were some wonderful limited-edition screen prints and etchings available.

A chance remark started it all. A friend asked if I knew anyone interested in premises not far from my home, close to a major crossroads where there are lots of passers-by, day and evening. I knew instantly that it was mine! I was very excited but nervous as well because it was a big step. Out of politeness I asked Mark and Mike if they wanted to be partners but in the end I did it all myself.

After a bottle of wine with some friends, I came up with the name 'Artbeat' and designed the sign in neon in my own handwriting. My shop window has always been very important; I sell what's in it many times over and it works for me 24 hours a day. I make sure it is well lit in the evenings when people walk or drive past to go to restaurants. I often have calls the next morning about things they have spotted, which is why the phone number is written large and clearly too.

A major element in Artbeat's success is customer care. People usually come in for advice about their framing and I will give them all the time they need. Long-term customers trust my judgement and frequently leave me to select frames and mounts for them. Sometimes people ask me to frame objects: baby shoes, jewellery, fabrics, even a golf ball (someone had a hole in one, so I backed the ball with astroturf and set it on a tee!).

Every year I go to the International Spring Gift Fair at the NEC in Birmingham to see the latest mouldings and images. I always select things for the shop to suit me but I know that I am good at catching the vibes. For instance, I don't just go shopping; it's more of a recce. Wherever I am and whatever I am doing, I am constantly picking up the trends in colour, fashion, music, style. I try to stay ahead and it's usually at least six months before anyone else catches on.

Artbeat has an enormous selection of cards and posters. I don't let the sales representatives guide me; I have confidence in my own judgement. You must know your customers. What will sell in Manchester won't sell in Fulham – and vice versa. I have a sale box for anything that doesn't move or I give the stock to a charity shop. But I don't buy in vast quantities, so if I have made a mistake – which is rare these days – I am not stuck with it.

Jill's advice:

Learn your craft or skill thoroughly so you are really confident in your ability. Never take on more than you can do properly because you will end up compromising your quality and you will lose faith in what you do. I would rather say I cannot fit something in than do it badly. Customers respect that. You cannot stick with the same stock: there is no point in displaying items that are dated. Things go in cycles: some styles will even go out and then come back in again.

Do not live to work. Enjoy what you do, but don't take it home. That's very hard to do when you first start. I worked seven days a week and every evening when I launched, but now when I close the shop, I leave it behind completely and have another life.

3

The Marketing Department

What does the market want? – what are your USPs? – being a sole practitioner is an excellent selling point – who are your likely customers – how to reach your target group: the personal touch, flyers & posters, advertising, brochures, workshops and other methods – selling online – cold calling – don't forget the rest of the world

The hardest thing for many would-be independents to grasp is that from now on they will have to go out to make contacts and find new work or customers, as well as doing whatever they do best. This is not a one-off activity; it is an integral, ongoing part of every business and cannot be skimped.

The reason is obvious. You can have the best designed, most innovative and useful products in the world or the most efficient, caring, creative and high-quality services, but if no one knows about them then you are very unlikely to succeed. This is where marketing, good publicity and effective networking come in.

Let's start with marketing. There is nothing mysterious about it. In essence it is extraordinarily simple: it is about presenting your business in the best possible light to the people most likely to be interested in it. But, like anything wrapped up in a nut-shell, this masks an entire culture. People take degrees in marketing. I am sorry to tell you that there's a lot to learn.

If you are a newcomer to marketing, set aside some time to study the subject and devise your own marketing plan. Part of your set-up expenses – in terms of both time and hard cash – should be related the promotion of your new venture. You owe it to yourself to give your new enterprise the best possible start. And, from now on, a percentage of your hard-won profit will probably have to be spent in keeping the work or the customers rolling in.

If you are wise, you will continue to keep some level of promotional budget. There are two distinct and very strong reasons for doing so:

(1) To bring in, maintain, and possibly to increase, a flow of clients or customers.
(2) To build your reputation.

By and large, people prefer to buy products or new services from someone they have had recommended to them or heard about previously. We are all prone to do this. If I need a plumber, I will ask friends to recommend someone who has done a good job for them in the past. I would rather go to a recommended supplier, even if they cost a bit more, than someone cheaper but who is an unknown quantity.

There is another reason for acquiring a good reputation. When you first start up on your own, you tend to accept any work or business offered to you, at the best price you can initially negotiate. As you grow in confidence and gain experience of working independently – and can therefore offer more – you should be able to raise your fees or income level. By continuing to promote yourself in appropriate ways, you start to build a reputation for what you do. People will then understand that they are paying for the best.

Even when you are well on your way, it is easy to fall into the trap of relying on one client or one major source of income. The all-your-eggs-in-one-basket syndrome is very dangerous: imagine what it would be like to lose that large customer or income channel. This might not be your fault: the business world is full of takeovers, relocations, key people moving on, and changes in the market atmosphere. The key question is, if it happened, could you survive? If not, you might wish to consider the pattern of your business, to see if it would be prudent to spread some of your eggs into other, maybe smaller, baskets. My own experience is that several small clients usually prove to be a lot more reliable than one large one. Lose one and the others will keep you afloat until you can replace it. So, difficult though it may be when you start to become busy, you need to keep on marketing and promoting your business.

Gradually you will refine your marketing plan, looking at where you can increase business without overloading yourself workwise. Or, it may be that you are taking the solo route initially, but you fully intend to expand your business in the longer term, taking on employees – and becoming a tycoon.

In the first instance you will need to devise a marketing campaign for the launch of your business. You should then formulate another for the following 12 months as you build it up, and finally, an ongoing programme to keep it going and growing. Be prepared to adapt and change your plans, as you learn more and develop confidence. You may have to alter your marketing plan to accommodate changes and new opportunities in the marketplace, or adapt it to the financial climate.

Right now, though, you must begin somewhere – and the starting point is not with you, but with the market.

What does the market want?

Begin not just with what you think *you* want to do, but also with the customer or client. What would he or she be attracted to: low prices, extra service, convenience, home delivery, tender loving attention? How would he or she like to be treated? What extras and incentives would appeal to your kind of customers? Would discounts be an ingredient in their decision to buy or would they prefer added value? To what extent would expert knowledge and in-depth experience be major factors in their choice? Do they require exclusivity? Originality? A new approach? Sir Richard Branson – who started out as an independent, of course – has this to say: 'All we really did was think what we'd like if we were our own customers.'* It certainly worked for him, and it can work for you.

Be creative in your approach. Make a list of the things which might give your enterprise added value; see if any of these would incur extra cost and, if so, whether that cost would be justifiable in terms of the business subsequently gained. Make sure that you revisit this list on a regular basis. People's attitudes and needs change, but most purchasers of goods or services are looking for the best value for their money. Only you can decide what that best

---

*Quote from a booklet entitled *Ideas of a Small Business Addict*, promoting Virgin mobile phones.

value is and see if you can meet it. Remember, most of us have champagne tastes on beer money!

Sir Richard Branson – who started out as an independent, of course – has this to say: 'All we really did was think what we'd like if we were our own customers.'

What are your USPs?

What are your USPs? This is true marketing jargon, meaning, what are your unique selling points? What are your particular talents and strengths? What can you bring to the market that no-one else can? What makes you special? There is very little point in duplicating something that someone else is already doing; the chances are that they are not perfect anyway. Take a good hard look at what you can offer that is an improvement in some way. This may be a specific skill you have developed or a talent you were born with. It might be about qualities such as attention to detail, insightfulness, or an ethical approach; or it might be the value of uncompromising high quality, labour-intensive hand-finishing or genuine best value. It may be your reliability, staying-power or off-the-wall creative innovation. Only you can decide what your special features are. Be honest at this point – not unduly modest, but not arrogant either.

If you come from a corporate background, you may be familiar with mission statements. If so, your list of USPs could well form the basis of your own personal mission statement. It is a good exercise to write one down. For example, the mission statement for a medical illustrator might read:

> Charlie provides a high-quality design service for medical, health and not-for-profit organisations. With long experience of clinical procedures and practice, he offers creative but knowledgeable solutions to design challenges, and he specialises in illustrations and graphics for publications and video for both medical professionals and lay audiences.

A public relations consultant might have a mission statement like:

> Valerie offers bespoke, marketing-orientated public relations campaigns for the food, wine and hotel industries. She is a specialist in media relations, sales promotions and events, and she is results-driven.

Whatever kind of promotion you are considering, you can check back to ensure that it is a 'fit' with your original mission statement.

Being a sole practitioner is an excellent selling point!

Ask yourself why clients might prefer to use independent practitioners rather than large organisations, companies, stores or agencies. Often the reason is price-driven. People assume, quite rightly, that you don't have the same, very expensive overheads as large businesses do in terms of lots of employees and shiny bright premises. As a result, there may also be some potential customers who, unfortunately, have a very unrealistic concept of what you may charge. In no way should you imply that you are the cheap route. By and large, cheap means shoddy or cheap equals someone who does not know their way around. If you plan to undercut your competitors as part of your business plan, you may well be wiser to use a term like 'unbeatable value'.

Whatever your business, you may find it advantageous to 'sell in' the value of using an independent. We have distinct pluses over larger, stodgy enterprises with over-inflated prices and – very frequently – an impersonal service. The advantages that independents can offer include:

- *Flexibility.* We can change our strategies quickly to meet our clients' various and latest challenges, or the latest marketing trend.
- *Novelty.* We are a breath of fresh air for most established organisations. Because we are out there in the wide, wide world on our little flat feet, we are often picking up trends, new ideas, contacts, and new solutions. This can be of immense value to stay-at-home clients or organisations where employees do not have the opportunity to move in the circles we call our own.
- *Good value.* We are cost-conscious and able to operate within a modest budget. Because we are used to managing on our own small budgets, we know where and how to save our clients

money, if that is part of the brief or is particularly appealing to them. We have low overheads: our clients and customers do not pay for teams of staff, the managers or directors of which they see only on the day they agree their contract. Nor do they pay for lavish offices and workrooms, with designer flower displays and acres of glass counters.

- *Commitment.* We are dedicated to our each and every client. We will be working directly on each client's or customer's behalf. We will not be handing the job over to someone more junior and less experienced.
- *Accessiblity.* We are available whenever required. Our clients and customers are never fobbed off with deputies and assistants. It's our talent and expertise that they will benefit from, and they know they can discuss every aspect of their project directly with us.
- *Accountability.* We are much more accountable. Our services are therefore bespoke, tailor-made, committed and personal. Our fees and charges reflect this highly dedicated service and, while they offer good value, our clients and customers must appreciate that **we are not cheap**!

Who are your likely customers?

Now you have worked out what you can offer, the next step is to select your target groups. These are the people most likely to be interested in what you – with your unique selling points and your care and commitment – are offering. It's tempting to wave your arms wide and say, 'The world.' If you are a hairdresser, solicitor, healthcare professional or trader, it is indeed true that most people could be your customers or clients at some point in their lives. However, unless you have an enormous and ongoing advertising spend, you may have to be more selective about the groups you promote to. Here are some examples:

- As a hairdresser, perhaps you specialise in young, cutting-edge fashions. In your target groups you may like to include the local clothes shops and department stores if they hold fashion shows. Businessmen and women would probably respond to early-morning or late-night hours – with a croissant and coffee and a manicure thrown in. Or you could offer a portable salon for house-bound or hospital patients.

- As a solicitor, you may specialise in conveyancing and will-making. In this instance, your target group might include estate agents, housing associations, property developers, members of the planning committee on the local council, building society managers and so on. You could add in the membership of the local Chamber of Commerce for good measure.
- Healthcare professionals might consider managers of health and sports centres, gyms, GP surgeries, company doctors and/or clinics. Chiropodists will probably want to contact the local branches of diabetic associations or Age Concern, as well as local swimming and other sports clubs. Sports therapists might list every gym, football, cricket, squash, hockey, diving and dance club in their area, both professional and amateur.
- If you are selling a service to big companies, your targets might be human resources managers, or engineering directors, or whoever is appropriate. Your task then is to identify the most likely companies, and then to discover the names and precise titles of these officers. Be very sure that each one is the person capable of commissioning you and is the decision-maker as far as budgets are concerned.

When identifying your target customers, think laterally and define your groups as tightly as possible. Then comes the next step: reaching them.

Reaching your target group(s)

How would your potential customers be most willing to hear about you? What might they read, where might they go and happen to see your information? What would attract them? These days we are bombarded with information and have become adept at 'editing out' what is not relevant to us. The smaller your budget, the more carefully you must select your means of communication.

By all means look at how competitors promote their businesses, and try to identify what channels are proving successful for them. You may wish to use some of the same routes but in a way that makes your business stand out – although obviously you should consider other routes too. Your competitors may not have researched this as thoroughly as you are doing!

Try several different methods and monitor them carefully. If one route brings no response, abandon it immediately. You probably don't have the budget to experiment, but be brave and follow your instincts occasionally. Whatever you choose, do it with a degree of style. You may only have one chance to impress a potential customer or client.

See if any of the following approaches might be appropriate to your target groups.

The personal touch

Personal, one-to-one contact

This is an excellent first step, particularly if you have recently been directly employed in your particular field. In the first instance, phone or preferably meet up with key contacts, usually people you know well or at least have met several times before. Invite them for lunch or a drink (wine bar or pub; it need not be grand) to brief them individually on your plans. Tell them that you intend to set up on your own and explain the services or products you will be offering. Make it clear that you are only talking to a limited number of important people at this stage – of which they are one. You might be surprised at the reaction. Some people will be envious; many will be admiring. Most will be appreciative that you have taken them into your confidence and be very helpful. Hopefully some will come up with leads or an offer of work.

If someone is supportive, keep in touch. Invite them to any launch party or exhibition, demonstration, workshop or talk that you are doing, or simply meet them from time to time. Someone who is interested in your enterprise may be unable to help initially but might come up with wonderful ideas or contacts later on.

a personal letter

Send a personal note or letter to former colleagues or contacts and potential clients to announce that you are setting up solo. You may not have an instant response but you can always follow up with a phone call to anyone who is likely to have work for you in the future. It does not have to be a long letter, just enough to explain what you are planning to do and how it might be relevant to the recipient. However, the letter should be individual and it should include all the chatty personal bits ('hope the holiday to Spain was great'/'love to Mandy and the kids' – or whatever).

an email newsletter

This is never as personal as a letter, even if you make it gossipy, but it can be very useful for keeping in touch with people who might at some stage require your services. Keep it short so as not to irritate the people who have to scan dozens of emails every morning. Make your title snappy or intriguing. You can send updates every now and again: these might contain information about your new services or new products, a special offer or even about a very prestigious new customer or assignment. But ensure that you have permission to quote the name of your new customer!

Flyers and posters

a mail shot

If you are hopeless at writing lots of letters or you want to contact people you don't know, then consider a mail shot. This could take the form of just one letter which can be duplicated, or a mini-poster, or even a version of an advert. It pays dividends to spend some time on the address list, because unless your mail shot lands on the right desk it will just be binned. If you don't know who the right person is, phone the organisation to check.

The art of mail shot letters is to grab attention right away. Don't waffle, be concise and tell everyone in the first few sentences why you are contacting them. Don't make them read to the end before finding out what it is all about – they won't. If they are not interested by the start of the second paragraph, you have lost them altogether.

This is no time to be a shrinking violet. For reference, look out for the letters/coupons/adverts that make an impact on you. Have no hesitation in copying the bits you like or think appropriate to what you are doing.

Always, *always* ask a friend or member of your family to read through any piece of written material to check for obvious omissions, misspellings and other howlers. You can probably use second-class mail for this kind of mail shot.

a house-to-house flyer drop

This could be the same material you use for a mail shot, or just a card or slip of paper. There are local firms who deliver from door to door, and the Royal Mail currently has a service (though it is quite expensive). Alternatively, you, your friends and family could pound the pavements in a relatively small area to see if this method has any impact.

Car windscreens

It drives me *nuts* when I dash into my car on a dark, rainy night, switch on the wipers and various bits of advertising literature start giving me a friendly wave. But I must admit that I have discovered a great local restaurant and new car shampoo place via under-wiper flyers.

Poster or card on a notice-board

Supermarkets, corner shops, libraries, sports clubs and gyms, social clubs, political clubs, companies and their leisure clubs, and even local coffee shops usually have notice boards. If it is appropriate to your business, consider making a mini-poster or card and doing the rounds. Some places may make a small charge. Make sure that your card is bright and snappy and, to prevent it looking grubby or battered after a week or so, consider having it heat-sealed in plastic. Most copying shops will do this for you.

advertising

advert in the local press

If it is appropriate to your business, it's worth checking out and comparing the rates in regional daily newspapers, weeklies, free sheets, local colour magazines, parish magazines and community newsletters. Paid-space advertising is particularly appropriate for local services such as hairdressers, sports and health therapists, solicitors, counsellors, shops and traders, private investigators, photographers, party organisers and anyone else who needs to remind people on a regular basis about their service.

Take time to decide how to make your advertising budget reach as many of your potential customers as possible. The value to you may not necessarily be based on the circulation of the newspaper or magazine. For example, some newspapers may have a huge circulation, but if few of your potential customers are likely to be readers, that's not the right place for you to advertise. However, maybe lots of people who take the local parish magazine are your target audience. So, although the parish magazine has a much smaller circulation, it will be a more effective place to advertise.

Spend a while putting together your words, ensuring that you are crisp and concise. If you have a natural bent for copywriting, fine – be cute or witty. If not, I suggest you play it fairly straight and just tell everyone what you have to offer.

If you have a generous publicity budget, put some of it aside for good-quality design from your chosen designer. If you are on a shoestring, you will find that most newspapers and magazines have very helpful staff who will help you design your own. They are doing this all the time and often have excellent ideas and suggestions.

Do remember that advertising-space salespeople usually have a lot of flexibility on their prices, so bargain as hard as you can. The rates come down substantially when you take a series of adverts.

Radio advertising

Local radio advertising can be surprisingly inexpensive, yet it can have enormous impact. It is certainly worth contacting your local station and asking for rates. Obviously the rates are higher for adverts which are within or close to the more popular programmes and peak listening times. Many stations will be able to give you a breakdown of what kind of listeners (teenagers/older people/ business people, etc.) tune in at certain times in the day and evening. Remember your target group(s); it may be that you don't need to advertise at peak times. A campaign of just a week or two, with short, snappy ads, might lift your business enormously.

The production costs are low, but you will need a professional to do the voice-over for you. The station itself will probably be able to help you construct the wording and recommend the right 'voices'.

Cinema advertising

This is probably too expensive for most independents but many small businesses have attracted local interest and customers by a 'short' at their local cinema. If you are opening a restaurant, a hair salon, a solicitor's practice, or sports/fitness therapies, you may wish to check out the costs of this form of advertising. The production costs would include some good photography, artwork and a voice-over, and you would probably need the input of an advertising agency to achieve something that looks professional.

Using your vehicle as an advertisement

I like this one! One of the funniest advertising ploys in recent years was from a small company, called Patel, who did asphalting and tarmacing. Their slogan, blazed on the back of their lorry, was 'You've tried the cowboys, now try the Indians!' Who could resist? Remember to make your contact phone number large and easy to read.

Website – as an advert

If your clients/customers are likely to search for your kind of product or service on the Internet, consider having a website as soon as you can afford it. This is just another form of advertising but it is only of value if people get to see it. You must therefore research the best search engines for your business and invest as much in them as in your site.

Unless you have a particular gift with web design, consider outsourcing this to a specialist. Also remember that nothing looks as tired and off-putting as out-of-date material, so budget for regular updates.

If you are considering selling via the web, *see* also 'Selling online' below.

Directories and listings

Sometimes it's useful to be on a list. Decide what is appropriate for your business: *Yellow Pages* (and Yell.com), *Thomson's Directories*, local shopping lists, and listings in professional and trade directories. Where there is the offer of free word-space, make every one of them count.

Brochures, workshops, cold calling – and other methods

Brochures

A lot of money can be wasted on having a glorious full-colour brochure, and then having nowhere to put it. Even more is wasted on brochures that quickly go out-of-date. Turn the consideration around. Is there a real need that only a brochure can fulfil? If you are running a guest house or a take-away food outlet, or a therapy that requires a lot of explanation, then by all means go ahead – but consider the following advice.

Be sure that you have the means to distribute your brochures: by mail or via dispensers in appropriate places. And take care when estimating how many you will require: too many and your money is tied up for too long; too few and you will quickly face reprint costs.

If you can afford it, have a graphic designer help you make your brochure the best of its kind. Remember that if it is going to sit in a dispenser, the top half of the front page is all that is visible initially, and therefore the most important part. You will also need a slightly heavier paper – light paper 'flops'. It is worth checking that your brochure has impact from a distance of three metres, as well as when you hold it in your hand.

Again, think about what your target audience wants to know, not just what you would like to tell them. Less is probably more. Don't overload a small brochure with tiny print: people simply won't bother to read it.

Brochures should have as long a life as possible, so keep that in mind when you are putting the words together. If you want to include a price list which may change after a few months, or information that will date, a cheap and cheerful insert may be the solution.

If the brochure is the most important means of promotion for your business, consider having it written professionally too, and set aside a proper photography budget. Nothing looks more amateur than poor-quality home photos in an otherwise well-designed brochure.

Editorial – a story or photograph in local newspapers

We will explore this further in Chapter 5, *The Publicity Department*, but don't forget that editorial space in newspapers and magazines has much more authority and impact than paid-space advertising.

Radio programmes

Many local radio stations keep a list of local 'authorities' to make comment on stories or provide advice for phone-in programmes. If you are a solicitor, osteopath, chiropodist or similar, and feel confident about speaking in simple lay terms about your subject, why not contact your local programme-makers. It is helpful if you know someone at the radio station or have a friend who can introduce you, but you can always write to the news editor offering your services.

Giving a demonstration or workshop

Some businesses lend themselves to demonstrations: hair and beauty therapies, crafts, yoga, dance teaching, and so on. These fit in well with fêtes and fairs, county shows, garden parties, or Christmas markets.

With a bit of thought, many other independents could give 'how to' workshops: an interior designer on creative soft furnishings; a florist on Christmas decorations; a singing teacher on how anyone can improve their singing; a car mechanic on how to look after your vehicle. Lots of clubs and organisations – if they fall within your target groups – may well be delighted at the offer of a workshop, and new business could result, if not immediately, then in time. Be sure to have hand-outs so people know where to find you in the future. I kept the card of a stylist whose workshop impressed me for three years before having the right opportunity to do some work with her.

Osteopath Kristian Wood, one of the case studies in this book, gave free 15-minute sessions to the members of a smart health club. People then understood how he could help them and many became his clients.

Giving a talk

Many organisations such as Rotary International, PROBUS (Professional and Business Club), some political clubs and ladies' clubs have lunch or after-dinner speakers. If the membership of these organisations falls into your target group, and you enjoy speaking in public, then this can be an excellent showcase for you.

Contact the secretary of the organisation and ask about what kinds of subjects they prefer and the ideal duration of a talk. Have some ideas ready to offer. Obviously they will be looking for something unusual – a topic that they haven't heard many times before. Remember that however serious your subject matter, most people attending will relish a little light relief. Make your talk fun as well as informative, and don't forget to explain what you do and find a way to demonstrate your expertise. Be sure to take lots of business cards or hand-outs. In fact, it is worth carrying your business cards everywhere, all the time. A stylish, well-designed card (*see* Chapter 4) which reflects your business will serve you well. And you never know when you will need it.

networking at events
This is such an important method of gaining business that there is a special chapter on *Networking* (*see* pp. 105–114). Almost any event is appropriate for meeting new people.

Special introductory offers and discounts
Well, why not? Everyone loves a bargain. You should certainly consider some kind of introductory offer for your launch and it may be appropriate to have special 'packages' throughout the year. It is a perfectly legitimate way to entice people to try your product or service. Make sure, however, that they understand that this is an introductory or special rate, and that normally the fees or prices are considerably higher.

Selling online
Selling via the Internet is such a major and fast-moving topic that it warrants a book on its own. Try the library but, because the Internet is growing and changing so rapidly, splash out on the latest books of advice from your local bookshop.

The obvious advantages to selling online are:

- Your customers can purchase your services 24 hours a day, seven days a week, from any time zone on earth.
- Your site does not require a salary, holidays, a pension scheme or perks.
- The customer base is vast.

There will be initial costs: your domain, service provider, web space, site design and content. You may decide to do this yourself but you should at least consider using an agency with a good track record of setting up sites. You will also have to budget for domain renewal, site maintenance, updates and new products.

There are also Internet marketing companies who have specialist expertise. Unless you are proficient in this field, you should investigate the possibility of consulting this kind of agency. Part of their remit would be to ensure that you do not become part of the 'spam' or virus cultures, and they would help you with issues such as security. It may be expensive but possibly not as expensive as your making major mistakes through lack of knowledge.

It is necessary to market the site in the same way as you would any other business. It's worth stressing again that no-one can buy from you if they don't know you are there. You may not want to rely solely on customers finding you via search engines; your site will need its own marketing plan and its own PR campaign. There are lots of on-line magazines, for example, who might take articles about your services or wares. There is a whole culture around referral from other sites, and the all-important links.

If you are selling products, you will also have to set up an ordering system that enables people to buy from you from anywhere in the world. In addition, you may require a system of packaging and mailing for a worldwide market, and a means of converting all kinds of currency into the one of your choice.

Cold calling

Very few people enjoy cold calling – telephoning people you don't know and trying to sell them your products or services. However, new business has been gained this way, so it could be worth developing the skill. The most effective approaches to cold calling are:

(1) Identify in advance the right person to talk to. This should be someone who has the authority to commission you or to make a purchase.

(2) Prepare. Have the details of your service, products, terms and all your contacts in front of you. Nothing is more embarrassing than going blank.

(3) Phone and ask for the person concerned. If a telephonist or PA asks why you wish to speak to this person, simply say that it is to do with a new business project. You have no need to sell yourself in at telephonist level.

(4) Smile (it will relax you) and then announce your name and the name of your company clearly: 'This is Henry Brown of Henry

Brown Services.' Remember, you are the chairman and managing director of your own enterprise. Speak with confidence!

(5) Announce what you do: 'We offer . . . '

(6) Ask in an unapologetic way if the person you are phoning ever requires services or products such as yours. If the response is totally negative, apologise cheerfully for taking this person's time and finish the call.

(7) If there is indecision, such as 'we sometimes buy . . . ' or 'we occasionally use freelance help but we don't need anyone at the moment', ask if you may send them your details/brochure/ career history in the hope that you may be considered in the future. If that is agreed, add your thanks – and send the material that same day by first-class mail. Add a note referring to your phone conversation.

(8) If you have a positive response, well done! Make a date for a meeting, and/or close the deal.

Don't forget the rest of the world

As an independent it is all too easy to think in very local terms. In fact, if you are good at what you do, or produce or sell goods that are attractive, good value and/or wildly creative, your market is as wide as you want it to be. It could be crowded in your own locality but there might be excellent opportunities in other parts of the country, or abroad.

Exporting goods and services is not complicated; finding the right contacts can be harder but is not impossible. A good way to dip your toe into this area is to talk to people who are already exporting, and to seek advice via your local Chamber of Commerce. Start scanning your trade press for any useful background information, or for products that would be appropriate to export.

There are a lot of international exhibitions, conferences and exchanges, both here and a Eurostar train journey away. It may be worth investing time in attending appropriate exhibitions in order to research what is currently available and who is already in the market. If there is a gap you can fill, or a better service that you can offer, go on to the next stage.

Exhibitors are there solely to answer questions, so ask away. Collect brochures from companies who might purchase your goods and services, and if possible, the cards of the people within those companies who may be purchasers or influencers. Write to them after the exhibition or conference. Most people in the international markets speak and read English these days, but if you speak another language fluently, by all means use this advantage.

Be prepared to speculate in a little travel in order to land the business, and be aware that subsequently it will be necessary to keep in touch. Email and faxes are marvellous but you will need to become familiar to and trusted by your new clients if the contact is to be sustained over a period of time. And nothing takes the place of face-to-face meetings to achieve a proper relationship.

Proceed as you would in your own area: ask for comprehensive briefings, have a proper contract or letter of agreement, decide the terms of payment and the currency you wish to be paid in, and away you go. Your bank will help you make the financial arrangements and there are lots of international carriers and courier companies who will handle the rest. If you are going outside the EU to work, check whether there are visa and trade restrictions and any tariffs or extra taxes. One way to find out is to contact the trade commission of whatever country you are interested in exporting to: most have representation in this country either as part of their embassy or separately. They are usually immensely helpful.

They are also useful if you are considering importing. In fact the major part of their remit is to help you find what you want, arrange introductions, and ease the way of importing. Again, unless you have already spotted goods when you were abroad, a good place to start looking for products is at international exhibitions or in your trade press.

As an independent, it is all too easy to think in very local terms. In fact, if you are good at what you do, or produce or sell goods that are attractive, good value and/or wildly creative, your market is as wide as you want it to be.

Keep track of your business leads

It is of enormous value to know what means of publicity or promotion has worked best for you and what has proved less successful. Find a way of asking your customers or clients how they heard about you and where they saw your name. Keep a note. When you are reviewing your publicity spend, you then have some evidence on which to base your next decisions.

If you are using paid-space advertising, invent a room number or an extra initial in your name for each ad. This way, you can identify the publication from which enquiries have resulted.

Things to do

- Look at what the market wants. Pretend to be your own customer and see what extras would be attractive.
- Identify your unique selling points.
- Decide who your target audiences are – that is, your most likely customers.
- Consider the best means to reach them. If you can afford it, use a mix of methods. Be creative. If possible, monitor each method that you choose, to see which are the most successful in bringing you clients or customers.
- Set aside a budget both for your launch and for ongoing promotion.
- Think big. Could your business expand into Europe or further afield?

Kristian Wood

'Even though there was just one lesson in the whole degree course about how to set up a business, I decided that had to be the way for me. I could have taken a job with someone else but somehow that just delayed setting up my own practice.'

Kristian Wood is an osteopath with practices in Shepherds Bush and Kensington, London.

At 15 I was spotted by Queen's Park Rangers Football Club. My grammar school took a rather dim view, but after my GCSEs I became a junior player in the youth team and in the reserves. Then, after two years, disaster struck: I was injured, with two prolapsed disks in my spine. Initially the only option was surgery but then it was suggested that I saw the legendary Eileen Drewery, the healer who was such an influence on Glen Hoddle. She lived in Broadstairs, opposite my grandfather, but I would have gone anywhere to see her. She was fantastic and reduced the pain. She also made me look at life very differently.

QPR offered to train me as a physiotherapist but I wanted more than that. The club supported me while I took two A levels in a year so I could apply for a four-year degree course in osteopathy. I liked the way that osteopathy treats everyone as an individual – there are no set solutions – and it's a holistic way of treating someone.

I wrote to the Football Association for sponsorship and they were amazing and came up with a yearly grant of £2000. My parents helped and I also took on student loans. Even so, by the time I qualified, I owed £13,000.

Even though there was just one lesson in the whole degree course about how to set up a business, I decided that had to be the way for me. I could have taken a job with someone else but somehow that just delayed setting up my own practice.

I had been giving massages to the staff at the PR company, Hall or Nothing, and the MD, Terri Hall, offered to rent me a room. My brother lent me enough to buy a desk and a phone,

and I arranged to pay for the bed – which is the most
expensive item – over a period of time.

QPR sent some of the players down to me which was not
only valuable business but a great selling point. I still look
after sportsmen. I worked at Watford for Gianluca Vialli not
long ago.

People like to be recommended to a health professional,
so other patients trickled in through friends of friends. I
thought it would be wise to be associated with a good health
club so I introduced myself to Holmes Place in Shepherds
Bush. They gave me two half-day clinics per week. I would
regularly give 15-minute free consultations, as a way of
introducing osteopathy to people. After a while it became
part of the package for any new member. Nowadays I have a
clinic in Holmes Place's flagship club in Kensington.

I've made plenty of mistakes. In the first year I felt guilty if I
wasn't working every minute. I started to open practices in
other places – a dental centre and with another osteopath –
but neither worked out.

I keep promoting what I do. I send mailings to existing
patients – anyone who uses a computer should have check-
ups every three to four months to nip any problems in the bud.
I also advertise on the back of the appointments' card for a
smart health centre. Now the Shepherds Bush practice is at the
point where I need help. I may ask my sister to take over the
administration, and I may bring in another osteopath part-
time.

There's a huge buzz when you help someone – maybe an
older lady who has suffered for years with arthritis – by loosen-
ing their muscles and lessening their pain. The one thing I
miss from the days when I played football is being in the open
air. So I recently finished a diploma course on equine
osteopathy, which will eventually lead to a degree. Then for
part of the week I can be in the countryside visiting riding
centres. The best way to build that business is through vet
referrals, so I am already spending weekends treating horses
for free, alongside local vets, so they can see what I can offer. I
can treat dogs too . . .

Kristian's advice:

The plus side of being independent is that you have the freedom to do what you want. Keep pushing your business around until you have the right mix and be sure you have a good quality of life too. It can be very stressful running a business on your own and you can wind up worrying a lot. You will need something to offset that.

Don't beat yourself up if at first you are not working flat out. Invest the time by meeting people, spreading the word and, if you can, demonstrating what you do – even if it is for free. It will pay dividends in the end.

Michael Austin

'There was one time when I told a client I would not work for him. I didn't set up on my own to work for people like that! If you are working for a large concern, you can have the client from hell but you cannot get rid of them.'

Michael Austin is a chartered accountant, and runs Blue Dot Consulting which specialises in the day-to-day financial management of small businesses.

I studied economics and accounting at Bristol University, mainly because I was interested in economics. It came as a shock to realise in my final year that 28 out of the other 29 students were lining up their first jobs with the major City companies. They all aspired to be senior partners in KPMG or PricewaterhouseCoopers. I didn't have that ambition and I agreed with someone who once said that most people become accountants because they don't know what else to do. That was me, but in the end I went to work for what is now Ernst & Young.

Some of the work was dull but I found that I enjoyed seeing what lay behind the figures, seeing why people invested in a product, the background to each enterprise, and the creativity.

Two of my six years there were in the training department, and that was the most interesting phase. But I preferred mixing with clients, I needed to get back to the coal face, so I left to become financial controller of an advertising agency. I found it fascinating how the most successful agencies marry the business and creative sides together. Then the late 1980s, early 1990s turn-down set in and I was made redundant.

I spent most of the 1990s in the business information sector in businesses supplying information on companies. The sector supplied its information online directly to clients and was, in fact, ahead of the Internet. Then came the time when I could either go for a major company again or do my own thing. I had so much practical knowledge which would be valuable to small companies and other people starting up that the choice seemed obvious.

I started with no customers at all, not one! And the phone wasn't ringing. I tried mail shots to medium-sized companies and some cold calling which I hated. Personal referral and word-of-mouth is still the best marketing in my area of business. What you have to do is go and and meet people. Build relationships, but don't try and sell. I joined the London Chamber of Commerce – it has a fabulous monthly meeting called Changing Places – and the Institute of Directors which is an excellent resource, and a breakfast networking club. Gradually the work started to come in, but it was about a year before I felt I had a real business. The amount of work was directly related to the number of people I had met.

There are two sets of clients. One set comes to me with specific problems. My aim for them is to become redundant because I have solved those problems. I enjoy taking people to places they otherwise would not reach. The other set is ongoing: I visit them two or three times a month to discuss business and look over the books. The mix means that I don't get bored.

There's already a growth issue – where I take my business next. I can stay at the current level, which is limited by the number of days in the week, or I can consider collaboration or

I can take the plunge and employ someone else. For the moment, I am involved in a joint venture and will see how that goes.

It's important to tell people how well you are doing. I built up a database, and I've started a programme of e-communications and also the traditional kind of direct mail shots. Even if your mail shot doesn't arrive on the day someone is looking for financial advice, the 'drip feed' may work. I've had several people say that they contacted me because they kept seeing my information. And direct mail is a good way to route people to your website. I've written features about the financial side of starting and maintaining a small business, and they have appeared on the websites of the umbrella organisations for various professions.

I enjoy being independent and I wake each morning without any feeling of dread about the day. I might make more money if I worked for a large financial organisation but I have a better quality of life this way.

Michael's advice:

Be very clear about what it is that you can do, what you are expert in, and what problems you can take away from your potential clients. Then go and put yourself in front of those people. Think of yourself as a product, then you will have some idea of how to market yourself.

It's well worth seeing what your professional or trade organisation can do to help. My Institute (the Institute of Chartered Accountants) is very supportive of small companies and sole practitioners. There are a number of helplines to sort out any technical queries. There's also advice on how members can grow their business, how to tackle their marketing and so on. There was far more than I ever thought.

The Public Affairs Department

*Your corporate design – shop fronts –
communications – answering the phone – your
address – staying in touch – accreditation and award
schemes – the influential client – dressing the part –
presenting yourself – making a 'pitch' – complaints
and mistakes*

The crafts of promotion and communication are brother and sister
to marketing and, like all siblings, demand equal attention. By
now, you will have decided what your product or service is; where
it differs from other products and services; who might like to buy
it, and the best way of communicating it to your potential
customers. Now you must show your product or service in a light
that will not just attract the customer, but also encourage them to
buy. This is like being an angler. You want to fish on a certain
stretch of water. You know what kind of fish are there. You select the
best rods and bait, and you cast expectantly. Now you have to land
the best fishes.

The way in which you present yourself to your 'community' –
your actual and potential customers or clients, your suppliers,
your competitors and rivals, and even your friends and family – is
vital to your future success. If you find this hard to believe, consider which of the following you would take on as a supplier:

- Someone who looks scruffy, in a dirty overall, with shabby
  equipment, *or* someone in a trim jumpsuit with a personal logo,
  clean equipment and a mobile on his/her clip belt?
- Someone who can't find a card so scribbles an illegible phone
  number on the back of an old envelope, *or* someone who hands
  you an attractive card and offers to email their career history
  and list of services – and does so?

- Someone you try to phone but find there's no reply, nor do you have an email address for them, *or* someone who has a bright answering machine or voice-mail message, and returns your call or email within a few hours.
- Someone with no visible work pedigree, *or* someone recommended to you, *or* about whom you see positive stories in the local paper?
- Someone who looks bored and whose clothes are dated, *or* someone who is brimming with enthusiasm, looks up-to-date, and raring to go?

Rather obvious, isn't it? But it happens all the time. People tell you that they are anxious for work, and that they have the right experience and bucket-loads of talent. It may be true but they just don't look the part or they are difficult to reach. Rightly or wrongly, we assume that they will be equally unreliable and sloppy about their work. Enthusiasm, willingness to make a special effort, and attractive design and surroundings are all great selling points. So where do you start?

Your corporate design

If you can possibly afford it, commission a graphic designer to design your corporate look. If you don't know of a good designer and none of your friends and contacts do either, one way forward is to find pieces of design work that you like. Collect brochures or cards that appeal to you and phone the companies or individuals they feature to ask who did the design and where you can find them.

Make an appointment and go to the designer's studio. Explain what you are looking for and ask for a design quote. Usually, a designer will put up several variations from which you can select the elements that are right for you. Ask for a separate quote for printing: this will be based on the kind of paper your designer intends to use, and the quantity you require.

If you are on a shoestring budget, ask your local copy shop to help you. They will have examples of card and letterhead designs. Take your time when considering these: it takes no more money to design an attractive card than it does a boring one. Look at cards that appeal to you and work out why. Integrate the elements that you feel are appropriate to what you do and the style in which you do it.

It is a good idea to have a business card with details that people can read easily. I have been given several cards on which the print size was so tiny that I could barely decipher it (and so didn't bother). I have been given other cards with a company name and the name of the bearer, but no indication of what the company does. Three months later, I will find the card and bin it because I can't remember what these people do.

When designing your business card, bear in mind that while novel or quirky shapes are fun and memorable if you are in a creative field, you still need to consider what people will do with your card. If they are likely to keep it in a purse or wallet, or a card-holder (if you are a healthcare professional, accountant or legal adviser), be sure it isn't so large that it won't fit. If you want to use your card to list opening times, or as a way to make an appointment or give background information, you could always opt for a double-sized card folded in half to normal card size.

Consider having a simple 'strapline' that goes under your name to remind people. Examples of straplines are:

Charlie Bates
Quality Painting and Decorating

or

Terry Humphries
Computer and Website Design Services

or

Katherine Smith
Legal Services in Conveyancing and Will Making

Your strapline does not need to be clever, just informative. Carry your design style through not only to your letterhead but also to your invoices (or use your headed paper for both) and your compliments slips. You can probably use the same 'look' for posters, flyers or leaflets. If you have to give written material for business proposals or even for presenting the final work, consider making the cover of your presentation folder fit in with your new overall corporate design.

If you use point-of-sale material such as brochure dispensers, price tags or signs, labels, tent cards, menus, wrapping paper and carrier bags, they should all reflect your overall corporate style.

If you wear overalls, tee shirts, a hard hat, kitchen whites, aprons and so on, consider having your name stencilled on them, or at least obtain them in your chosen company colour.

Shop fronts, interiors and vehicle design

This kind of design is not for amateurs. Too much of the success of a shop, restaurant or hair salon rests on their look to risk making a mistake. Find an experienced professional designer and work with them to develop your style.

Communications

You simply have to be available. If you are not, you risk irritating your current clients as well as losing new business. It is therefore well worth spending some time working out the best ways for existing customers and new business enquiries to reach you quickly. A mobile phone may be the perfect solution for some businesses, but not at all suited to others – particularly if you do a lot of driving or you are constantly in meetings, or you are likely to forget to recharge it regularly. Instead, it may be better to ask people to call your answering machine back at base and leave a message. Check your messages on a regular basis and return calls as soon as possible. Have a cheerful, reassuring outgoing message and change it regularly. One freelance bookkeeper who works from her various clients' offices leaves a different message every day to say where she is.

When you receive a message, you may not have time to deal with the problem immediately. But clients always assume that you work for them and only them. It is therefore good practice to do a holding operation and let them know that you have received their message, and will be attending to it as soon as possible.

If you are unavailable for a day or more, or on holiday, say so. Leave a message such as, 'This office is closed for holiday until 6th January but please leave me a message, and I'll call you straight back on the 7th!'

Emails can be life-saving but only if you are in a position to check them regularly. Ensure that you can access messages from your laptop as well as your office computer, in case at some point you can't reach the mother ship.

Only give people your out-of-hours number if there is no other way. We all have a private life and even clients need to know that. At the same time, be there for them in their emergencies.

Answering the phone

If you work from home and any other member of your family is likely to answer the phone for you, *train them*! Give them forms to fill in with the name of who called, at what time, the number to respond to and an outline of the query. If they are teenagers, turn them into a sales team. Impress on them that their contribution might mean more business for you, which in turn might improve their own financial status.

On a number of occasions I have phoned a freelance photographer or a designer working from home, only to be greeted by a bored-sounding youngster who didn't know where his father was, couldn't say when he would be back, was unable to find a pen, let alone any paper – and by that time I knew that any message he took down would be lost anyway. If this was someone I hadn't worked with before and I had other names, I would move on. Droopy teenagers can lose you business. If the training doesn't work, stick to the answering machine.

Your address

If you work from home and you don't want your clients or customers to know it, don't forget that there are excellent High Street business centres which offer mail box and monitoring services. You can use their address on your cards and even arrange for them to post on your mail and faxes. Some offer a phone answering service too.

Staying in touch

Of course, even when a piece of work is completed, you will want to stay in regular contact with your customers or clients. It is well worth building a client database. This does not have to be computer-based, although if you have the technology it is a good investment in terms of time to set one up. Your list can even be kept handwritten in a notebook. You should also make a note of any likely work your client may have coming up in the next year, along with details of their particular likes, dislikes or any potential minefields. However you choose to keep your list, you must also keep in touch. Identify ways to use the whole or part of your list at regular intervals. If you are a dentist or car mechanic, you can send half-year reminders about check-ups, or MOTs and servicing. Whatever your business, you should always send a card at Christmas or your major religious festival. Drop a note and an invitation if you are giving a talk or a demonstration somewhere. Send a flyer if you have a special offer or discount. Consider e-newsletters. *See* Chapter 5, *The Publicity Department* for other ideas. Gentle reminders of your excellent service should ensure that your clients come back to you again and again.

Accreditation and award schemes

Potential clients and customers will be reassured by your professional qualifications and membership of any relevant trade and professional bodies. There are many reasons for joining all the pertinent organisations. One of them is to be able to display on cards, letterheads and brochures, all your accreditations – these being the letters after your name or the line which says 'Member of (and the full name of trade organisation)'.

Whether I am commissioning an electrician or a sub-editor, I like to know that they have been properly trained and have sufficient respect for their own industry to be subscribing members. This is part of building your reputation for excellence and, it is worth repeating, can often be reflected in your fee and price levels.

For the same reason of customer recognition, consider entering any suitable award schemes. It's better still if you win, of course! To be a recent or current holder of a local or national award gives kudos, and an opportunity for some local press activity.

If you don't have an appropriate acknowledgement, you can even consider making your own. This is not a suggestion of any-thing fraudulent: an example is the Jubilee Market in London's Covent Garden. When it was set up in the 1980s, the stall-holders were aware that some customers were reluctant to purchase goods in case they were faulty, on the assumption that they could not return them or the stalls were temporary and wouldn't be there if they went back. Therefore many traders displayed a bronze plaque stating that their stalls were leasehold and that they subscribed to the Consumer Protection Act.

The influential client

Look for other kinds of endorsement. If customers or clients write thank-you letters, consider quoting them on your publicity material. When an important client compliments you, ask them if they would be prepared to be quoted. The more important the client, the more impressive the endorsement and the more weight it will carry. Don't be shy about asking; people are often flattered to be considered as an authority.

When an important client compliments you, ask them if they would be prepared to be quoted. The more important the client, the more impressive the endorsement and the more weight it will carry.

Dressing the part

'Most people dress to belong. The spare room tycoon must dress to bill.' So says the American James Chan in his book, *Spare Room Tycoon*. He is correct, whatever side of the Atlantic you view it from. People will only pay high fees to someone who looks the part. Would you pay top prices at a butcher's shop where the meat was piled on metal trays and the butcher wore a bloodstained apron and a two-day stubble? Probably not. But you might pay more if the butcher was in immaculate whites, with a straw boater and a big grin, presenting you with choice morsels on a china platter, decorated with Mediterranean parsley.

It's the same at every level. Don't forget that you are the sole representative of your own standards. Many independent practitioners keep a 'client getting' wardrobe: this usually comprises a very smart suit or well-cut jacket, up-to-date, brushed and pressed, with good shoes and, if you use one, a briefcase, shined and ready to go. When I started out I was on a very tight budget but always kept money aside for a decent haircut, good-quality dry cleaning, and the most elegant shoes I could afford.

Dressing for success can be a worry if you haven't done it before. If you are aware that this is now an element in your business but feel unsure about how to meet the challenge, consider going to a style consultant. It could prove to be a wise investment. Carol

Spenser, the UK's leading style consultant, has guided many men and women through the minefield of their personal style. When she first started in 1991, almost all of her clients were women – since, by and large, women have always known that effort is called for if you want to look good. But at about that time, many companies started to realise that the appearance of their employees – male and female – was just as important to their image as their products, brochures, advertising and office décor, and Carol is now regularly called in to advise executives in all spheres. Men in the public eye – such as politicians – are especially aware of how their looks can affect public response and give them enormous power on the world stage.

Carol often laughs about an experiment she uses to demonstrate how much emphasis we put on appearance in our initial judgements of people. When she is conducting a seminar or consultation, she will often ask her clients to guess, based on her own appearance, where she comes from, what her father did for a living, her marital status and what her job was before she became a style consultant. The majority assume that she comes from the South East of England, that her father is probably an office manager, that she is single or divorced, and that previously she was either a hairdresser or an airline stewardess. In fact, Carol was born on a council estate in Liverpool, has a good degree in English, is married with children, and used to be in public relations work. She can also assume a great Scouse accent when the mood takes her.

So where does this leave you? Carol offers the following advice:

If you are a man

Hair, glasses and necklines
Your face is the focal point of your whole appearance. People you meet look at your face first, then their eyes travel rapidly up and down your body before returning to your face again. Your face, hair, glasses, collar and tie make an extremely important contribution to the viewer's opinion of you. Having a 1970s collar-curling hairstyle or 1980s brightly framed, owl-like glasses indicates a sad attempt to hold onto youth. Research shows that men who look old-fashioned are often regarded as being outdated in their knowledge, abilities and attitudes.

What suits you by way of hairstyle, glasses and necklines depends on your face shape and whether your features are soft or sharp. If you are unsure, a good hairdresser should be able to help you decide what is most flattering.

Most men prefer shorter hair but in certain industries – music, advertising, media, fashion, theatre and so on – longer hair is very acceptable. It is also worth remembering that it requires much higher maintenance.

A practised optician may be able to help you choose glasses, but for a balanced look, remember that the top of the frame should follow your eyebrows, just on or just below, to avoid a look of surprise. The sides of the frames should not extend beyond the sides of your face, unless you wish to look like Brains in *Thunderbirds*; and the bottom of the frames should definitely not touch your cheek. If you have a small or light bone structure, select a lightweight or frameless style.

If your features are 'curved' rather than 'angular', look for details such as standard or rounded collars, necklines and jacket lapels. Opt for plain fabrics or blended stripes, soft checks, swirls and paisley tie designs or even polka dots. If your features are more angular, look for pin, tab or crisp button-down collars, notched or peaked lapels, V-necks, turtle-necks and zip-up necklines and patterns that are sharp stripes, bold checks, geometrics or zigzags.

Body shape

There are basically three male body shapes: triangular (where the shoulder measurement is much bigger than that of the waist and hips); rectangular (with a straight but slim body outline); and contoured (still rectangular but with much softer, rounded edges). Carol has strong guidelines for each of these groups, but in short: 'triangular' men should be careful not to overemphasise their shoulders, and unconstructed loose clothes will camouflage their shape. Instead they should be looking for wider lapels on suits, short casual jackets, tucked-in tops and figure-hugging jeans.

'Rectangular' men look better with slight shoulder pads in suits, double-breasted jackets if you are slim and single-breasted if you are tubbier. Casual jackets are best worn straight or slightly below waist length. The 'contoured' figure is flattered by an easy, unconstructed suit rather than by a sharply angular 'gangster' look – and avoid double-breasted suits at all costs. Casual jackets should also be roomy and trousers should be flat-fronted, not pleated.

Colouring

Check your colouring: the stronger this is, the deeper and more intense the colours that will flatter you. If your colouring is light, you can be overwhelmed by very dark and sombre colours near your face and you should consider lighter and more pastel shades. Silver and grey hair is often very 'cool' in appearance and you can pick icy colours such as blues, lilacs and pinks. Redheads suit the opposite colours – warm shades of beige, rust and olive.

The way in which you interpret these guidelines depends on the sort of life you lead and the kind of personality that you have. But remember, you are the chairman and managing director of your own enterprise and that should be reflected in every aspect of your appearance in whatever way is appropriate. Be brave, toss out the old wedding suit and step out as today's man!

If you are a woman

Don't get stuck in a time-warp or become a professional mother. We all have the tendency to take the 'safe', familiar option, even those of us who once keenly followed fashion. But just as Princess Diana, Margaret Thatcher and Hilary Clinton reinvented them-selves, so you too can emerge as a bright entrepreneurial woman.

Face, hairstyles, and glasses

Research shows that men notice your figure first, while other women notice your clothes. However, it is your face that has the overall greatest impact, especially when you meet someone for the first time. So, in the same way as the men, you need to create a frame for the picture by assessing your face shape, and whether your features are soft or angular.

A good hairdresser should be able to help you decide if your face is oval, round, heart-shaped, pear (all curved outlines) or rect-angular, square or diamond-shaped (all angular shapes). From this – and from the thickness and texture of your hair – you can make decisions about the hairstyle that is most flattering to you.

If you have had the same specs for ten years or more – or you have been putting off buying a pair altogether for fear of looking old or frumpy – go down to one of the new spectacle shops and have fun picking out some new, fashionable glasses. You are bound to find at least a few flattering styles which, believe it or not, can add to a stylish look rather than detract from it. Take account of the tips Carol has given the men (*see* pp. 69–71).

Body shape

There are four basic body types for women: straight (long, straight ribcage, little or no waist, flat hips and thighs); tapered (short ribcage, visible waistline, rounded hips and thighs); curved (long ribcage/high bust, obvious waistline, flared hips/thighs, hips low); and fuller (full bust, wide ribcage, little or no waistline, full hips/thighs).

The straight figure, like that of Princess Diana and many models, is flattered by straight, lean, tailored shapes in crisp and geometric fabrics. It suits pencil skirts, shift dresses, boxy suits and straight-leg trousers but not waisted garments.

The tapered figure looks better in fit'n'flare dresses, princess-line coats and semi-fitted jackets. Tucked-in tops and belts, in particular, should be avoided.

Curved figures can take lots of emphasis on the waist: wide belts, tucked-in tops, full skirts and soft drapey fabrics. Straighter styles can make this figure look too wide.

The fuller shape does *not* require bigger sizes, and wide, full skirts should be avoided. Instead look for long, straight jackets and tunics over straight skirts, trousers and dresses. Aim to keep the silhouette narrow.

Look for vertical lines if you wish to appear taller and slimmer; horizontal lines can be widening. Shiny fabrics reflect light and draw attention to themselves, and this can make the wearer look bigger; this includes blouses, tights and stockings. Matt fabrics absorb light and are therefore more body-friendly for those who want to look slimmer.

All these guidelines – and many more – appear in Carol Spenser's two marvellous books, *Style Directions for Men* and *Style Directions for Women*. (For details *see* the Resources section pp. 234–8.)

Presenting yourself

In design, advertising, public relations, and many other services, clients often ask for several agencies or consultants to 'pitch' for their business. Most successful people will promptly come up with good ideas and present them well. But who wins the business? I believe that two of the winning ingredients are enthusiasm, and a team or a consultant that the client thinks they can work with. No client or customer is going to choose someone that they feel uncomfortable with or intimidated by.

Figures vary slightly, but the findings are that what we look like accounts for 60 per cent of someone's first reaction to us. In this instance, it is not a matter of our height, leg length or the evenness of our features, but more to do with an assessment of our charisma. What we sound like takes a further 30 per cent and the content of what we say only about 10 per cent. This explains a lot about politics and politicians!

But we don't tend to like many politicians, possibly because we don't find them very believable. The people we find charismatic, by and large, are those who come across as genuine and authentic.

The other part of your personal appeal will be your keen interest in the task in hand. This does not mean that you have to be over the top or ingratiating, just don't be afraid to let the client know that you really do want to do the work because it is exciting/ interesting/worthwhile/a great opportunity.

What we look like accounts for 60 per cent of someone's first reaction to us. What we sound like takes a further 30 per cent, and the content of what we say only about 10 per cent . . .

Making a 'pitch'

There are a thousand variations, and maybe more, of how you should make a pitch in your particular sector of business. There's a culture which applies to each individual area, but there are also some aspects you may wish to consider that are common to most of us. The following represents not only my own experience but also the accumulated wisdom of a number of independents who regularly go out and win – and sometimes lose – the job.

Homework

I recommend that you start by asking as many questions as possible to establish what your potential customer really wants, the time span or deadline for the project, the budget, what else is happening around the project, whether it is part of a bigger event or campaign, and who will be your contact or manager. If you are pitching for a major contract, request a briefing meeting. Be brazen and ask if it is going to be a competitive pitch. If so, ask how many others are pitching against you.

It is always worth taking time to do your homework; this may well prove a key element in your success. If the pitch is related to a company or organisation, see what you can find out about its background, development, product range, customers, competitors, particular strengths and potential problem areas. Ask other suppliers about it. Check the website; pick up brochures. Check who the directors or main managers are and, if possible, ask around to see what your friends and contacts know about them. In your pitch, demonstrate in an appropriate way how thoroughly you have done your research, and how you plan to use it to the new client's best advantage.

Your presentation

By all means suggest that a client may benefit from following your advice, but it is probably a mistake to decry or scoff at their previous courses of action. In the same way, be sensitive to what they think they need now: they may be wrong in your opinion, but take care how you explain that. Gentle coaxing of your client into better practice could prove the better way.

At the same time, you don't have to tell your clients how great you are. Assume that they know, and let your career history and reputation speak for you. By all means give examples of other clients' problems or challenges that you have successfully solved; however, if you are in a creative field, beware of implying that you give exactly the same solutions to all your clients. Each one will wish to be regarded as highly individual; every one of them believes his or her problems to be unique (even though they rarely are!). For example, if you are an interior designer and cream-on-ivory is this year's vogue, don't assume that everyone will want to subscribe to the fashion. If they have children or pets, or want your design to outlast the current trend, you can assume that cream-on-ivory probably won't appeal.

Plan how you are going to make your pitch with care. Will you be presenting ideas? How will you illustrate your presentation? Computer presentations can be a distraction: be aware that it's *you* that people are attracted to, not a piece of software. And remember that computer presentations frequently work magically at a rehearsal but seize up immediately the potential new client is present. You will lessen the risk, and your tension, by leaving the computer back at base.

Part of your pitch preparation should be to consider what questions are likely to be asked. It may be prudent to decide how to field the questions you *don't* want to answer, as well as those you do.

If you are pitching for a big contract, find out how many people will be attending the pitch and who they are. Arrange to go to the venue early and set the room out as you would like it. Ensure that you are comfortable in the surroundings and that you can be heard by everyone. Check the lighting and, if you are using any aids, where the plug points are.

Spend some time deciding what you wish to leave with your potential new client. It may be a simple estimate or it could be a full proposal document with your ideas, a budget breakdown, your career profile and a list of your current clients. Remember to make it attractive enough to leap out of the pile but not sufficiently detailed that it becomes a do-it-yourself guide.

Standing up

When you are presenting, try not to give what comes across as a 'spiel'; you are not a door-to-door salesman with a set patter. Remember that your potential client has approached you because you have knowledge, skills and experience that the client doesn't have.

Rehearse. The bathroom mirror is ideal and mine has heard many a 'pitch'. Have your notes in bullet points rather than as a script that you stand and read: script-writing is an art, and so is delivering one. Instead, just talk naturally to your would-be client, and make a point of checking your list rather than being furtive about it. Make it part of your presentation: perhaps say 'Now, have I covered everything that I want to tell you . . . ?'

Remember to 'interview' your client too – albeit gently. You must be sure that they will make good clients, and that you will enjoy working with them. We often forget this, but it is a two-way affair!

Decide what three things you would like your potential new client to remember after the pitch. Concentrate on those and be succinct. Watch for any signs that boredom is setting in; if someone yawns or you can see that they have 'switched off', turn up your energy. If that fails, you can assume that they are either disinterested in you or were at a very good party the night before.

Sometimes you will have a tough interview or receive a negative reaction. If you are aware that this sometimes happens, you will not be taken by surprise. What comes with more experience is the ability to walk away unscathed when it doesn't work. Ask any actor or stand-up comedian: there are times when an audience is totally unresponsive and nothing you can do will help the situation.

But, however desperate you feel the situation has become, it is unwise to attempt to befriend, flirt or manipulate. You don't need to resort to seduction techniques. You will have been asked to pitch because of your reputation and skills, so try to establish a good professional relationship from the outset.

If you regularly pitch for work, consider taking personal development and communications training. It is expensive but may well turn out to be the best investment you have ever made. Your ability to be an authentic and effective communicator may be the deciding factor in whether or not you win the kind of new business you long for.

Complaints and mistakes

They happen: we are members of the human race. Sometimes the goods prove faulty, the delivery goes awry, there's a glaring error in the calculations, the written work has a spelling mistake that a child wouldn't make, the cake doesn't rise, the hairstyle flops. You have let your client or customer down. Oh *dear*!

Sometimes that's it, you have blown it and nothing can retrieve the situation. But in the majority of cases I believe that a complaint well handled can give you a client or customer for life. If you own up, take the responsibility and do everything you can to rectify the error, people will respect you for your honesty. More, they know they can trust you in future to come clean if there are any other problems. Everyone knows that Marks & Spencer never make a fuss about changing something or refunding the money. The policy has added to their reputation. This is much the same principle.

However you decide to handle the matter, do it quickly. If you cannot resolve the issue right away, respond immediately with a phone call or letter, not just apologising but also reassuring the recipient that you will be taking action within the shortest possible time. Here are a few more suggestions:

- Give people space to be angry. It's a stressful world and ineffi- ciencies rattle everyone these days. Once they know that their voices are being heard, most reasonable people will calm down, particularly if they see that you are willing to make amends.
- Occasionally someone will be totally unreasonable in their complaint. You know it and possibly they do too. However, before you send them away with a flea in their ear, consider if they are likely to spread negative gossip about you or even go to the local press with their grievance. Even though it has nothing to do with fairness or justice, sometimes you have to take the wider view and deal with their complaint as though it were legitimate. It may make your eyes water, but in the long run, it's possible that this route will serve you best and cost less.
- Deal with the complaint in the way you would wish to be dealt with were you the one complaining. A young man, driving too fast, ran his car into my mother's garden, damaging a wall and ruining some of her favourite plants. The garden was put right under the insurance settlement, but the young man, realising that my mother was upset by the hassle and the loss of her dracena, brought her a huge bunch of flowers the morning after the accident. Corny? Well, yes, but he had acknowledged her angst and made a special effort. She was pleased and now thinks he is a charming young man. He feels gallant for flat- tering an older lady. Everyone has won. This is not a business example, just a gentle reminder about the power of flowers.

Things to do

- Find a graphic designer or a good print shop to help with your corporate design for letterheads and business cards.
- Decide how you can best stay in touch with your clients and how they can most easily reach you.
- Ensure that everyone in your household knows how to handle your business calls, or use an answer service.
- If you have professional or trade qualifications, find the most appropriate way to display them.
- Ask influential clients to endorse your service.
- Take a long hard look at how your clients perceive you and ensure that you dress for success.
- Take time to develop your presentation skills.
- If you pitch for new business, consider carefully your business presentation.
- Deal with any complaints and mistakes quickly and with due care.

Robert Carslaw

'Don't distance yourself with lots of secretaries and assistants. Particularly in a business like mine, clients want to deal with you, and talk directly to you, not to employees.'

Robert Carslaw is an interior designer. Though based in London and Cornwall, he works all over the country.

As a small child, as young as three or four, I wanted to be an architect. I loved building houses with Lego bricks. When I was 12 my father pointed out that, as I was badly dyslexic, training as an architect was unrealistic, but I wanted to stay in that direction. My mother had a friend in London with an interior design practice. She wrote at length to warn me against the business. That's when I knew it was for me!

After taking a foundation course at Salisbury College of Art, I did a three-year course at the London School of Furniture. It was all theory and offered no preparation for the outside world at all. There was certainly nothing on how to run a business.

For the following three years I worked for a well-known interior designer in Knightsbridge. It wasn't easy; he was moody and jealous of other people's talents, although he was gifted himself. Looking back, I realise that I was badly bullied. In the end I simply walked away. I was already beginning to build up a following of wealthy clients, and one of them gave me two pieces of advice which I have followed to this day. The first was never to take a partner – not only because you are then financially involved but also in terms of the division of work. You always feel that the partner doesn't work as hard, which causes resentment. Instead, make your own decisions, be your own boss and do what you feel is right. Secondly, don't distance yourself with lots of secretaries and assistants. Particularly in a business like mine, clients want to deal with you, and talk directly to you, not to employees.

I've been on my own since 1991. My wonderful aunt, the theatrical agent Sheelagh O'Donovan, believed in me and helped to sponsor me financially for the first year. She thought I would be up and running by then, and I was. She was also very interested in my business, and became an early form of mentor, always giving me sound advice such as asking for enough in advance from a client to fund a project properly.

My work is mainly domestic. People come to an interior designer for something out of the ordinary, otherwise they would simply go to a department store and pick things that are immediately available. My work varies: younger clients want something contemporary; the more staid clients like the traditional – although I always incorporate at least one contemporary element, if only a painting.

Most of my work comes through networking and recommendation, and many clients come back to me again and again. I advertise in *House & Garden*. It's the only magazine that brings me business; I've tried other interior design magazines but to no effect. Advertising doesn't always have instant impact. One client contacted me in April having seen my ad the previous September.

It's true that the rich and aristocratic are not like the rest of us. Occasionally I have to put up with some very bad behaviour. I treat these clients as if they were spoilt children, keeping calm and giving them a lot of rope until I am really cross, and then I let it show. There are also the clients who are immensely wealthy but capable of being incredibly mean. They are always looking for bargains and always want a discount. I've had to fight for reasonable fees for my craftsmen before now.

When life becomes tiresome because of ghastly clients, I have a pool of friends in similar businesses that I call on. They call on me too. We have lunches and take it in turns to moan and groan. This is very necessary when you work on your own.

But I still get an enormous high, a real satisfaction out of what I do: maybe designing a piece of furniture or creating an atmosphere with the right fittings and positioning of lights. And I enjoy being thanked too. I've had delightful letters, champagne and even presents from pleased clients.

Robert's advice:

Be vigilant, don't let people take advantage of you. It can easily happen when you are inexperienced. Lots of people want something for nothing. You must command respect from your clients: after all, they cannot achieve what we are capable of doing, otherwise they would not have come to us. Refuse to be bullied. Insist that they speak to you as they would to their solicitor.

Estimate for *everything*! I didn't do this initially but I'm older and wiser now. I send pages of detailed estimates, with each item listed separately. Then I ask for immediate payment. I always ask for deposits and I require 50 per cent of the estimated costs up front. Fees are billed monthly in arrears. For projects like mine that may take months, you need a flow of cash to fund the business, to pay people, purchase goods – and to pay yourself. Keep on top of your accounts. Don't be artistic and airy fairy when it comes to the accounting and business side!

Jem Davis

'I am quite impulsive but I trust my own intuition. If I'm in doubt I talk to someone more analytical and I listen hard to their feedback.'

Jem Davis qualified in the UK as a barrister and solicitor and currently practises as a legal consultant.

I grew up in Bermuda and graduated from Bermuda College at 18. I became interested in law after a careers adviser suggested it. Even so, I was not yet ready to leave Bermuda and so spent the next five years working in banking and the hotel industry. Bermuda is a beautiful island and you can have a very good life there, but with a population of just 60,000 people, I knew that I wanted a bigger stage.

I moved to the UK to study for my law degree. During that time I also qualified as an aerobics teacher, which I thought would be fun as well as helping to subsidise university costs. It was important to have an outside interest to offset the rigours of studying. After my law degree I went to Bar School and qualified as a barrister, after passing my Bar exams on my first sitting. But I continued teaching aerobics; it ensured a good balance between work and play.

I was fortunate: I undertook a period of pupillage (a pupillage is rather like a form of apprenticeship, where you learn from an experienced barrister) based at Middle Temple. During this time my pupil master suggested that I consider qualifying as a solicitor, as it's extremely difficult to make a living during the first few years of practice as a barrister. I applied to the huge, prestigious international law firm, Clifford Chance, and was delighted to be offered employment. It was a wonderful place to cut my teeth and while I was there I also qualified as a solicitor. Some people are particularly suited to private practice in a law firm but I decided that it wasn't for me, and accepted an interesting offer at an investment bank.

During this period I developed an interest in contract law and in particular, IT, technology and computing law. After five years of working in the City I began to want more variety. A friend who is a senior partner in a City law firm suggested I consider legal consultancy. I am quite impulsive but I trust my own intuition. If I'm in doubt I talk to someone more analytical and I listen hard to their feedback. In this instance, I knew immediately that this was the way forward for me, and my friend eventually helped me to land my first major client.

The decision to become a legal consultant and use all my collective work and life experience felt right: it was time for me to move on to doing my own thing. I no longer have to identify myself as either a barrister or a solicitor and legal consulting gives me the diversity and commercial environment that I relish. I love the challenge of living and working in London, with all the variety and quality of work that can be found here. People ask me if I think being a woman makes a difference: I believe that things like this only make a difference if you let them. When you go into business for yourself, you should not underestimate the value of tenacity and determination to succeed.

The initial part of setting up my consultancy practice was hard. You must wear lots of hats. For example, sometimes you're a salesperson, at other times you're a bookkeeper, and all the time you must focus on actually making a living. You also need to discuss money and terms of business with your clients and the sooner you do it, the better. Networking is vital. You soon realise that the more you talk about what you're doing, the more you'll convey how much you enjoy what you do, and that inspires confidence both in you and in the client.

My clients require daily attention, but I ensure that my work does not take over my life. Fitness remains important, which is why I now spend my spare time running, either at my local gym, in the neighbourhood or out and about at races.

I still miss teaching aerobics classes. You know, it's a real achievement to get a room of 50 English people dancing, clapping and jumping in the air!

Jem's advice:

Create a balance. When you go solo, it's the perfect time to improve your overall quality of life. You do not need to become a slave to the clock. I firmly believe that it is not necessary to work long hours on a day-to-day basis. Provided you focus and work effectively, you will have enough time in the day not only to work but also to play too!

Be yourself. Be straightforward, direct and clear. This is very different from being rude and I believe that clients appreciate knowing exactly where they stand. This will also help you to set boundaries early on in the relationship. For example, if you find that a client is asking for too much free time or advice, gently ask to whom the consultation invoice should be sent.

5

The Publicity Department – and Your Launch

The Press Office: why press coverage is so powerful – the DIY press campaign – what makes a news story – news releases – future press opportunities – other ways into your local press – radio – television – trade press – consumer magazines – Exhibiting: going on show – the importance of a good site – exhibition wheezes – Becoming a sponsor . . . your launch

In addition to straight advertising and promotion, there are other channels of promotion, well worth exploiting, that may be suitable for publicising your enterprise. They fall into three main groups: press campaigns, exhibitions and sponsorship. The first is not costly, although a media campaign takes time and effort to put together. The other two are more expensive but, depending on the type of your business, can pay extremely good dividends if you plan with care and take proper advantage of all the opportunities such promotions offer.

The Press Office

Why press coverage is so powerful

Britain is amazingly well-off for news providers. Despite the fact that we take most of our headline news from national radio or television, we have the choice of at least nine national daily newspapers plus all the weekend papers. In addition, there are about 100 regional daily newspapers, all with loyal local readerships. Then there are weekly newspapers and all the free sheets, not to mention the county magazines, the 'what's on' magazines and, a force in themselves, parish magazines. And that's just on the print side! We also have regional television with its own local programmes and lots of local radio stations.

With the exception of the nationals, all these thrive on local news. If you can provide something newsworthy, you stand a good chance of obtaining free editorial coverage. In the PR business, we will tell you that editorial mention is worth three to four times the same space in the advertising columns because people read the news sections much more thoroughly than they do the ads. Editorial coverage also has 'third party endorsement'; the newspaper has chosen to cover your story and has therefore endorsed it by doing so – hence all those reviews outside theatres and on the back of books that proclaim *'brilliant, witty and perceptive, says* The Times'.

It is also true that, whereas people may be a little (or even highly) skeptical about some of the things they read in the national press, by and large they believe what their local papers tell them.

The DIY press campaign

With the right snippet of news you can take advantage of the influence and impact offered by the media. Most businesses are likely to benefit – if not directly, through gaining new business, then indirectly by enhancing their reputations. Certainly, people prefer to buy goods and services that they have heard of.

Start by researching your local media (*see* page 92 for advice on trade media). Coverage is really only worthwhile if it is read by your potential customers, so revisit your target groups and consider what those groups might read locally. Take at least two issues of the newspapers or magazines you think might be appropriate, so you can identify which columns and features are regular items. Alternatively, visit your local reference library; they should have up-to-date copies of most of your local press. Then, look at the kind of news these newspapers or magazines feature. Look at the sort of photographs they use, check the letters page, the advice section, the special columns, the women's and family health pages – whatever is appropriate to your business.

When preparing for your DIY press campaign it is a good idea to make up a press target list in advance, with all the relevant names, addresses, phone and email numbers. This will save you time when there's a rush for you to put a news story out. For the contacts, look in the magazines or newspapers themselves; they should give you the editor's name and the appropriate telephone number(s). If they have a website, and you have access to it, look them up there. If you get stuck, contact directory enquiries.

Be aware of deadlines. Magazines often work one to two months in advance; weeklies usually have an editorial deadline on a Tuesday or Wednesday and bring their papers out on a Thursday or Friday. Morning papers have a late-night deadline and evening papers complete in early afternoon. You could add the deadline for each publication onto your press target list. Bear in mind that if you have urgent front-page news you can be closer to the deadline. If not, you need to approach the press much, much earlier!

What makes a news story?

Unless you are trying for national coverage – in which case you should consider commissioning a good freelance press specialist – you are likely to be seeking local (or trade magazine) news. News by its very nature must be immediate and exciting. Your piece might be about winning a challenge or some unusual new business, or it might be a celebrity client or a link to charity. Consider some of the following:

LOCAL SOLICITOR RAISES CHARITY £3000 IN LONDON MARATHON

LOCAL COMPANY WINS MIDDLE EAST CONTRACT

LOCAL HAIRDRESSERS GAIN NATIONAL PRIZE

LOCAL PHYSIO TO HELP [LOCAL] FOOTBALL TEAM

(They probably won't use the word 'local' but the place name instead.) These are all examples of how people have achieved something noteworthy. It will add to each business's reputation to have good press coverage of the story.

Be aware that the editorial side of newspapers, trade magazines and broadcast media is *news*-based but will not be interested in *advertising* you, your company, goods or services. The acid test is to ask yourself if *you* would be interested in this story. Would you mention it to a chum in the pub or a member of your family? If even you find it dull, bin it. If it holds your attention – or makes you laugh – give it a go.

Press releases

If your news is about something that is happening now or has just happened, it is important to inform the media quickly: *old news is no news*. If it is really exciting and likely to be of interest to the whole area, simply pick up the phone and call the news desks of all your local media. Be prepared to back your call up with written information – faxed or emailed – within the hour.

If it is good stuff but not necessarily front-page news, you may have time to write a press release – but again, be sure to put it out quickly. For example, you are running in the Flora London Marathon under the name of your business but raising funds for charity. You can always prepare your press release *in advance*. The event is held on a Sunday morning. Arrange for friends to hand-deliver your release to the regional daily newspaper offices on the Sunday afternoon (immediately after you have phoned them to say that you have completed the run). The newspaper can then use it on the Monday. If they only receive it on Monday, it cannot be used until Tuesday and that's already too late for a daily. You might still get something in a weekly paper, however.

The press release should be on your new headed paper and:

- carry the date at the top;
- have a punchy, short headline;
- tell the main drive of the story very simply in the first paragraph: who did what, when they did it and where. Then follow that information with a why.

Always give full names and full addresses at the bottom of your release, and include your daytime, mobile and evening telephone numbers so reporters can call you for further information or comment. Avoid 'techno-speak': keep your release in plain, clear English. If you need to use a technical term, explain it in brackets. If you are not sure what level is acceptable, imagine that you are explaining your news story to your children. Remember that journalists receive *hundreds* of press releases every day. They haven't the time to work hard at understanding yours.

Remember that all national and regional daily newspapers are made up of departments. Therefore, you should send:

- a news items to the news editor
- a business item to the financial editor
- medical items to the health correspondent
- shopping, beauty and family health items to the women's editor
- sports stories and sponsorships to the sports editor

If you are contacting a regional daily newspaper, they will almost certainly have an email address for their news desk and different email addresses for the specialist writers. If you have access, send an email as well as a hard copy as this saves the journalist having to type out the information. Phone and check the appropriate email address for the section of the paper you want.

Weekly papers have a smaller staff, so address everything except sport (which goes to the sports editor) to the editor or news editor.

Future press opportunities
Newspapers, radio stations and television companies live by their diaries. They plan each day around what is in the diary, assigning reporters, photographers and camera teams at the beginning of each day or working session.

When you know in advance that a news story will be happening – a special event or presentation, workshop or fashion show – the procedure is similar to that for post-event news. Write your press alert as before, following the format of a punchy headline plus the who, what, where and when. Post it first-class to newspapers, radio and television about one week to ten days in advance. Any earlier and they will lose it; any later and you will go to the bottom of the list! Then, a day or two beforehand, phone and check that your 'happening' is in their diary. If it is not, ask how they would like the information: fax or email.

If a newspaper phones and tells you that a reporter and/or a photographer will be attending the event, make sure that someone is detailed to look after them if you are unable to do so yourself. Journalists are used to walking into new situations and working out quickly what is going on, but you will score high marks for making it easy for them. Ensure that they have a good view of anything you wish them to see and introduce them to anyone important to the story. Have some notes ready giving any relevant name spellings and any suitable background information.

Do not be crushed if:

- Your story appears with a silly or fatuous headline. This is not the journalist's fault. The headlines are created by the sub-editors who design the pages. It is well known that they have a very short attention-span and frequently only glance at the story.
- Your story doesn't appear at all. There's no such thing as a sure-fire news story. Something else may have extra appeal on the day for no obvious reason. It's very arbitrary but that is the nature of editorial work, I'm afraid. Sometimes you receive lots of coverage for a fairly minor story and nothing at all about what you consider to be crucial. Keep trying anyway. This is what makes gaining any editorial coverage so valuable.

Other ways into your local press

There are other routes to good press coverage. If you have strong opinions about local issues, write letters to the editor from your business address, expressing your views. Some newspapers, particularly the weeklies and parish magazines, welcome larger contributions, and especially opinion pieces. In some instances you may even be able to gain a commission to write an advice column. This is an opportunity for you to present authoritatively your particular skill, be it gardening, catering, the law, baby care, fashion, or whatever you do within your business.

Radio

Start listening to your local radio station. Are the people you are trying to reach likely to be regular listeners? If so, what would they listen to? Daytime radio is mainly heard by people in their cars or at home – many of them pensioners, mothers with young children, the unemployed and shift workers. Breakfast and early evening shows have a fairly universal listenership.

By and large, most local stations divide their programmes up into one- or two-hour chunks, interspersed by national and local news. Each section then has its own presenter who will probably make up his or her show from a mixture of music, competitions, interviews and discussions, or they might follow a talk-show format. Some of the larger radio stations have specialist programmes covering business, farming, health, personal finance and legal affairs. This offers local businesses the following opportunities: local news items, discussions which tie in with your business, you acting as an authority to a 'phone in', and the sponsorship of a prize for a competition.

The only way to find out what opportunities there are for you and your business in radio is to check the schedules in your local paper – and *listen to the station*. Get to know the names of the regular presenters and what elements they like to feature in their shows. If you have something that you think will make an interesting item or discussion, write to the presenter of the programme. It will almost certainly be a researcher who opens your letter, but at least you are selecting the appropriate programme for you and your market.

If you are asked to speak on radio, be it in the radio station's studio or at your own premises, the following guidelines may be useful:

- Ask who else will be taking part in the programme or news piece and what the main drive of the story is. Only then decide if you are willing to participate.
- Never agree to speak off the cuff about things you don't really know about. You will almost certainly be caught out and sound silly.
- Know what you want to say. Yes, of course, the interviewer will be asking you questions but remember that you have an opportunity to speak here – not just to him or her, but to all the listeners. Have a very clear idea of what you want to put across.
- Don't try to make what you say into an advert. If you push your company or brand too hard, the station will not use the piece at all and will never ask you to take part again.
- Ask if you are being recorded or going live. If it is a 'prerecord' and you fluff something, you can ask the interviewer for a second try. If it's live and you do 'fluff', don't worry and, if you possibly can, have a sense of humour about your gaff. To the listener you will sound like a real person rather than just slick!
- Ask the interviewer what the first question will be.
- Keep it simple. Speak clearly in short sharp sentences and try not to waffle. If you are trying to explain a complex subject, avoid becoming bogged down in technical terms and pretend (to yourself) that you are explaining to a child.

- Don't forget to breathe. Before the interview starts, practise breathing slowly and deeply. That way you won't squeak when you start to speak.

Television

Television will only be interested in your story if there are strong visual elements that will make a good film. Obviously, you will need to tell the TV station about your news well in advance so that a film crew can be assigned to cover it. Address your press alert to the Forward Planning Desk.

If you receive a call to tell you that a television crew is coming, ensure that there is assigned parking – they have heavy equipment to carry. Make someone responsible for looking after them and introducing them to you and/or to any other key players in the story, and ensure that any relevant background information is available for them.

If you are asked for any reason to go into a television station to be interviewed – for example you may be asked to be an authority on something or comment about a news story – ensure that you know exactly what you are being asked to do. You are entitled to know who will be interviewing you, and who else will be interviewed or taking part in the programme. Only then should you decide whether or not you are willing to take part. You can also ask how long you will be needed for. If you are required to attend early in the morning, late at night or in the local rush hour, ask the station to send a car or arrange a taxi for you – so that if you are late it is their fault, not yours!

For interviews, dress simply. When in doubt don't wear wide stripes, or fabric or ornaments that shine or glitter, or anything bright red. Avoid having an alcoholic drink until after the broadcast – some skins look flushed. Do accept the offer of a powder puff to cut down a shiny face.

If you are seated, ensure that you are comfortable but beware of snuggling into a sofa: the viewer will just see your head and shoulders and it can look odd if you are scrunched up. Jackets tend to ride up and look like a lion's mane. Men should take hold of their jackets at the centre back and pull them downwards.

Again, remember to breathe deeply and evenly: it will relax you. Above all, remember what it is you want to put across and do it with your whole heart.

If you are likely to be called upon regularly to broadcast on either radio or television, media training would be an excellent and very wise investment. At the very least, you will become acquainted with all the technology (how to cope with a phone interview or what's known as 'down-the-line' – that is, from one studio to another – or an outside broadcast).

Trade press

We have the most amazing selection of trade magazines and professional journals in this country. Almost every kind of human activity, work and pleasure, is represented by some kind of specialist press. Whatever you do, the chances are that there is a magazine which represents your 'industry'. There may be value in having coverage in this magazine, if only to tell competitors that you have arrived and are flourishing!

There may also be a trade press which services your potential clients. If you are a farrier, then horse breeding and farming magazines would offer appropriate readerships. If you are a painter or tiler, then the trades read by interior designers would be perfect press targets for you. If you are not sure what your customers read, look in their office reception areas, or around their offices – or ask them.

Most trade and professional magazines are usually monthly or bimonthly; only a few are weekly. Check them out on the Internet, most will have a page listing their forthcoming features. If you have a service or new product that is a natural fit, write in to the features editor and tell them what you do. Use the guidelines for writing a press release and be sure to include your contact numbers. If the magazine is interested, a journalist will contact you for more information. Be sure to tell them if you have good photographs available: trade journals are always short of illustrations. Attach a caption to your photograph and include your name and phone number.

Consumer magazines

In the same way, check out which generally available magazines are read by your potential customers. Take yourself into a major high street newsagent and spend an hour looking at the range of weekly and monthly titles. Take note – or better still, buy a copy – of anything that looks appropriate to you. This might be the local city or county magazine or a specialist title, or one of the many women's magazines. It's usually fairly obvious what age range and income level they are trying to reach. Remember that all require an endless stream of news, but they are also targeted by some of the best press relations professionals in the country. Despite this, when you see pages of news items, or a column, or a regular feature that covers services or products similar to yours, add these titles to your press list.

You may find that the larger local libraries will have a copy of *Willings Press Guide* or *Benn's Media Directory*, which list every publication in the UK, showing the circulation and the target readership for each one. They are well worth a browse.

Exhibiting

Going on show

If you have goods, from craft items to gadgets, or offer certain kinds of services including therapies and consultancies, you may find that there are appropriate annual trade shows which might lead you into all kinds of new business arenas. Local producers and services have made the leap into national and even international markets by meeting the right kind of buyers at the larger shows. This is where buyers are seeking what is new, high quality and innovative. There are often excellent consumer shows too and these will give you a chance to meet potential customers face to face.

It is worth checking out what shows are potentially most appropriate to your business. Attend them, talk to current exhibitors, ask them how valuable the show is to them, whether there is a steady flow of 'buying' visitors and how well attended their stand is over the whole duration of the show. Regional shows can be very profitable, but don't be afraid to consider the major exhibitions. There is only a limited number of exhibitions any one buyer can attend, so they are likely to opt for the major venues.

The organisers will usually have packs of information at one show ready for the following year. Some exhibitors automatically book their stand from one year to the next; you will therefore need to make your decision early if you are to obtain a good site. In making your decision, be aware that the cost of the stand will only represent about half of the actual budget you will need. The rest of your money will be spent on travel and accommodation for the duration of the show, staffing, insurance, lighting and decoration of your stand, giveaways and literature.

One way to decide whether an exhibition is going to be viable is to work out how many orders you will have take to bring you into profit. However, don't just consider the short-term benefits – look ahead.

The importance of a good site

You may not necessarily need a large stand but it is worth paying a little extra for a good position. Ask the organisers for a site plan and consider it very carefully. Traditionally the best sites are *en route* to the coffee bars or restaurants, the conference or lecture rooms, where aisles cross (that is, corner sites), and other areas where there is likely to be a constant flow of visitors.

The poor sites are the ones tucked along a back aisle – however much the exhibition organisers will try to tell you differently! If there is the option, see if you could get onto a group stand or share part of someone else's larger stand. Negotiate hard for the best section.

Local producers and services have made the leap into national and even international markets by meeting the right kind of buyers at the larger shows.

Exhibition wheezes

Publicising your stand
There are lots of ways you can promote your stand, some of which you can do in advance:

- Always fill in the free entry in the catalogue and make your stand and presentation sound attractive, not just a list of products. This is a mini ad, so you can be imaginative.
- Most major exhibitions have a press office. Make sure you have quantities of press releases available and check throughout the show that they are in a prominent position. You might also be able to tuck flyers into dispensers in the lobbies of the hotels where delegates are staying.

- If the organisers are putting together 'goodie bags' for delegates, offer a flyer or brochure. Be sparing with samples, however; keep these for visitors to your stand who look likely to order in the future.
- Some exhibitions, such as the Spring Fair in Birmingham, have a tie-in with a local regional daily newspaper which produces a special show edition. Many trade shows link up with a trade magazine which also does a special exhibition issue. These special issues are usually prepared well in advance, so check early when the editorial deadlines are and supply a press release (and even a photo of your product if that's appropriate) in good time.

Making the stand work for you

Even if your space is tiny, give it some impact. Make it one strong colour or have one bold but simple image. Good lighting will help bring it alive and it is worth the extra money to have a few extra halogens. I recommend that you have a table and at least two chairs: visitors who have been walking around an exhibition for some hours are thrilled at the prospect that, while they talk to you, they can sit down for a few minutes. It is also worth considering having a small fridge and supplies of juice and wine, and a hide-away (under the tablecloth) for coats, bags and packaging.

It is extremely important to have enough people to help you. You will want to spend some time visiting other parts of the exhibition, both for ideas and to meet fellow exhibitors who may be potential clients, customers or associates. You will also need the odd break because exhibition work is very tiring. If you are a woman, take two pairs of shoes with different heel heights to ease the burden of standing for most of the day. This is an old trick taught to me by the girls who demonstrate at the *Daily Mail* Ideal Home Exhibition – and it works!

Make sure that anyone who is helping you either knows enough about your business to deputise properly, or is able to take names, addresses and enquiries competently. You can also ask your helpers to hand out flyers at coffee points.

I strongly recommend that you buy a large book, lots of pens and a glue stick. You can then stick in people's business cards and write extra information and requests alongside as you go along. This is absolutely invaluable after the exhibition when you come to do the essential follow-up. You can also design yourself some enquiry forms.

Scatter them around your stand so that, if you are busy talking to one visitor, another can fill in a form and leave it for you to follow up later.

The work starts afterwards

Attending the exhibition is only half of the work. The really valuable part starts when you return to your desk with your book full of all those business cards and enquiries. Wise exhibitors write within a few days of the event to everyone they met. Sometimes you may not have the information that visitors have asked for: write and tell them that you are in the process of obtaining that information and will contact them again shortly.

It is always fascinating to see who finally places an order. You may never hear again from some of the people who sounded as though they would be absolute certainties, while others, whom you barely registered at the time, become regular clients or customers. Much of it rests on your enthusiastic follow-up.

Become a sponsor

There is yet another way of placing your name, or that of your company, goods or service in front of potential customers. Sponsorship is not just the preserve of rich corporations underwriting motor racing and arts events. And you are not just giving your money away; sponsorship is different from donation. If you give an amount as a donor, you do not expect a return. With sponsorship, however, you can expect some form of promotional advantage. It can be an excellent way of gaining both advertising space and sometimes free editorial as well.

The art of effective sponsorship is to find something that is complementary to your business and that puts your name in an appropriate way in front of potential new customers. All kinds of organisations, events and individuals are seeking sponsorship. These might include charities, churches or schools, associations or clubs, or special events (usually related to endurance or athletic prowess). Most seek either an overall sponsor – in which case the whole event will bear the sponsor's name – or break down their requirements and seek lots of smaller sponsors.

You might consider a part-sponsorship initially to see how useful a marketing opportunity it is for you, either in terms of awareness-raising or new business.

Let's consider some examples:

- A hairdresser might support a charity fashion show, throwing in hairdos for the models and a raffle prize of a session at his/her salon.
- If you run a bookshop or stall, you might consider giving a book prize to the local technical college.
- An insurance agent might consider supporting a charity adventure event such as climbing Kilimanjaro.
- A cheese-maker or creamery might sponsor a major cookery demonstration and ask for a sampling opportunity or discount vouchers to be given out at the same time.
- If you repair or sell cars, you might sponsor a cup at a charity car rally.

If you decide that sponsorship is an avenue worth exploring, don't be afraid to ask for your name to be used prominently. If there is the right opportunity, ask if you can also display a banner, poster or flag with your name on it. Be prepared to hang it yourself (and take it away afterwards).

If there are programmes for the event, confirm that your contribution will be acknowledged and also ask if you might have free advertising space. Supply the words yourself. It would probably be appropriate to wish the sponsored organisation or individual good luck in their endeavour. Don't forget to mention what you and your business do at the same time. Remember, this is a form of advertising. You are still after clients and customers.

Your launch

Start as you mean to go on and, if you can possibly afford it, give yourself a launch party. You can make it a very personal celebration of this new chapter in your life or you can go for a high-profile promotional affair. Either way, make it a notable occasion. This is a rite of passage in life, just as much as gaining a degree or getting married. It is a major change and you should celebrate it properly. If you do nothing else, tie a bow on the dog's collar and invite some friends around to share a very nice bottle of wine. But you could – and probably should – do more.

There are all kinds of people who are important to your success: your new accountant, bank manager, landlord (if you are in an office space), first clients or customers, the support team (family and friends), associates and suppliers. If you have a shop, treatment rooms, workshop or gallery, go and fish out the Christmas lights and buy lots of balloons. Invite anyone you think might add to your business now and in the future. You don't have to be lavish or even particularly imaginative; unless of course you are involved in catering, glasses of wine and some pretzels will be perfectly acceptable.

If it is appropriate, put up an exhibition of what you do or give a demonstration, and have a special launch offer or a discount.

Whatever the format, have a quantity of price lists – with your name and phone number(s) emblazoned at the top – or lots of business cards available for everyone to take away.

If you have never organised an event before and feel nervous or unprepared, act out being a guest. When I am a guest, I like to know the following: how to get to the event, where to hang up my coat when I arrive, where I can put a wet umbrella, and how to find the ladies' loo. I would like to be greeted by my host/hostess, be given a drink and introduced to someone I might like to talk to. This tells you, the organiser, to have a map or travel instructions on your invitations, place a coat rack and a wastebin (for the wet brollies) near to the door, put a sign on the loos, and be ready to meet, greet and mingle. Think of it as looking after people, just as you would if they were coming to your home.

Always recruit lots of chums or trusted family members (probably not small children or teenagers unless they are very responsible) to hand around the wine and nibbles, and later to help remove glasses and empty ashtrays. If you plan to have music, be courteous and warn any neighbours. Better still, invite them!

Your launch is a rite of passage in life, just as much as gaining a degree or getting married. It is a major change and you should celebrate it properly.

The bigger event

Some kinds of businesses lend themselves to an even splashier launch. If you are starting a high street business in a small town, for example, and want everyone to know about it, you can let your imagination rip . . . at least to the extent of your chosen budget. You may opt for sandwich-board men or clowns giving hand-outs to passers-by. On a big budget, how about a hot air balloon or a bus, dray horses or a vintage car hired for the day and decorated with flags and banners? Be sure to tell the local press; some of these ideas also offer good photo opportunities.

Alternatively, if you are a solicitor or accountant, you might prefer to give a rather smart lunch party in a good local restaurant or golf clubhouse for local opinion-formers and businessmen – or 'bigwigs' as we used to call them.

However you decide to launch yourself, do it with panache and have fun at the same time!

Things to do

- Research your local media and decide what your target audiences are most likely to read, listen to and watch.
- Be alert for any news stories about your business which may appeal to your local media.
- If you prepare a press release, do it quickly – because old news is no news.
- Keep the news-alert simple but have background information ready.
- See if you can become a local expert and have articles or columns in your local magazines and newspapers, or even on local radio.
- If you are considering taking part in major exhibitions, do your research first; then gain the best possible site for your stand.
- Publicise your stand, have lots of well-briefed helpers and follow up every sales lead afterwards.
- Consider becoming a sponsor but make sure that your name and message are displayed prominently.
- Make a splash, big or small, to launch your new business – and enjoy it!

Peter Fox

'Despite it all, it is very satisfying to know that the money I earn is mine. If it's sometimes worrying being on your own, it is also exciting.'

Peter Fox has run his own car service and repair business, PEC Mobile, in central Birmingham since 1983.

I was employed for nine years in the motor trade. I have always been grateful to my employer for giving me an opportunity to learn the business because I had few paper qualifications when he took me on. But in the 1970s the recession bit hard and I was on short-time. Someone I had grown up and worked with approached me to help him start his own business, so I handed in my notice and went into partnership with him. It worked well at first but, like so many partnerships, it became more and more difficult. I was an equal partner and I had put money into the business, but when my friend's marriage broke up his involvement became far less. We had two options: to split the business, or for one of us to buy the other out. We had premises – a good workshop – and customers. So, although I had a mortgage, bills and a two year-old son, I agreed to be the purchaser. I had had enough of working my socks off for other people, and I had a good client base of my own.

It was very tough at first, not least because I inherited my former partner's debts. For instance, I had no idea that he hadn't been paying our National Insurance contributions. My mother, who was the secretary for a small transport company, helped me sort things out. I arranged an interview with the DHSS and they proved very efficient. They worked out how I could repay the outstanding contributions over a period of a year so it wouldn't affect my pension in the long term. Although I am glad now that I did that, it made the beginning even harder.

It took two or three years to pull it round. My wife, Liz, returned to her career in a bank which also helped to even out the finances. But there were plenty of other problems along the way. I had a landlord who went bankrupt, then a fire next door to my workshop which set me back for a time.

I have never advertised, although I once sponsored the strip for my son's under-14 football team. My company name appeared on first and reserve team shirts and there were several enquiries from the other fathers after each match. But almost all of my work comes through word of mouth. People phone all the time, recommended to me by established customers. I have had some of my customers since I started on my own. This means they must be satisfied with the quality of the work and the service I give.

I always try to be fair. I will contact a customer if I find something seriously wrong with their car but I never do work that is unnecessary. However, I will put a report on the bottom of the customer's invoice telling them about any work they may need doing at some future stage – for instance, that they will need new brake pads when their mileage reaches a particular level.

Right now the business is flourishing but I would worry about employing other people. My work is of a high standard but employees may not have the same pride in what they do or the same commitment. At the end of the day, any unsafe or shoddy work would be my responsibility, not theirs. I would spend all my time checking what they do. I don't want that.

Despite it all, it is very satisfying to know that the money I earn is mine. If it's sometimes worrying being on your own, it is also exciting. I think of myself as an entrepreneur. I don't move mountains but I don't rely on anyone else – and I do this because I want to do it.

Peter's advice:

Some partnerships work well but they are few and far between. For me, it was a real learning curve! I would urge anyone considering a partnership to think very carefully. If possible, consider ways to go on your own from the start.

Learn to present yourself properly and speak with authority. Always explain things in laymen's terms so your customers will really understand and have confidence in what you can do for them. Be genuine and honest: people quickly 'suss' if you are trying to pull the wool over their eyes.

You have to be prepared to graft and put in the hours. I frequently work late but I always take my holidays. You don't drive a car in top gear all the time; the engine wouldn't cope with the pressure and would simply stop!

althea Wilson

'I have always believed firmly in promotion and, through friends, have met journalists and editors. The result has been spreads in international interior design magazines and colour supplements.'

Althea Wilson is an artist, designer and ceramic maker living in Chelsea, London.

I grew up in Nigeria and, although I went to school in England, considered Africa my home. I realised when I was 11 that I wanted to be a painter and I had my first exhibition in a Lagos gallery, sponsored by the Nigerian Arts Council, when I was 16. But my father felt that art did not constitute a career and so reluctantly I took a secretarial course.

I worked as a PA in various embassies in Lagos. The hours – from 8.00 a.m. to 2.00 p.m. – meant that I could paint in the afternoons and soon the paintings were selling before they were dry.

In 1974, I came to England with no money and no career. I found a job as a telephonist through an agency but after two hours knew I had to leave. I knew about antiques so, to learn about the trade side, I took a cleaning job in an antiques shop in Hampshire. Then I rented half a shop, doing odd jobs for friends and relatives in order to buy stock. I briefly became a buyer for a pine and antiques business where part of my salary was a pick of the antiques at buying-in prices. Six months later I sold my house and opened my own shop in Alresford – famous for its antiques shops – and the following year, I doubled the space by buying the adjacent shop.

I spent the next 12 years there but towards the end started painting again. It was hard; I had lost my techniques. I rented the shop out and spent time practising and re-building my skills. Then I started doing special finishes and effects. In 1984 a friend found a property for me in Chelsea. I loved it and completely renovated it. My motto is 'don't pay someone to do what you can do yourself', so I did the demolition work. It became not only my home but a showroom, gallery and studio workshop too. I started to create lifestyle designs, painting not just the picture but the frame, the walls, the ceilings, the tiles, the fabrics and upholstery. At the same time I took contract work such as restoring antique painted furniture for Lord Rendlesham's antiques business.

Gradually, I gained really exciting commissions, such as designing wallpapers for a prestigious French company, Nobilis, and I was still doing murals and designing fabric. The paintings continued to sell and I had several exhibitions in Cork Street. Commissions took me to the USA, the Caribbean and Italy and I won a prize to design a collection of tableware for Shiseido in Japan. Sometimes they were for work in private homes; in other instances they were corporate projects.

I also wrote two books, *Paintworks* and *Stencil Genius*. Both sold well but did not make huge amounts of money. What they did achieve was to give me a pedigree, and potential clients the confidence to commission my work.

Some years ago I took pottery lessons – something I had been promising myself I would do. I had always loved Michael Cardew's work and some of the African pots I was brought up with. Now I have invested in my own kiln and I produce 'couture' ceramics. Some pieces have been cast in bronze to make sculptural wash basins and fire baskets. This is where my main interest lies at the moment, although I am planning another book. I also work for interior designers as a colour, furniture and design consultant.

Like most people, I don't enjoy some forms of selling. When it comes to cold calling, I find it difficult to sell my own work. I have always believed firmly in promotion and, through friends, have met journalists and editors. The result has been spreads in international interior design magazines and colour supplements. I have also taken part in several television programmes about designing your home.

My other main selling method is to hold exhibitions, either in my own home or someone else's, networking along the way. I held an exhibition a few years ago in the Kensington home of the French fashion designer, Roland Klein.

Since childhood I have been training for the career I have now. Everything I have done has been linked to a style of living and interior design.

Althea's advice:

People cannot buy if they don't know you are there. I will consider any PR or promotion that is offered. Grab any chance for publicising what you do. Sometimes your efforts won't bring you work immediately, but it all adds to building awareness of your business. I recently had an offer of work from the USA because people had seen my first book – and yet it was published in 1988. It's still having an impact!

I learned my PR skills from the Yoruba, one of the three largest tribes in Nigeria. They believe in show. They will have a Mercedes but live in a hovel. If you look successful, people will assume you are a success and will buy into that. Act successful, and you probably will be.

6

networking

*Who do you know? – who do they know? – painting
with a broader brush – join where there might be
new business – your trade or professional association
– breakfast clubs & networking clubs – events –
create your own event – good networking manners –
Sharon's tip – cards – passing the favours on –
keeping track*

There's a famous old-fashioned saying that to be successful, it's not
what you know but who you know. The reason it has lasted so well
is because there is a nub of truth in it. Your marketing plan, advertising, PR and promotion should be assisting you to enhance your
reputation and to bring in business prospects, but there is another
tried and tested way to increase your business: 'networking', or
making contacts. This can be the life blood of the independent lifestyle and, for many people, it's very pleasurable. At the same time
as providing new work for you, good networks will also bring you
potential associates, interesting new suppliers and fresh ideas.
Hopefully, some of these new contacts will become friends and
acquaintances as well.

Nowadays, some people make a career out of networking. These
professional networkers are approached by large companies or
organisations who commission them to seek out certain influential
people or groups. A big company may wish to meet opinion-
formers, politicians or even celebrities who can help them in some
sphere of their activities. The networker makes the links with the
right people and arranges the introductions.

Who do you know?

You might be surprised by how many people you know already. Your Christmas card list will give you a starting point, but during our lives we make many more contacts than that. It is quite revealing to write a list of all the people you know and meet more than twice a year: relatives, neighbours and friends, old school and college mates, former colleagues, former bosses, other members of the clubs and associations you belong to, people you play sport with, people you drink with at the pub (not to mention the landlord), people who service your car, your hairdresser, newsagent and dry cleaner.

Who do *they* know?

Everyone on your list knows at least 50 more people whom you do not: these include their neighbours and friends, former school mates, colleagues, bosses, and so on. Among their contacts are people that you may like to meet.

Don't forget your suppliers. Who else do they supply? Would any of their customers make customers or clients for you? If you are in a workspace outside your home, don't forget to check who else has space in the same building and the immediate locality. Some may be businesses that are complementary to yours. Call in and introduce yourself. Wave every time you pass. Chat to everyone at the reception point.

People rarely volunteer to make introductions, not because they are being mean-spirited but because they are busy and it simply does not occur to them. If you were to tell them exactly what you are doing and ask them directly who they know and who might be interested – as potential customers or suppliers – you might well be astonished at the people they suggest.

If they are well acquainted with someone you would like to know, why not ask if they would fix up a casual meeting or a drink so you can meet them? Or, if appropriate, ask for the contact's phone number with view to calling them direct. Don't forget to confirm that you can use your friend's name by way of an introduction.

Painting with a broader brush

Your sports or social club is no longer just somewhere you work out or have fun; it has now become a networking opportunity! One interior designer I know gains all her new business through her gym. She simply mentions what she does to the other women in the changing room or while she is pedalling away on a bike, and before long someone is sure to seek her advice and then ask to see her portfolio. In a not dissimilar way, quite a number of orthopaedic surgeons build their private practices – all those hip and knee replacements – from the fellow players they meet on the golf green.

Your church, golf or yacht club, darts or football team, political association, Masonic lodge, reading circle, women's group or even the local adult education centre are all places where you can mix and mingle, not to mention the local pub or wine bar.

Join where there might be new business

You may not be a natural 'joiner'. Often, the kind of people who opt for an independent lifestyle are not. But in the interests of your new enterprise, it could be enormously valuable to join appropriate kinds of groups, purely in terms of networking. It may be a hedge against the isolation of working alone too. Get involved. Don't just join the organisation; in due course, perhaps you could volunteer for the committee as well. This extends the opportunity for really getting to know other members in a relatively short time.

Chambers of commerce are excellent places to network for new business – and in fact the people who attend their regular events would be very surprised if you didn't! You might also like to consider the British Lions, Rotary International, the Royal Order of Buffaloes, Ladies' Circles and so forth. These not only introduce you to influential people in your area but also have the added bonus of working for local charities at the same time.

If you are a sports injury therapist, it makes sense to join a major gym and become a 'friend' of the local football association. If you are a photographer specialising in family portraits, you should certainly join your children's parent-teacher association. Picture framers might want to belong to local arts clubs or take soft furnishing classes.

Try to pick something that you will actually be interested in. Consider the local history society, walking clubs, local action committees, the parish council, residents' associations, and luncheon clubs such as Probus or Soroptimist International.

Your trade or professional association

Local branches of your own trade and professional organisations may not sound like obvious stomping grounds for new business, but they can have other advantages for you, such as:

- informing you about the latest regulations and trends
- helping you to become known within your own trade or profession
- confirming what other people charge, and where and how they promote their businesses
- introducing you to potential associates for that rare but wonderful occasion when you are offered a job too large for you to handle on your own – or to someone who can act as a 'locum' should you be sick or on holiday when an urgent piece of work suddenly comes in
- possibly linking you up so you can benefit from recommendations by other independents and small companies when they have an overload
- enabling you to check the creditworthiness or the reputations for quality of local suppliers

There are few disadvantages to belonging and attending meetings and events. Many associations have their own codes of practice and advice channels which could also prove useful to you. At the very least, you may pick up some good wheezes and make some valuable friends as well.

Breakfast clubs & networking clubs

Recently there has been a boom in clubs that are specifically designed for networking. One or two are national networks – or plan to be. Some are breakfast clubs, which may or may not suit you; some are just for women; others are for small businesses. Many try to attract just one person from each area of business, so you don't wind up with a glut of solicitors or publicists. And most have a fee which is about the same or even less than the membership of a decent health club, so joining may be well worth the investment. After all, you would only need a few bits of business to cover your outlay.

Events

You can also seek out events and exhibitions where new business contacts might lurk. Here are some possibilities:

dinner and drinks parties
county shows
gallery previews and opening nights
trade exhibitions
journeys on trains, planes and long-distance coaches
church fêtes and village fayres
charity events

professional & trade conferences
Christmas bazaars
annual dinners (sports and social clubs)
holiday (or business stay) hotels
your clients' events
any open day or event held by your suppliers

You can probably identify many more events. Look yet again at your target groups: where might they go both on business and for fun? Can you go too?

Create your own event

Much along the same lines as we discussed for your launch, there is nothing to prevent you from holding your own events for relationship-building. The phenomenal networker Carole Stone has for several years now held a weekly 'salon'. For more than ten years Carole was producer of BBC Radio 4's flagship current affairs discussion programme, *Any Questions?*. It was there she learned the skills of putting very different people together to bring out the best in all of them.

When she left the BBC, Carole decided she would try to keep in touch with some of the interesting people she had met by inviting them to one of the simple salad lunches she organised twice-weekly at her flat. They came, they enjoyed it, and then one of her guests asked if Carole could organise lunches like that for his company, on a professional basis. Soon Carole found herself with a networking business, putting together journalists, politicians, people from 'think tanks' and senior business people to discuss issues of common concern. She now has 21,000 friends and business contacts on her database.

These days Carole's annual Christmas party is legendary, with around 1300 guests gathering together (a 'salon' on a grand scale) in central London. Many of the faces there are well known: newscasters, radio and television journalists, editors of national newspapers, MPs and government ministers, academics and captains of industry. Some guests are involved with the charities Carole supports, and others will be members of her family, or just friends. The noise level is high as everyone follows the order of the day, which is to meet and talk to as many people as possible.

Carole's philosophy is as follows: 'Making friends is a continuous business, whatever your age and situation in life. There are always people out there who will be glad of a chance to get to know you and who in turn will enrich your life. When you are shy and socially awkward, it's difficult to imagine that anyone else can feel the same – that they can be just as insecure inside as you are. You may think that they can't have any need of you or your friendship. My experience is that they do. We all need each other if we are to make the best of our lives.'

Carole's bulging contacts book (actually now an electronic database which she carries with her on a little personal computer) is the result of hard work: keeping track of the people she meets and makes friends with. Her advice is:

- Whatever the occasion, always be ready to make a friend.
- The best way to make a friend is to take an interest in other people.
- Don't be possessive – share your friends with other friends.
- Keep your friendships in good repair – nurture your network.
- Accept your friends for what they are – nobody's perfect!
- Network your friends – and watch them benefit from it.

You can read more of Carole's advice in her book, *Networking – The Art of Making Friends* (Vermilion, 2001).

Good networking manners

Because you have such a strong incentive to make new contacts, you will find that, with practice, you too can overcome your shyness or reservations about speaking to people you do not know well. Even so, it's quite obvious that you cannot march up to strangers and announce that you are a consultant/plumber/ health professional and you are looking for new work. People would be embarrassed and no-one wants to feel under pressure or used. So all networking opportunities are about making new acquaintances who *may* at some stage – who knows? – become customers or clients, or who may recommend you to others. In the meantime, enjoy them as interesting people and potential friends. That makes for a comfortable and mutual flow of information when you meet.

You are not necessarily required to be very good at small talk, but be aware that most people adore the opportunity to talk about themselves. If you put a few key questions to them, away they go! And given half a chance, they will tell you the most amazing things about themselves. I believe that we should develop skills in how to listen and be empathic, rather than trying to make empty party chatter.

Of course, part of the exercise is to remember who it is you have met and what they do. We have all had the experience of being introduced to someone and not catching – or rather, not retaining – their name. Somehow you just don't hear it. Make a real point of listening out for the name of anyone you meet and make a mental note of what they do. It's so flattering when someone you have met only once before greets you by name and remembers details about your life or interests.

Sharon's tip

If you sometimes blank out someone's name, you can expect that they will also do the same when they meet you. The other half of the networking task is to ensure that people remember who *you* are, and what *you* do. Sharon Levinson's advice is therefore partic- ularly useful to the budding networker.

Sharon is a casting director for television and films, and she is currently working for *Spotlight*, the famous casting directory for actors and directors. She meets literally thousands of established and aspiring actors over the period of a year. She finds that a large majority of them expect her to remember their names and acting pedigree, simply because they were once introduced to her or have sent her their career histories. 'I remember the most outstanding, of course, but to remember everyone is a very tall order,' she says.

Sharon suggests that you follow the examples of actors like Dame Judi Dench who, despite being so well known, never assume that you will remember who they are. They make a point of repeating their names whenever you meet them ('Hello, I'm Judi Dench. We've met before . . .'), so you are not in that awful 'I know the face but . . . ' syndrome.

The late Sir John Gielgud did the same, as do many politicians, including Bill Clinton, the former US President. This is very sensible, because it helps people learn your name at the same time as giving you a chance to remind them what you do.

Cards

Be sure to have a supply of business cards in your sports bag, your jacket pockets and handbags, and in your car as well as in your briefcase. Don't push them onto people, but you can always ask if they would like to keep in touch. As important, ask for their card or contact numbers. As soon as possible afterwards, scribble notes on the back of the cards for future reference. You might jot down where and how you met, or the name of the person you met through, the kind of work they do, anyone they mentioned that you would like to know, and anything you may have promised to do.

Passing the favours on

In the firm belief that whatever you put out in life in one direction, comes back to you from another, why not build a reputation as an information broker? Be the person who knows where to find the really useful things: supplies, emergency plumbers, the best take-away services, the best-value stationers, and so on. It gives people the chance to contact you.

Always repeat good news and *never* fail to pass on potential business leads if you cannot use them yourself. This is so important. It is what you are hoping others will do for you. Start the ball rolling . . .

Keeping track

Start some kind of filing system for the contacts you are making. Most address books will not be big enough, but you can convert a scrapbook or keep a card index or use an electronic address system. If you choose the latter, be sure to back it up: losing years of carefully gathered contacts into the ether doesn't bear thinking about. Whatever system you use, make an effort to keep it up-to-date. It should be a highly valuable, self-assembled and personalised marketing tool.

If you meet someone that you think might be very important to you, consider dropping them a little note saying how much you enjoyed meeting them and asking if they might be available for a drink or even lunch. Then phone after a few days. Send them details of what you do only if it is appropriate. It might take a couple of contacts with them before you can be so bold as to make a business move or sales pitch.

Always repeat good news and never fail to pass on potential business leads if you cannot use them yourself. This is so important. It is what you are hoping others will do for you.

networks for marketing

Your contacts system is very important both to your ongoing marketing campaign, and also when you decide to do a new business push. The system can form the basis of a mailing list or the starting point for a major phone-round. You should certainly go through each and every listing when you are making up your business Christmas (or Jewish New Year or other festivals') card list.

These are the people you should invite to any party or open day you are holding and workshop or demonstration you are giving. You may like to consider some of them for an e-newsletter or regular update. If you know them well, add a little handwritten note saying that you thought they might be interested to know why you are so busy at the moment, but intend to call them soon about a quiet drink.

If marketing has never before been part of your remit, you may feel daunted at first. If at all possible, attend a workshop or an evening course in marketing and selling: it might help you avoid expensive mistakes. Learn everything you can about the basics of the subject and then gradually build up your programme so it works well for you. As you go along you will probably refine your plans again and again, expand them, and – as you see what works for your business – become braver. After a while it becomes second-nature to see the opportunities for new business and networking.

Things to do

- Start making a master list of everyone you know who might be able to help you in your new business, or who may know others you would like to meet.
- Create an electronic and/or hard copy filing system for your contacts.
- Look at opportunities to meet or mail your contacts singly or in groups.
- Consider where you might meet new contacts in the area(s) appropriate to you.
- Bite the bullet and join clubs and organisations where potential new clients might also be members.
- Consider one of the new business networking clubs.
- Always carry your cards.
- Lighten up and enjoy meeting new people.

Jack Jewers

'The art is to believe in yourself. That's the most important thing.'

Jack Jewers is a film director, currently based in London.

Someone lent me a video camera to make my first film. I still have the film: it has a proper story and all my friends were in it. I was six. By 12, I knew I wanted to direct rather than produce. That may sound precocious but both my parents were actors, so it didn't seem strange.

In the midst of taking my A levels I made a 'short', called *Future Imperfect*. I used a directory to find the right people – camera, sound, editing and so on – and I contacted them to ask if they would participate. I didn't have any money; it was all on a wing and a prayer! I worked on the principle that people could only say no – but that some would say yes. It became a half-hour film which went to the small festivals and helped me get into the film and television course at the University of Wales.

That was where I learned the theory and also the craft side of directing. You must be technically skilled, not just motivated. The people there were amazing: John Hefin, former head of drama for BBC Wales, was particularly encouraging. One of the films I made won the Royal Television Society Student Award. It was a short documentary about the discovery of a three-hour feature film, made in black and white in 1918, about the Prime Minister, David Lloyd George. This film was suppressed by the government of the time and went missing for 75 years before turning up in the tool shed of Lloyd George's grandson, Lord Tenby.

I also made a ten-minute film for the Welsh Film Archive about their activities, which went on limited cinema release. I felt that this piece must be both lyrical and creative, so I interviewed actors and directors about what mattered to them.

In my final year I made short films mainly on location. Kodak, which has a genuinely progressive attitude to training, sponsored me and VFG Hire Company lent me equipment for free. The whole project came under threat from Foot and Mouth Disease, then rampant, but I managed to gain special dispensation from the Home Office to film on some Forestry Commission property. Even so, we had to disinfect everyone and everything, including a tank, that come onto or left the site! The film's story – which is true – was about a group of Allied soldiers stranded on the Russian border in World War II. They worked their passage home doing all kinds of odd jobs, including putting up advertising hoardings. The film, *Storm*, was previewed at BAFTA (British Academy of Film and Television Arts) in London. I asked everyone I knew and some I didn't, to the preview. I expected 50 or so, but 250 came, including someone who has since become my agent. And I am very proud that the film won a BAFTA nomination for the Best Short Film (Wales).

I then took myself off to the Cannes Film Festival, just to see what it was really like, and to network. I had a couple of contacts but no official pass. Somehow that didn't matter and I was invited to a few of the parties. The whole scene was surreal – glamorous but cynical – but I met a number of people that I have stayed in touch with, including one mad young producer, hungry but hugely talented, with whom I am now co-writing.

I keep in contact with the heads of development in film companies – even if I have nothing to offer at the moment – and various producers. Few people mind being approached because they all want to know where the new talent is! I've a number of projects under development and I am not sure which will take the lead. I'm due to start work on my first feature film soon, and I've been working on both a short and a documentary film series. I'm also co-writing another film. The art is to believe in yourself. That's the most important thing.

Jack's advice:

People can be wonderfully supportive if you approach them for help in the right way. I am always completely honest about what I have to offer and brazenly point out that potential such as mine is well worth supporting!

You must be prepared to put everything into what you do – no half measures. If you don't have the courage of your convictions, and don't project an image of success and commitment, how can anyone else take you seriously and 'buy' into whatever it is that you do? At the same time, when you are young, you will put up with almost anything to get a start. People may well then take advantage. You must know where to draw the line. After all, you are the professional.

Miti Ampoma

'I once pitched via an agency for a large European project and later found I'd been paid a tiny fraction of the overall fee. It taught me not to work through other people but to do the work direct.'

Miti Ampoma is a journalist and public relations consultant, based in North West London.

I was born in Ghana. My father was an educationalist and diplomat. He greatly respected English education and so sent all his children to private schools here. At 11, I went to Edgehill College in Bideford, Devon, a staunchly Methodist school. I wasn't impressed initially: it was so cold! I had chilblains for years.

When I was 16 my father suffered a heart attack and funds became stretched. Very lonely, I obtained a grant and took my A levels at Tottenham Technical College, which at the time was awash with racism, something I hadn't met before. I realised that I could either become deeply upset, or find a way of managing it. I wept for a while but, as I needed the qualifications, decided to make things happen for myself.

Afterwards I went to Kent University to study politics and international relations, and followed on with postgraduate studies in journalism at City University. I won the LBC Radio Award for the Best Radio Documentary while I was there. It was about bulimia, unheard of then. It took me to the BBC Radio News Room, where I wrote news bulletins for Radios 2, 3 and 4. Later I became a reporter for Radio Sussex.

I wrote hundreds of letters trying to get into television. Then I saw a documentary about the relationship between Africa and the UK. I wrote about how I would improve the programme to the executive producer, Bill Greaves, marking the envelope 'personal and private' so he saw it himself. He had just become Head of BBC North England and he invited me to Leeds, and offered me a job on the arts programme.

After a short stint as a political researcher for Lord Bethell, then as head of an All Party Committee on the Cyprus question, I was headhunted for TV South (now Meridian). I went through the ranks, covering news, current affairs, 24-hour marathons and even religious programmes. LWT then asked me to work for them. Breakfast television was in its infancy and I was offered a job as a producer, but suddenly my father died. I therefore returned to Ghana for a while.

On returning, I became Head of PR at Surrey University. I enjoyed creating a national profile for them but I was aware that higher education was not my ultimate goal. I travelled for a time, then temped, but I finally went back into TV as a freelance, producing everything from *Dispatches, Kilroy, Without Walls*, the *No. 10 Show* and *Channel 4 News*.

Television was playing safe, only commissioning the tried and tested. I felt that I was unlikely to realise my full potential in this environment, so bit the bullet and set up on my own as a PR and communications consultant. I thought that not only could I make a good income, but also have immense fun as well. Through my networks, I heard that the British Council was looking for PR support: I went along for a discussion and came away with my first client! Then I added Eutelsat, Europe's largest satellite operator and I've had contracts with Railtrack, First National, the BBC, Westminster City Council and Halifax Bank of Scotland Financial Services.

If you're an independent consultant, you have to be a cut above the rest. Often the big agencies gain work simply because they are well-known; they then put junior staff onto the account and wonder why the clients don't stay with them.

What clients really need is a customised programme, not some tired old formula. Having worked as a print and broadcast journalist, I have a real understanding of how UK media works, and how to put together successful stories. There's a lot of waffle and pontificating in public relations these days. I enjoy cutting through all that and making it work.

I was very green to start off with. One client tried to halve the agreed fee after I had started work. I needed the job but felt so resentful that I wrote and said 'thanks but no thanks' at being railroaded. My fee was reinstated. I once pitched via an agency for a large European project and later found I'd been paid a tiny fraction of the overall fee. It taught me not to work through other people but to do the work direct.

Miti's advice:

Make sure that the client sees your worth immediately. Be sure that you are happy with the client, and that each party understands the boundaries and scope of your job.

If there's work you cannot handle, be generous, pass it on. There's plenty for all of us. Entrepreneurs like us are a breed who thrive on hitting the ground running. So let's all enjoy it!

7

The Production Department

*Motivation – starting the engine – time-wasters –
good practice – TCB (Typical Client Behaviour) – 'make
it purple' – feast . . . or famine – the big project –
the ability to let go – keep your eye on the business,
not just the work – don't put all your eggs – stay
flexible – have a fall-back – mix and match*

You have made the decision, done your research, drafted out a
marketing plan, sketched out a publicity drive, and made your first
decisions about budgeting and finance. You may even have your
first clients or customers within sight. Whoopee, you are on your
way. Time to ease up a little? Of course not. You have to put it all
into daily practice, and that's yet another challenge.

Motivation

This is not a problem I have ever faced. There's something about
that big, shaggy grey wolf sitting at my front door, his nose in the
air, howling and keening, which raises the hairs on my arms. He
certainly ensures that I am motivated! Bills that have turned red
and inflamed are another very good incentive for rolling up the
sleeves.

However, some people really do find it difficult getting started in
the mornings when there is no boss wagging a finger if they are late.
One playwright I met many years ago would do almost anything
rather than get down to work on a script. Although he was properly
commissioned and had a firm and impending deadline, he threw up
every kind of work evasion strategy. London was too distracting,
with too many friends, previews and parties, so he moved to a farmhouse in deep countryside in the region where his story was set.
Unfortunately, from the study windows he could see the postman,
horse riders, cows on their way to be milked, ramblers and the local

busybody, all so very distracting. He therefore moved into a caravan at the end of the garden. But then he could see the leaves growing, caterpillars and birds, and the change of light as the sun moved through the sky. In desperation, he painted the windows white. Then each morning, he would go into his little white office, read the instructions on back of the fire extinguisher a couple of times, and finally sit down to write. He eventually won a television award for his play.

Another writer, this time of children's books, admits that she uses displacement activities before getting down to work. She reads the newspaper *and* all the supplements, then vacuums, dusts and tidies, and makes coffee until guilt drives her to her desk.

'The fear of getting started is the fear of having nothing to say, of drying up, of failure, maybe of being found out, that you have no real talent,' explains counselling psychologist Nick Gundry. 'Motivation and self-esteem are closely linked. At its most acute, some people can have this feeling that they are safer working on their own where is no-one watching them. At the same time, they are testing themselves to see whether they are good enough and strong enough to make the whole thing work. Self-esteem is boosted by getting it right, being punctual, making the deadline, and so being in control,' he continues.

Doing what you are good at and fascinated by is also a spur to motivation. I have been fortunate in my journalistic career to interview people who have been at the peak of their careers, at the very top of their chosen spheres. These included the Formula One driver who subsequently owned his own airline, an American film and cabaret singer, several internationally renowned novelists, a famous war correspondent and the highly academic wife of a notorious Tory peer. Their backgrounds and interests could not have been more different. Yet, there were strong similarities. The two common threads were their focus and their unstinting energy. Each and every one of them was interested in their subject to the point of passion. They gave their careers 110 per cent of their attention and were completely tunnel-visioned, brooking no diversions. By and large, they were all perfectionists and would go to infinite lengths to get something absolutely right. There were no half or even three-quarter measures.

Now, in some cases, this mega-interest meant that they were not good friend material, and made even worse marriage partners or parents. Most of them had two or three marriages behind them. Everything was sacrificed to their talent and progress.

Because of their intense involvement, they had all become very successful. And almost as a by-product of that, they had all become rich as well – yet quite clearly not one of them had ever sat down and thought 'How do I become rich?' There was a natural flow: super-interest, the strongest motivation, driving energy, success and finally, wealth and recognition.

This is not to make a case for workaholism or perfectionism, and certainly not to that extent. It's simply that I believe firmly that you must do something in life that you are truly interested in. Life is too short to spend hours doing something that bores you or that you actively dislike. By going on your own, you have the opportunity to angle for the work or projects that most interest you. If you are fascinated enough in whatever it is, you will become good at it and therefore success and good fortune will follow.

Starting the engine

If getting started each day is a battle, you must create devices and routines to help you. Various friends and associates have offered the following accumulated advice:

- If you work at home, be sure to get dressed properly in the morning. You don't need to be wearing a suit, but do not slop about in baggy sweaters and slippers. Be in role, as if someone might knock on your office door at any moment.
- Have distinct working times, as if you were in a formal office – even if you are a part-timer. More important, keep to those hours! Be on time every day.
- Kick-start the day by making your appointments first thing.
- If you work at home, have a designated working area, preferably one with a door that you can close on the rest of the house. If you have a young family, encourage them to understand that your office is not an extension of their play area. This is *your* space and it's where you do important work. There should be no toys or domestic items in your work area.
- If possible, keep your computer solely for your work, and don't make it available to the rest of the family for their computer games and Internet usage. Don't put *your* computer games on

your computer either, not even for the occasional, necessary break from duty. Not only might you never get back to work, but you also risk losing information that's important to your business, since games can use up a lot of your computer's memory.

- Make your working area attractive with pictures, photos or plants. Ensure that it is warm but with a good air flow. Have a comfortable ergonomic chair, good clear lighting and proper trays for paperwork. You may well spend many hours in this place so it must be conducive to constructive thought, planning and work. The same applies if you have a studio or workshop: plan it so that it is easy to work in. Have plenty of light where you need it most, and your working gear laid out neatly, with the things you use frequently in the most accessible positions. Wherever you work have a decent coffee-maker and attractive cups and mugs. Keep a supply of good quality coffee and teas and, if you lunch in your workspace, a mini fridge. Make it an executive dining space, not a canteen.

- If possible, have two phone numbers if you work from home: one for business (calls, fax and email) and another for personal use. (Maybe one will be a mobile.) Be strict with yourself about not answering the personal phone during office hours, except in emergencies. Do not use your business line for personal calls and try very hard not to give your business number out to friends and family. Have an answering facility on both.

- If you are better at working to deadlines, create some! Tell a client or customer that you will produce the work or the goods by a set time, then you know you simply must achieve that. At the same time, be aware that unrealistic deadlines are demotivating: you are setting yourself up to fail, which is foolish and unproductive. If you are creating deadlines, be sure that they are achievable within a reasonable time span. There is no point in losing sleep unless you have to.

- Some people work best using lists. Make a realistic list every day and do everything on it. Aim to finish the day with a clear desk and prepare a list ready for the following day. However, if some of the chores go over to the next day, be philosophical.

- Do the thing you least want to do *first*. If there is a project, a piece of work or even a phone call that is in any way difficult or even mildly worrying, do it first thing. The rest of the day is then a breeze.

If motivation remains a major problem, you may have to consider whether the independent route is really suitable for you. One reason for going solo is to find a way of working that enhances your lifestyle. If it becomes a daily battle to get down to work, there is no enhancement. If you don't feel motivated, there may be an issue of poor self-worth affecting your self-discipline. Perhaps at some level you don't feel that you and your ideas are worth making a effort for. Alternatively, it may be that the loneliness of working on your own is weighing you down and you would be happier, more creative and more productive working in a team.

It could also just be that you are very tired and in need of a holiday. If you think your lack of motivation is just a temporary 'blockage', consider the services of a counsellor who will give you feedback and support and to help you structure a change. If you think there is a problem in the way you structure your working patterns, you might consider a mentor (*see* 'Mentoring' in Chapter 12, *The Human Resources Department*).

One reason for going solo is to find a way of working that enhances your lifestyle. If it becomes a daily battle to get down to work, there is no enhancement.

Time-wasters

You owe it to yourself to cut out the time-wasters. For an independent, time not spent working is time not earning. But time spent planning, caring for your clients or customers, or looking after the staff (in other words, you!) is not time-wasting; these activities are good investments.

Keep to an absolute minimum the time taken up by non-productive, don't-add-to-your-life-at-all things. Everyone can sit down and write a list of time-wasters. Scribble down the obvious ones and start a campaign to eliminate them from your new life. Consider the following:

- There is no need to see advertising space salesmen. Even if you are buying, you can probably do all that is necessary over the phone.

- There is no need to see financial advisers, unless you are desperate for a new approach to saving and investment.
- Explain to the representatives of suppliers you use regularly that you are pushed for time and and can only spare them ten minutes. You will be amazed at how focused they become. Explain that you don't expect a personal visit every time you make a repeat order; it can still be credited to their commission without the 'personal interface'.
- Purchase a phone with a hands-free device. Then, when you are 'in a queue' but 'your call is important' to them (and, more particularly, important to you), you can get on with other tasks while you are waiting for a human being to talk to.
- Find a way to convince your friends and family that even though you are independent, you are working and therefore cannot spent time gossiping or doing errands. One way to do this is to suggest an alternative time for socialising or domestic chores, and pointedly make it outside of business hours.
- Develop a way of doubling up on the unproductive parts of your business. For instance, go to the post office, the bank and a supplier in one run instead of three. Avoid rush-hour appointments so you won't spend hours stuck in traffic. If you make a medium to long train journey, take appropriate paperwork or your laptop with you. You can set up your office in some train compartments these days.
- Make specific times to see customers or clients and keep to the schedule. Sometimes clients assume that because you are independent, you have time to spare. They will ask you to wait or cancel appointments at very short notice in the most cavalier way. Try to train them that your time is accountable. If they repeatedly offend in this way you can always imply that wasted time may even have to go on the bill.
- If you get an unprecedented amount of junk mail on your email – SPAM – let your Internet server know. There may be a way to have it filtered out.
- Never spend time on what is obviously junk mail. Dump it into the bin unopened.
- Do not 'chat' online. No-one expects you to answer all your emails immediately. It's the fastest way to communicate but remember that in many countries, what you say in an email is

legally binding. Take the necessary time to answer properly.

- By all means take trade magazines, but only if you read them *religiously* from cover to cover. If, like the rest of us, you find yourself with a pile of journals and newspaper articles that you promise yourself you will get around to reading, accept now that you probably won't. Bin this pile on a regular basis and refuse to feel guilty about it.

- If your work comprises a series of projects, keep the paperwork for each one in a separate file or box of files. When the project is complete, label, date and store it. If you have the time, prune down the paperwork in each box and retrieve any useful contacts for future use. Within a year or so you will find that there is very little of value to file anyway.

- Be ruthless about what you will really need in the future. Your working space can easily become littered with things you believe that you might just need at some vague unspecified time (but probably never will) to the extent that you wind up hunting for hours to find the things you are working on now.

- Be on your guard for the clients who treat independents as a free 'advice and ideas' service. We have all had the experience of being asked to put forward proposals and solutions and, excited at the prospect of a new piece of business, have worked for days putting together ground-breaking and innovative ideas for the project, all wrapped up in a gorgeous presentation folder. Later it has become apparent that the client had no intention what-soever of commissioning work, but went to two or three independents for free creative solutions. The word 'theft' (in terms of time, experience and expertise) springs to mind. As a result, many consultants do not hand out full proposals these days but instead give potential clients a bullet-pointed aide memoir, rather than a free do-it-yourself guide.

- Most of us have to spend a certain amount of time pitching for new business, and we don't always win it. There's not a lot we can do about this, because frequently the 'pitch' that looks as though it is virtually in the bag doesn't come off, and another – on which we think we are probably wasting time and effort – brings in a client that will be treasured for years. You therefore have to put your heart into every pitch – but even so, it is worth looking for the obvious ways to cut down on the time spent preparing them: keep recent good case studies to show your pedigree as you go along, ensure that your CV or job history is up-to-date, and smarten up your portfolio regularly.

Good practice

Taking the brief

When you are first invited to undertake a piece of work, large or small – be it cutting someone's hair or creating a publicity campaign or designing a table – make sure that you have all the information you need from your client or customer. In addition to negotiating the costs, fees and expenses for a piece of work, you require a comprehensive brief in order to function efficiently. Few clients will object if you question them closely about their expectations. This can even be flattering, since you are performing a task which is for them and them alone and they will appreciate your care and attention to detail. For *you*, the brief can be a very necessary safeguard against any misinterpretations which could lead to later disputes, loss of future business and even, in some cases, compensation claims.

Be sure you are clear about both what the client wants and, as important, *when* they want it. Negotiate on a deadline which you believe to be unrealistic. There may be reasons why a client appears to be giving you too short notice, but if the timescale is completely unachievable it is better to point this out initially than to be panicked into poor work further down the line. Where appropriate, be sure you know to whom you should report your progress.

All of the above may form part of the initial contract or agreement, examined in detail in 'Quotations, agreements and contracts' in Chapter 9, *The Finance & Legal Department*. But no matter how small the task, establish precisely what your responsibilities are, what background information you need (and who will source it – you or the client), the resources you require, the support you may need, the approvals that must be acquired and the deadlines for different stages of the job (as well as for final completion). It may prove useful to keep a written memorandum of the brief/agreement; date it and give a copy to your client.

Ongoing professionalism

However friendly you may become with your clients, it is worth remembering that, at the end of the day, they are still your clients. Don't rely on friendship when it comes to business matters. It may win you time to explain any mistakes but you cannot presume that it will overcome any disputes. Stay professional.

Experience suggests that it is also wise to document your progress with a client. This demonstrates exactly what activities you are undertaking on their behalf, how long each one has taken, and where you expect support from them. You can also chart any changes in your client's brief, and this may prove useful in the event of any confusion or dispute later on. Progress is usually recorded via time sheets, contact reports and activity reports. You may also need expenses sheets.

Time sheets

You can design these yourself. Give every client a separate time sheet for each project, or for each week or month, depending on which way you have agreed to bill them. Have a column for the date, another for the hours you have worked and a third for describing briefly the activity you have spent those hours working on.

Time sheets are an excellent way of demonstrating to your customer how long each procedure has taken. You may never need to show them – but they are there if you do. Clients are often surprised but usually impressed that you are so well organised. Some people also like to back up their time sheets by keeping a diary showing each day's output.

Activity reports

If you have ongoing work for a client, it is worthwhile (as well as impressive) to give them a regular update of your progress on the agreed programme of activities. You can attach this to a project or monthly invoice, to remind your client why they are paying you so well! The report shouldn't be too long and detailed, or no-one will have the time to read it. A succinct, bullet-pointed list will probably be sufficient.

Contact reports

After meeting a customer or client, it is often of great value to make out a contact report and circulate it to everyone present. This does not have to resemble 'minutes' with long paragraphs about your discussions; it is often more useful just to have a list of the decisions made, with a column on the right-hand side entitled 'Action Required By' and showing the initials of those who will be responsible for each task, along with the completion deadline. This forestalls the situation when clients say, 'Oh, but I thought you were doing such and such.' One freelance consultant I know calls this client-speak for 'I forgot to do this, so I'll blame you.' What a cynic!

Expenses sheets

Keep a running list for each client or each individual project, showing any expense(s) for which you will be recharging, such as phone calls and faxes, postage, photocopies, travel and subsistence. Much of my business is spent on the phone so I keep a list just for phone calls and postage. It has a date column, a 'call made to/postage to' column for the names of the people I have been in contact with, then 'tick columns' for local phone calls, long-distance calls and first-class stamps. Any other expenses are listed on a separate sheet.

Don't forget to keep receipts for your clients or customers to show where you have spent money on their behalf. This includes receipts for taxis, stamps (the Post Office issues these on request), train tickets (ask the travel agent or station ticket office) and car park (attendants have a voucher scheme). Send them attached to your expenses sheet with your recharge invoice.

TCB

This stands for Typical Client Behaviour and is endemic in every sector of industry and commerce. Anyone who has been independent for a while will be giving a wry smile at this point, because we have all suffered from it. The examples below have a thousand variations and after 20 years I am still finding new ones. I mention TCB only because there is comfort in knowing you are not, *not*, the only person to have experienced such scenarios:

- You break your neck to complete a job by a tight deadline. You give up theatre tickets, move a holiday ferry booking, miss your child's birthday party or school play, work through the weekend and into the night. Triumphantly you present your work or present the goods/service ready for collection on time. The client then sits on the work or fails to collect it for weeks for no known reason. Murder in your heart, you smile sweetly and thank them for the opportunity to work for them.

- Having given 110 per cent to the project, you present your invoice, prepared to enjoy the fruits of your hard graft. Then: the client loses the invoice/the only cheque signatory goes on holiday or snaps a bone in his wrist/the auditors are in (I've never quite worked out why this makes a difference, but apparently it does)/your payment is on the computer rota and no-one knows how to 'do a manual' (odd, then, that they manage to write a cheque for their own employees' expenses). In other words, they pay late. This is a common form of TCB and you must just grit your teeth and transfer money from your slush fund to keep you going until they finally stump up.

- 'Could you just . . . ' is always a worrying phrase. Could-you-justs can run to anything from an extra hour to several days' hard work. There are several tried and true responses, all of which start 'Yes, of course, delighted to help, but I'm afraid that the implications are: that your request may take us outside your timeframe/we may no longer be able to meet the deadline/this takes us over the budget on both fees and expenses/this will probably add a further amount of . . .' Alternatively, you say: 'I think I can probably just about squeeze the extra work in and still make the deadline/keep within the budget – as it is for *you*.' Does this ensure a grateful client? Sometimes, it does.

'Make it purple'

Sometimes clients want to do something entirely tasteless, not in their best interests or even downright bad for them. You must remember that as an independent, you can only advise – you cannot insist. So advise them. By all means do so robustly, but you will have to accept that they are (a) the client (b) grown-ups and (c) paying the bill. Therefore, if they really want it purple, purple it shall be.

If the client's decision is one you disagree with to the extent that you feel undermined or compromised, you may have to consider your ongoing relationship with that client. If the decision is one on which your reputation hangs, you may even have to consider resigning the job. You will not be the first, or last, person to do this. It frequently happens that you will be vindicated in the fullness of time. Unfortunately you may have had to live thin for a while in order to prove your point.

If the client's decision is one you disagree with to the extent that you feel undermined or compromised, you may have to consider your ongoing relationship with that client.

Feast . . .

One of the hardest things to deal with on the independent roller-coaster is the eternal cycle of feast or famine. This takes any number of forms, the most problematic being when your clients all have their busy times or major crises at the same time. Of course, such periods are very gratifying in terms of income: it pays to keep your head. Even so, evaluating each of your clients' degrees of neediness, and fitting everything into a day which persists in being only 24 hours, is an art that no-one can teach you.

Take a deep breath. Accept that you may not be able to do it all. Prioritise. Take an hour out and plan properly. Make a list of the clients and the work, the most urgent project being at the top. Contact the clients or customers half-way down the list and below, and tell them that you will deal with their dilemma or urgent project as soon as possible, within whatever is a realistic deadline. If you think that these clients will understand, explain why they must wait. They will know that in the future, when they have something vitally urgent, you will clear the decks for them. Reassure them that this is so.

Work at a pace which, while in top gear, is not the desperate gallop that attracts mistakes. *Never forget this*: panic engenders silly errors, and these are inevitably the time-consuming, loss-of-face variety that lose you your hard-won customers. It's better to be honest and try to buy the time you need to work sensibly.

In such circumstances, knowing other independent practitioners can become a lifeline. As part of your networking, you will probably have met someone else doing the same or similar kinds of work as you. If the panic is a major one, consider bringing in some extra help (see 'Making it grow' and 'Outsourcing' in Chapter 11, *The Long-Term Planning Department*).

The senior anaesthetist of a major London teaching hospital, which has a large Accident & Emergency department, is faced on occasions with a major incident – a bomb blast or train crash – as a result of which dozens or even hundreds of casualties arrive in a short space of time, each one needing urgently to be assessed and treated. Sometimes, a patient with a broken wrist must be treated immediately because they are in deep, life-threatening shock, ahead of someone who is screaming with pain from burns but whose vital signs are strong. Every time I face a wall of client demands and my heart begins to pound, I remember Dr John Goldstone and his team at University College Hospital London, and it all falls into perspective. However heavy, my workload is a breeze by comparison.

. . . or famine

There will also be times when you are not so busy and this can also be a source of great anxiety. When will the next project or customer arrive? Will the phone ever ring again? What happens if it doesn't? Nasty little whispers, these, but we all hear them. It does not matter how long you have been in business for yourself or how often your skin has been saved, you never feel comfortable when the workbook is looking thin.

Common sense doesn't come into it either. It matters not that you have done all the right things: you have a good marketing plan, you have continued to scout for work, you know your business backwards and you are proud of your work record and achievements. If you are not fully extended, somehow, a feeling of failure and guilt creeps in. Insecurity lives? Not okay!

This is where independents show their mettle; this is the definition of courage. Use your time, but not just to nibble your nails to the quick – the phone isn't going to ring because you are sitting and watching it. Here is the opportunity for you to brush up your publicity plans, go on a training course, start a networking drive, do the boring old filing, paint the workspace, order the stationery, go out and have coffee with friends, walk the dog, go swimming. It takes nerve to carry on regardless but nothing is going to happen while you hide under your desk. Get on out there . . . you never know what's around the corner, and it could well be the big one.

The big project

It is wonderful when you land a major piece of work or a massive order. It's bonanza time, although when you are working on your own, a large project can also be very daunting. The first decision to make is whether you are really able to take the project on and do it successfully, without losing the rest of your business.

Sometimes, the wise decision is either to hand the project on to a larger concern – you may even be eligible for a commission for doing so – or to form a group with trusted associates and share both the work and the profits. Only you will know if this major project will be worthwhile in the longer term.

Let's suppose that you firmly believe that you should be able to undertake this new work. You want to do it and, what's more, however apprehensive you are, you want to do it on your own. This is not the time to be losing sleep: you need your energy. Start, therefore, to plan carefully: time invested in good planning is time very well spent. You will then feel organised and in control.

Make lists

I find large pieces of paper and giant, coloured felt-tips very useful. Start by making lists and, when necessary, revise them as you go along. The first list should be based on your diary and cover *everything* that you are already committed to. It's extraordinary how often big projects come in just when you are also trying to organise a family wedding or anniversary party, or have visitors from overseas booked to come and stay, or have offspring facing major examinations. It's necessary to start your planning by ensuring that everything is running smoothly domestically. Pull in any help that you need to make it happen.

Be ruthless and start cutting down where you can: cancel having the car serviced unless the MOT and tax are running out or the car is making strange noises; postpone non-client dinner parties and other social jollies. For once, forget the gym or the golf club. They will all still be there when you have completed your project.

Take a good look at all your other work. See what can be deferred and what still has to be done. Identify any tasks that can be done by others. Draft in family and friends, if only to run to the Post Office and collect materials from stockists for you.

If other clients call wanting you to do something for them (and you can be sure that they will), I recommend that you tell them – with due pride – that you have just been awarded a major contract and are therefore against a very tight deadline. Tell them (realistically) when you will be free to help them, and ask if there is any way in which they can wait. There's a good chance that your other clients will be impressed that you are bringing in work or orders of a high calibre. Everyone likes to be associated with success.

Then comes the planning of the project itself. Again, this initial work can save you time later on. It should be your main reference point for the duration of the project and it should be updated regularly as you progress. The list will probably include:

- a detailed list of the work/order
- equipment/transport/packaging needed
- the other people or services you need
- a comprehensive schedule, as detailed as possible, about what has to be done, by whom, and by when

Bring the project or order down to bite-sized pieces, and always allow time for things to be late or to go wrong. Make a chart, accurately timed and with action in bullet points. Tick off the items as they are obtained or the various elements are completed. My chart for researching and writing this book is in red, blue and black and covers a considerable area of my office wall.

If you are going to bring in other people to help, allow sufficient time to brief them properly and to oversee their work. Make sure that there is adequate time to consult and update your client or customer. When there is a big project, there are usually reputations to be made or lost – and not only yours. Do not be a nuisance – the client might just want you to take it all away – but at the same time, keep your client reassured that everything is in hand and that you can deliver on time.

If it's appropriate, document the project as you go along. There are two reasons for doing this. The first is that your list/plan may serve as a blueprint for when you next face a major project. Secondly, you may be able to use this project as a 'case study' for when you are pitching for other new business.

The ability to let go

Timing is everything. There are ideas or projects which flourish even though you are not making a particular effort, and there are others that refuse to make progress no matter how much effort you put into them. When a lot of obstacles – the kind you can do little about – start to litter your path, then stand back and see if there is something basically wrong with the concept. Everything has teething troubles. The art form is to know when the gums are rotten.

Business leaders the world over would love to have a guideline about when to cut their losses, but no-one can really teach you or help you in this. By all means check with friends whose judgement you respect, and there is no harm in buying professional advice. But do it sooner, rather than later, and then listen very hard to the little voice inside your head. It is usually fairly accurate.

There is no loss of face or prestige here; it's better to let the project or the client go before the consequences are serious. We are always being told that we learn by our mistakes. Maybe there will be lessons to be learned from the instances when you cannot make something work.

When you are directly employed, you have just the work in hand to concern you. As an independent business person, you must also stand back and take a thorough look at the overall pattern of your business.

Keep your eye on the business – not just the work

This is a new concept for people starting out on their own. When you are directly employed, you just have the work in hand to concern you. As an independent business person, you must also stand back and take a thorough look at the overall pattern of your business. Ask yourself:

- Is it remaining profitable? If not, why not?
- Is it revenue-driven – that is, work accepted at any price just to increase the turnover? Or better still, is it profit-driven? This may

mean not only reviewing your prices or fees at regular intervals but also ensuring that your expenses are not rising unnecessarily.

- Are you taking note of what parts of the business bring most profit, and which parts don't?
- If some part of your work is not earning its keep, do you continue to offer this service or product? Sometimes, if that work is bringing you particular pleasure or more business or good publicity, its value is beyond its profit and so you should keep it. If it doesn't have 'legs' on any level, it makes sense to drop that part of the business and concentrate on what does.
- Do you need to look for new business, even when you are at your busiest? The answer to the last question is always *yes*. When you are busy (feast time), it is very hard to find the time to continue promoting your business – but if you don't, famine will certainly follow.

Don't put all your eggs . . .

If you have found a niche market and the right level of customers within that market, it's very easy to feel comfortable and so miss the signs of any outside incidents, trends and influences that might bring adverse changes to your business.

There are some things that you cannot anticipate and would find very difficult to guard against. Who could have anticipated that in 2001 the holiday industry in Britain would be so negatively affected firstly by Foot and Mouth Disease, and then by the lack of US tourists following the 11th September atrocity?

But other trends you can spot, and take action to avoid. This is where reading the business pages of both national and regional newspapers as well as your trade journals may prove invaluable. At the same time, your networks may help you pick up on how the market is faring. Do other small businesses report that customers are drawing in their horns? In a recession, for example, people look for very good value but may not buy extravagant items. Some clients may look at outsourcing certain of their services to cut costs.

Equally, keeping abreast of current fashions and trends can offer you not only warnings, but also opportunities. One example is that when house prices in a certain area soar, people may not be able to afford to move and so will spend their spare income on improving the home they already have. This offers opportunities for garden designers, decorators, tilers and bathroom fitters, and interior designers.

Never become so comfortable – and it's easy to do when the pockets are full – that you fail to pick up the scent on the air.

Stay flexible

One of the great benefits of being a sole practitioner is that you have immense flexibility. You can alter your business, products and services and your prices instantly in response to new circumstances or information. You have no need to wait for board decisions, meetings, committee reactions or group consultations. The only person who has to approve such changes is you!

By all means test the market and seek the advice of people whose opinions you respect. Otherwise you can make any changes overnight if necessary. A friend described it like this: 'When you work for a large organisation, you are like a liner or super tanker; stopping or changing course quickly is very difficult and takes valuable time. If you are independent you are like a speedboat, you can swiftly turn in any direction, avoid the storms, and head for more promising water.'

No matter how busy you are, keep your head up. You must be your own early warning system. Watch for the trends but at the same time, listen to and trust your instincts. Develop the extra antennae that will keep you ahead of the game.

Have a fall-back

In some ways, independents are more secure than people who are directly employed. After all, if an employee loses his or her job, they lose all of it. As independents, the chances are that if we lose a few customers or even one major client, we probably still have at least a good part of our business left.

Not all of us can do this, but for those who can, it may be worth developing a safety net for the more desperate 'famine' situations. One friend has a spare room which she lets out when her business is slow. Another has a secondary line in cooking for other people's dinner parties. She will also take their cars for servicing, their dogs to be shampooed, collects their dry cleaning, buys their partners' birthday presents and interviews new cleaning ladies. Her clients are busy, she is not, and they will pay for her very competent support.

Actors are past masters at having alternative income sources, because their work can be particularly intermittent. One friend is regularly seen in character roles both in the theatre and on television, but he never knows what is – or is not – coming up next and he has school-age children. He therefore tops up his income as a tourist guide (lucky tourists; he's very entertaining) and has taught himself to be a website designer. Another young actor frequently hosts murder mystery weekends and acts as a Master of Ceremonies at celebrity parties.

If my PR work takes a dive or the work being offered to me isn't suitable or appealing, I revert very happily to being a journalist. It doesn't usually attract the same income level but I enjoy being paid to ask questions and it keeps my bills covered until the phone rings and another wonderful opportunity presents itself. Optimism is all.

In some ways, independents are more secure than people who are directly employed. After all, if an employee loses his or her job, they lose all of it. As independents, the chances are that if we lose a few customers or one major client, we probably still have at least a good part of our business left.

Mix and match

If it suits you and your personality, you can regularly mix and match to make up your income. You are not obliged to do just one thing any more; that's for employees. Many independents choose to have a 'portfolio' of involvement. You might decide to take one-third of your income from one kind of work, perhaps with a contract for one or two days a week. Then you might add another day of advisory or consultancy work, or spent supervising a project. Finally you might top up the week with work that is completely different – maybe in a new area, but something you have always wanted to tackle.

You could work towards having a 'dripping roast' income such as the rent from part of your workspace or from a letting property. This might enable you to cut down your active working time, or to take less well paid but particularly satisfying or experimental work, or to undertake a training course.

At the end of the day, you can push your work programme into any shape you like – the one that best serves your purpose. This is one of the big bonuses of independence: *you* decide how it's going to be.

Things to do

- If motivation is a problem at the start of each day, develop strategies for kick-starting yourself.
- Invest (a short) time in tackling and eliminating diversions and time-wasters.
- Decide how you will monitor and keep track of the work you do for clients.
- Accept that there is likely to be 'feast or famine' in your work pattern and therefore in your income too. This is just part of the ride.
- When the big project comes in, don't panic – start planning.
- No matter how demanding your clients or customers are, keep a watch on how your business is developing and sustaining itself.
- If something refuses to work, let it go.
- Mix and match if you wish to. Have a portfolio of projects and use all your talents.
- Be philosophical when your clients make unlikely choices or silly demands; be kind. They are worthy of your tolerance. But if they compromise or undermine you, fire them!

Richard Bailey

'The rents help to even my income out. One of the benefits of being freelance is that when I am not taking photographs, I have time for the property projects. actually, I don't think of either photography or the renovating as work. If anything, the work element creeps in only when I have to find new business, which is the part I don't particularly enjoy.'

Richard Bailey is a photographer living in north London.

I have always wanted to be a photographer. My father gave me a camera when I was very young and I suppose that's what started me off. I took a Foundation Course at my local art college and then took a degree in Photography, Film and Television at what is now Westminster University.

The course taught me many aspects of photography, but not how to run a business, so I had no idea of how to set up on my own. The usual route is to become a photographer's assistant, but it never really occurred to me to work for any-one else, and at the time I wanted to travel. Over the next three years I went to Borneo, South East Asia, Mongolia, Russia, China and South America. I took photographs in all these places of course, and when I came back I placed them with picture libraries. That didn't bring in enough to live on, or to continue the travelling, so I subsidised myself by taking odd jobs – mainly driving.

During this period I was asked to do the photography for a glossy brochure. It was very well paid and I thought similar work would come easily. Bits and pieces continued, mainly through design agencies, but it didn't take off at that stage.

In 1995 I spent three months in Paraguay and the following year, I was commissioned to photograph the British athletes taking part in the Paralympics, which was held in Atlanta, USA. The results were published in a book, *The Road to Glory*, and there was an exhibition of the photographs which toured Britain. I didn't make much money, but did gain a lot of exposure.

I decided afterwards that I had better take advantage of that exposure to establish myself, so I sent out some mail shots to design companies. I also developed a website fairly early on. Since then work has come in regularly. Some of my clients are long-standing. I have been working with a number of universities, including City University, for about 10 years, producing images for their graduate brochures. I have also enjoyed taking photographs for Great Ormond Street Hospital for the past five years and likewise the Radio Authority.

I specialise in taking pictures of people, including children, and several jobs recently – such as one for Business Link and another for Ribena – were shot in South Africa. Both involved taking photographs of kids and both were great fun.

Most of my work comes through recommendation. Lots of my clients become friends and I enjoy staying in touch whether I am working with them or not. Some years ago my wife, Fiona, and I decided that we would buy a property rather than carry on paying rent. We couldn't afford much. The place we bought had had a fire so needed a lot of work on it. We enjoyed doing it and of course, along the way we increased its value. We sold it and took another property that needed renovation. When we had finished it, we had the idea of renting that property out while we took on yet another to do up. Now we have the house we live in and two flats we rent out. I am toying with the idea of maybe another one!

The rents help to even my income out. One of the benefits of being freelance is that when I am not taking photographs, I have time for the property projects. Actually, I don't think of either photography or the renovating as work. If anything, the work element creeps in only when I have to find new business which is the part I don't particularly enjoy.

The other great advantage is that photography, although a crowded field, can be very well paid. So, if there is work coming in, I can take days off around it. Unlike someone in a big corporation, I can spend more time with my wife and my children. That's one of the best things. I am able to see my children growing up and play a full part in that.

Richard's advice:

If you can, have a fall-back. It doesn't have to be a rental property, it could be anything that supplements your freelance income and fills in during the lean times. The most important thing is to keep going. Treat every job, no matter how big or small, or whoever the client may be, as special and important.

Do not lose your nerve if you are not working every day. Have a balanced life instead! Have personal projects. In my case it's taking more photos. In this way I am building a body of work that might make a book or an exhibition in the future. It's also important to make use of any slack time to experiment, try out different aspects of what you do, so you can offer more to clients in the future. That's what keeps you ahead.

Andie Airfix

'One of the biggest lessons I learned early on was to have confidence in my own talent. If you have confidence in what you do, your clients will too. They will instinctively trust you.'

Andie Airfix of Satori is a graphic designer based in Chelsea, working mainly for the music industry.

I travelled on and off for about ten years, latterly in India. On my return to London I was invited to hold an exhibition of my paintings in Country Cousin, the first American-style supper club to open in London. Afterwards I was asked to do the in-house graphics, something I had never done before. I also met someone through the club who was building stage sets. We decided to team up, and our first job was to design and build the interior of Blitz, the coolest club in London in the early 1980s, frequented by David Bowie, Mick Jagger, and the New Romantics like Boy George.

Some of these people asked me to do work for them but it wasn't appropriate to the partnership, which was focusing on the interiors of clubs and restaurants. The partnership lasted three years, and it was a relief to us both when my partner decided to pursue other interests. By this time, I longed to do more graphics – I had been learning my trade on the run – but, although my friends said I should go it alone, I was apprehensive.

I started with design contracts for various fashionable venues and met some very influential people. The break came when Tom Robinson asked me to do an album cover for him. The Thomson Twins followed, then Dead or Alive and Def Leppard.

A merchandising company who had seen my work contacted me and it was then that things really took off, with world tour brochures and merchandising for Bonjovi, the Stones and Paul McCartney. There were many others – Guns'n'Roses, Tears for Fears, Page and Plant and Metallica – and soon the bands themselves were asking me directly to design covers for them.

I also developed some corporate work with clients like De Beers and the Disney Corporation. At one point I had much more work than I could handle, and so I worked out some criteria. I chose the work which was likely to be ongoing, was the most profitable, the least stressful and, preferably, for people I enjoyed working with.

The music business is frenetic and full of egos. One of the biggest lessons I learned early on was to have confidence in my own talent. If you have confidence in what you do, your clients will too. They will instinctively trust you. I will not receive briefs from managers or record companies, but only from the artists themselves. This saves time and avoids misinterpretation of ideas. I am hired because clients cannot do the job themselves: they need my expertise. If they want to change something, I tell them that they, as clients, can have anything they want – I am here simply to advise them. It usually works!

I was delighted to work with Robert Plant again last year, first for his individual work, then back with him and Jimmy Paige for Led Zeppelin. Recently I undertook one of the largest projects I have ever done. It was for Time-Warner and was the design for Led Zeppelin's 'DVD' and 'VHS'. The job comprised a two-box set for the DVD, a two-box set for the videos, the posters, magazine adverts and preview invitations, and I was dealing with people in the US and Japan as well as the UK, and as well as the artists themselves. I found that it was very important to talk to the key players by phone, not just by email. If you are dealing with personalities, you have to get to know them, then emails hit the right note later on.

Andie's advice:

Always establish deadlines with the most senior person possible: avoid the scenario where someone creates an unrealistic deadline just to impress their boss! Clarify your quotes. Overestimate slightly on costs (you can always reduce them) and double the time you think it will take (usually about right). I always add to my estimate the phrase 'based on information received'. This way, you have bargaining power if the brief is changed or expanded. And always, *always* put it in writing at the time!

Asking for an advance payment usually sorts out any time-wasters, and covers expenditure if anything goes wrong. It is standard practice so do not be afraid to ask; it will only gain you respect for your practical business sense.

I mostly do large, complicated projects and they almost always grow along the way. I always inform the client when there are items – either work or expenses – that none of us predicted. But when I come to do the billing, I invoice the initial agreed amounts and then the extra separately. If there is any query about the additional costs, at least the main payment should be going through and won't be held up.

My other advice is to train your clients! Teach them to collect their thoughts and give one brief in one email, not lots of scattered emails that contradict one another. Try to persuade them to title them properly too, not keep replying on the same title which doesn't fit the subject matter any more. One of my major nightmares has been managing emails. Print out a file, it's an education!

8

The Purchasing Department

*Shopping – setting up your office or workshop –
services – goods – credit – bulk buying – receipts
and guarantees – complaining*

It seems simple enough. You need something; you have the money,
so you go and buy it. Of course – but there are hints and tips to pass
on which may be useful if you have not previously purchased
goods or services for your work.

Shopping

Because you now have so much to do, it is very easy to cut short the
shopping time and grab what is nearest and most convenient.
Inevitably, you will rue such shortcuts. You need to source the best
equipment at best-value prices, with a competent back-up service
should you be likely to require it. You may be able to save a few
pounds buying your computer from a discount store but, if you
need support in setting it up and then keeping the wretched thing
on track, you'd probably be wiser to buy it from a specialist
computer centre which has a team of bright bunnies who like
nothing better than sorting it out.

Setting up your office or workshop

There are things which you should economise on, and others
which you should not. You will need a desk or table – it does not
have to be antique maple – and an appropriate and comfortable
chair. You must have decent lighting; probably a few shelves for
reference books; and storage, possibly a filing cabinet, for both
your business and financial records and for clients' and customers'
current records. In due time you will require further storage: the
Inland Revenue requires that you keep all your records for six
years, and you may have to store completed client work.

You will probably need a phone with an answering facility, a mobile phone, and a computer with email, perhaps served by broadband. You may also find a fax machine useful if you have to transmit diagrams, plans or maps, although nowadays there are laptops which have sketchpads. Ask friends and former colleagues for advice, take the appropriate *Which?* guides and visit phone shops and computer centres before making your choices. Be guided as much by how appropriate they are to your business requirements as by the price.

If you are planning a studio or workshop, take time to make it as energy- and labour-efficient as possible. Hopefully you will have so much work that you won't have time for re-planning for a very long while. Make sketches, invest in a few fittings so you can reach everything you use regularly. Make it the workshop of your dreams!

When you are starting up, probably on a tight budget, it is tempting to choose the cheapest and hope that it will do. In fact, it may be the penny-wise-but-pound-foolish choice. So if you are likely to require something bigger and better within a year, grit your teeth and buy the bigger and better now. However, if you are getting carried away by the sheer gorgeousness of the design, get a grip and head back to the most practical. Elegance comes later.

Services

Let's suppose that you require a printer for your stationery or a brochure, or a designer for a website, or a builder or decorator for your premises. The normal order of progress is:

- Write down a proper brief. Be very specific about what you require.
- Look at several different suppliers. If you are not sure where to find the right kind of supplier, check in directories such as *Thomson Local* or *Yellow Pages* (or the online version, Yell.com) or ask people whose judgement you trust. Alternatively, you can take or note down examples of work that you like, and ask whoever commissioned that work for the contact details of their supplier.
- Ask each supplier for a quote, based on the brief you have given (and possibly discussed with) them.
- When you receive the quotes, be aware that the cheapest may not necessarily be the best. If one is very much cheaper than the

others, it may be worth checking to see whether quality is being compromised. If there is something you don't understand, do not hesitate to phone up and ask. Some suppliers will use terminology that is gobbledygook to the rest of us. It is very important that you understand exactly what you are agreeing to and buying.

- When you have decided on your supplier, make an agreement. Where appropriate this may include a delivery time and the terms and manner of payment. If a large sum of money is involved, have a written agreement signed by both parties. Don't be shy about this. It can save a lot of time, stress and money later on.
- In some instances you must be prepared to pay a deposit or some of the expenses up front. Occasionally you will receive a Pro Forma invoice which means that you pay the entire amount up front.
- If goods such as printed items – letterheads, invoices, brochures or leaflets – are involved, check them thoroughly as soon as they arrive. Have someone proof-read them for you and be sure that the size, paper (and weight of paper) and colour(s) are exactly what you agreed and expected.
- Some suppliers may require your credit rating. If you are unsure about your credit rating, you can contact Experian. If, for some reason, you wish to check another business's rating, you can contact Experian or Dunn and Bradstreet.
- Ensure that you have a full receipt for all work, goods or services ready for your books.

When you are starting up, probably on a tight budget, it is tempting to choose the cheapest and hope that it will do. In fact, it may be the penny-wise-but-pound-foolish choice.

Goods

Many of the same rules apply to goods as to services. Always shop around, and blatantly negotiate on the price whenever you can. Check delivery times: if you need something urgently, this may influence your choice of supplier.

If you are making a major purchase, always send confirmation by email or as hard copy, even if you have ordered in person or over the phone. Your accountant will require the original receipt for these items, but always take a photocopy for your own records and file it carefully along with any guarantees.

Look at service agreements and warranties very carefully. Most goods are covered by the normal consumer protection regulations for at least 12 months. For some items, which depreciate rapidly, it may be better to take a risk after that period. Buying a new item can actually be cheaper than buying these expensive service contracts.

If you are considering hire purchase on a large investment, look at the various ways of financing the purchase. Where possible, look for low-interest or interest-free deals. Find out the real cost of the manufacturer's or retailer's best offer. Try negotiating. Then, if you are unhappy about what it is costing you, consider other methods. Would it be cheaper to pay in two or three instalments on a credit card? Would a bank loan be too expensive? Can you raise the money in some other way?

You may also find it worthwhile to consider leasing equipment, which is then serviced by the company which owns it, rather than making a straight purchase.

Credit

You may have to make a major purchase which is just too large an investment to pay for in one fell swoop. Sometimes the suppliers will offer you a way to buy in instalments, but even so it is worth shopping around – some of the rates of interest on repayment are quite scandalous. It is true that you will receive tax relief on the interest, but there is still no point in paying more than you need to. Check with your bank or building society and check with your trade organisation. There may be schemes in your area of business which are advantageous.

Bulk buying

You are now eligible for trade buying. This means that you can purchase your supplies from, for example, wholesale office furnishers, wholesale stationers or art suppliers, caterers, cash-and-carries, and trade-only equipment shops.

Sometimes there will be a catalogue, a phone or online ordering system, and free delivery for orders above a certain value. If you only need small quantities, consider linking up with other people and purchasing in bulk together. I know of two picture framers who have entirely separate businesses but purchase certain mouldings together. It keeps the expenses low and the profit margins higher. That's the spirit!

Receipts and guarantees

Keep all receipts, guarantees and lease or service agreements, along with instruction books, in a separate office file, neatly labelled 'Equipment'. This can save hours of hunting around at a later stage.

You will require your receipts for your accounts. In some instances, your receipt also acts as the guarantee. Be sure to photocopy your receipt twice in this instance: you then have a spare should you need to complain.

Complaining

Just as we looked at your mistakes and slip-ups in Chapter 4, *The Public Affairs Department*, it is worth revisiting what you should do if something goes wrong with one of your suppliers:

- Sort it out immediately, not weeks later.
- Be reasonable and pleasant; everyone makes slip-ups.
- If you are phoning, ask to speak to someone at management level and try to be matter-of-fact, even if you feel angry.
- Explain that you run your own business, that the mistake is causing you inconvenience, and ask what can be done. Sometimes, shops or suppliers will offer to collect and replace. But always ask for alternative solutions. It may be more convenient to you to receive a refund than wait for replacement goods.
- If you are writing, be sure to send a photocopy of the receipt.
- If a complaint is dealt with well, don't forget to say so. If it isn't, contact the managing director (do not forget, you are a managing director too).

Things to do

- If you are commissioning a service, give a clear brief and put your agreement(s) in writing.
- When purchasing goods, always do your homework, and know precisely what you are looking for.
- Shop around and negotiate prices where possible.
- Consider leasing major equipment.
- Keep all receipts for your accountant.
- Retain copies of receipts and all guarantees and agreements in a designated file.
- If you have to complain, be firm but pleasant. Life is too short to have endless hassles.

Richard Brassey

'I know what I will be doing for the next two to three years which, as books take so long to produce, is reassuring. But at some stage soon I need to stand back and review where I am going.'

Richard Brassey is a children's author and illustrator.

As a child I loved the illustrations in books: Babar, Tenneil's drawings for Lewis Carroll, Edmund Dulac and many less famous illustrators who were just as wonderful. At school, I was involved with editing and the layout of school magazines. I then went on to the London School of Printing where I studied graphic design. Afterwards I worked for a publisher.

It was when my daughter was small that I put my first book together. She didn't particularly like it but, for some reason, she requested a book about a famous lion. So that's what I called the next book. I gave it to a family friend who ran a bookshop where it was seen by the sales rep for Jonathan Cape. He ran off with it and shortly afterwards I was summoned to see the great editor, Tom Maschler, who took the book on. When the children's catalogue came out, I was placed somewhere between Nicola Bailey, Quentin Blake and Roald Dahl: I thought I was made!

In fact, the book didn't do all that well. I took another idea in to Tom Maschler but he wasn't interested. I put it in a drawer for the next few years and took odd jobs in graphic design and worked on improving my house and selling flats.

You need time and a lot of self-confidence to put together an illustrated book. Eventually, I took the manuscript out of the drawer and took it to another publisher. This one loved it but already had a very similar story. It did encourage me to start again. There were several false starts. One publisher was just about to sign a contract when it was taken over, and the new people weren't interested.

Then I met Judith Elliott who was starting the children's book department at Orion, as she had done previously for Orchard Books. I have been with her for years now. Because it is a relatively small publisher, she is able to give a decision quickly, rather than it going to endless committees, and she believes in developing someone who shows promise.

I have had books that seriously bombed; one in particular was very expensive to produce. But others have flourished. A particularly successful book was one I did relatively quickly. It's called *Nessie, the Loch Ness Monster* and it sells almost exclusively in Scotland. It has sold over 150,000 copies so far and is still selling about 20,000 to 30,000 a year. I have done other books linked to Scotland: *Greyfriar's Bobby* and *The Story of Scotland*. I won two awards for the latter, one from the Scottish Arts Council, the other The TES Saltire Award.

Most of my work at the moment is in non-fiction. I have done *The Story of Ireland* and now I'm working on *The Story of London* and a series called *Brilliant Brits*. A few years ago, I was thrilled to be asked to collaborate with the award-winning author, Geraldine McCaughrean, on *Britannia: stories from British history*. It meant two illustrations for each of the 300 pages – and I did it in just nine months. It's recently been issued in paperback and was nominated for a Blue Peter award.

Illustrating is very intensive work, very tiring. I know what I will be doing for the next two to three years which, as books take so long to produce, is reassuring. But at some stage soon I need to stand back and review what I am doing. I would like to return to fiction.

The market has changed over the years: at one time any UK picture book would automatically be sold in the USA, but now the US has more home-grown illustrators and there is a real cultural divide. So, it is important to look at other markets. My work has sold well in Scandinavia, for instance, and the Far East is opening up.

It can be lonely but I never was a team player. Occasionally I go to the Society of Authors' conferences and things like that and we all moan about how little we are getting paid and how much J K Rowling is making! When a book is in production, I will work regularly alongside my editor and public relations people. It's wonderful when you have success, seeing your books in the bookshops, the signings and the awards but mainly knowing that people are reading them.

Richard's advice:

Only a handful of people are truly successful in this field, although lots are scraping by. The Society of Authors did a survey and found that only a few per cent of authors make a living from their work.

But if someone really wants to do it, they should try. If they feel they have the ability, it's up to them to prove it. You need to be tenacious and appreciate that doing any book, even if it is not exactly what you want to do, is good experience.

Many people think they can write as well as – let's say, Beatrix Potter or J K Rowling – but, even if that is true, there is no point. That has already been done. The publishers are looking for something different, something that they haven't seen before.

The Finance & Legal Department

*Starting out – grants and loans – business plans –
'drop dead funds' – other considerations –
insurances – pensions – taking business from
previous employers – codes of practice – quotations,
agreements and contracts – standard terms of
agreement – jury service*

The tightrope of independence looks higher if there is no safety net. It feels dangerous, and it is. No wise person would set out along the wire unless they knew there was some provision for their future health and wellbeing, should they become dizzy and unfortunate enough to slip. For an independent, this means securing financial continuity and ensuring that you are working well within the laws and regulations governing your area of enterprise.

Starting out

For the majority of independents starting out, the ideal safety net will probably take the form of a soft and comfy cushion of savings to carry you over the first stage of your journey. Every freelance and independent practitioner has found the reality of no regular income an immense shock to their system.

The size your cushion needs to be depends on the nature of your business. If you are in a cash business, you may have some return fairly quickly. If you are in the kind of career where you receive a retainer, you need only keep a fund against the possibility of your client suddenly cancelling your contract, or you being unable to work for some reason.

For most people, who must complete the work before presenting an invoice, and then wait for that invoice to be paid, I recommend a cushion that equates to five or six months' required income (that is, sufficient to cover all your known bills, plus living expenses).

That way, you can be paid late and still not suffer. You may even have a small sum left over which you can keep for another rainy day, or add into your funds for publicity or extra equipment.

Your safety cushion should be separate from and additional to your start-up budget. Start-up funds cover your marketing and launch, and initial purchases (stationery, for example) as well as any advances for materials, equipment and, for some people, production expenses and deposits and initial rental on work spaces.

Every freelance and independent practitioner has found the reality of no regular income an immense shock to their system.

Loans and grants
Where such funding is beyond your capacity, but you know you have a marvellous idea that will generate a good business, you will have to consider a loan or grant. The most obvious sources to try are the banks. People under 30 may also like to investigate grants from the Prince's Trust and Shell Livewire.

The Prince's Trust or Prince's Scottish Youth Business
These marvellous organisations 'exist to help young people fulfil their potential'. They work with anyone aged between 14 and 30, unemployed or part-time, and unable to find funding from elsewhere. There is financial support – normally in the form of a low-interest loan or a small grant – for people with viable business ideas and the commitment to see it through. Each successful applicant is assigned a business mentor who acts as support on a monthly basis (*see* 'Mentoring' in Chapter 12, *The Human Resources Department*). Since it was set up in 1983, the Prince's Trust has helped to establish more than 40,000 small businesses. Of these, more than half were still trading after three years or more.

Shell Livewire
Sponsored by Shell UK Ltd., this trust offers a similar service, again on a regional basis, to would-be entrepreneurs aged between 16 and 30. It offers business start-up information packs, funding,

business plan development, access to professional specialist advice and ongoing support. There is also an annual Young Entrepreneur of the Year award with a £10,000 prize for the winner.

For most people starting up, the major likely sources are:

- *A loan from a family member or long-term friend.* If you go down this road, it may be wise, and will defuse future tensions, to have a properly constituted letter of agreement about the terms and the timeframe of the loan. For instance, you might agree to refund any interest your family member or friend loses as a result of making this loan to you. If so, add it into the letter. The more businesslike you are about this kind of loan, the less concerned your family member or friend will be.
- *An overdraft.* If it is a relatively small amount that you require, over a matter of weeks or a few months, consider approaching your bank for an overdraft facility. By and large, overdrafts are an expensive way to borrow money but they allow you flexibility and you can repay them in one lump or several chunks, to suit you.
- *An extension of your mortgage.* For example, if you have an outstanding loan of £70,000 against a property which is currently valued at £150,000, you may be able to arrange to extend your mortgage to, say, £85,000, releasing £15,000 for your business needs. This kind of loan can prove to be the cheapest way of borrowing money.
- *A business partner.* Consider bringing in a long-term business partner who provides financial support but doesn't necessarily work actively within the business. Obviously, they will expect to benefit from your profit.
- *A business angel.* 'Angels' may be willing to invest in your business for a given time but then will expect a good return on their money.
- *Venture capital.* If you need the investment of a large amount for a high-turnover/high-income business, consider involving a venture capitalist or a venture capital trust. You will need to form a limited company and 'sell' the shares in return for investment in the business. Investors will expect the shares to increase in value over time and will then sell them in order to

make their profit – often within just a few years. You will need specialist investment advice before going down this road.

Be aware when applying for most kinds of loan that you will be asked to give some form of personal guarantee. Consider very carefully before putting your home up as security; instead, see if there is a way to start more slowly and less ambitiously. For most of these routes, your first step will be to produce an attractive and comprehensive business plan (*see* below). You may also wish to have a contingency plan in case you are turned down.

Consider very carefully before putting your home up as security; instead, see if there is a way to start more slowly and less ambitiously.

Business plans

All banks and organisations you may apply to for a grant or loan will require a business plan. These are fiddly things and require some leaps of faith and imagination for a business that has not yet started. It is worth making a special effort, though: once you have created a plan, the framework may well serve, with updates, for many years.

If you are seeking a large sum of money, you may need to take advice on how to present this document. Business Link has advisers for the marketing side, and an accountant or financial adviser will help you prepare the figures and charts.

The usual format for a plan is as follows:

a summary

A one- or two-page summary of your plan, covering the nature of your business, the market, the potential for your product or service, the likely profit, and how much money you are asking for. Try to reflect how fascinating your business idea is. Make it sound exciting and worthy of the lender's investment. Remember that your enthusiasm will be a strong selling point because it will demonstrate your commitment to your new venture.

your pedigree

This will probably cover your career history, qualifications, experience and achievements. If you have been in business for a while, include details of your past performance with trading figures. Also give the details and qualifications of anyone who might be working with you.

your product or service

Give an exact description, explaining why it is special, different from and better than other services or products in your market – in other words, how you stand out from the competition.

Marketing

Give more details about your market, its potential for growth, who the potential customers are, the size and shape of the competition. Then outline your marketing, launch and publicity plan.

Operating

Explain how and where you will run your business, describe the premises, cover the quality of your work and how you will deliver to your clients and customers.

Financial projections

This is where you will need your cash flow statements and a financial forecast for up to three years. You might also be expected to list any risk elements or potential weaknesses, as well as your strengths.

Prospects

Give your objectives and aims for the future, both in the short and long term, with a timetable and, if appropriate, deadlines.

Exit route

Show how you can make enough money from the business to repay all of the borrowings. If there are other investors in the business, show how the business might be sold to new owners or floated on the stock exchange (because, for instance, this is how venture capitalists make their money).

Accepted wisdom is that you should be generous in your requirement. Most people are reluctant to take on a big loan, but it is self-defeating if you don't ask for enough money to operate properly; don't skimp for the sake of it. Remember too that suppliers' prices will rise over two or three years so you may require a margin on your budget for supplies. And give yourself enough time to pay back without impeding the growth of your business. Of course, it would be wonderful to pay your loan off quickly, and certainly pay back early if you are able to, but beware of being a slave to the loan. You have to live reasonably in the meantime.

The document need not be wordy; it can even be in succinct bullet points. Keep it to ten pages or fewer if possible. It should be clearly presented and easy to read. Your bank manager will have to scan many such documents in the course of a year and will welcome you making his job easier. It doesn't have to be multi-coloured and brimming with charts, but it should reflect the quality of all your work. Put it into a smart folder and wear the suit when you go to present it.

'Drop dead funds'

Real independence is not just about being your own boss, but about being in the position to refuse work which is unsuitable or demeaning. In extreme circumstances, you should be able to fire your client.

Obviously, there will always be some tasks that are less exciting than others, but where there is sufficient financial benefit or there is kudos to be gained, it may well be worth accepting the job. There are other occasions on which it is highly gratifying to be able to turn work away. This is considerably easier to do if you have a healthy 'drop dead fund'. As soon as the business can sustain it, consider building this security blanket and putting the money in a fund that is easily accessible.

Other considerations

Now that you are in the grown-up world, do as all other 'corporations' do and seek the best professional financial advice you can find. By all means consult several advisers but be sure that they are independent and not tied to a fixed set of financial product providers. You are most likely to need advice in the areas of savings, mortgaging, insurances and pensions. There is a wide variety of products available, with new ones being launched all the time. Unless you are fascinated by these subjects and have time to make a regular study, you are best served by people who are familiar with the markets and work within them on a daily basis.

Most advisers seem to agree that for independent practitioners, particularly when they are starting up, it is worth considering a flexi-mortgage on your property, rather than a straight repayment or endowment arrangement. Flexis allow you to make overpayments when you are in funds, so paying off the mortgage quicker, but also to take a payment holiday when the cash flow is against you.

You may also wish to revise your savings and investments in light of your new venture, to ensure that they are available should you need them suddenly. In the early stages, it may be wise to have at least a part of your savings in an accessible fund or even in cash. Overall, if your income is likely to be irregular, this is not the time to be tying funds up or risk-taking.

Insurances

There are lots of insurances available to the independent practitioner, and you could spend much of your profit on premiums. Take a careful look at what is essential to your business but after that, take a view. Life is risky. You cannot insure against everything.

Health & income protection

When you leave a company or organisation to go out on your own, you will lose various benefits including paid sick leave. It is therefore prudent to consider some level of insurance cover in case you are sick for any length of time.

There are two main kinds of cover. The first is accident, sickness and unemployment insurance which will cover your mortgage payments for up to one year. The other is income protection insurance, also known as permanent health insurance, which will kick in after several months but, if necessary, will continue until your retirement.

Private health cover

If you have been in a company scheme for private health care, be prepared to be mildly shocked when you ask about rates as an individual. Companies usually buy health insurance schemes at a vast discount. The premiums vary, so it is worth shopping around.

Employer's liability

If you are likely to have someone working with or for you, you must consider employer's liability insurance and display the certificate in your workplace. This will cover you for any disease or physical injury your employees sustain as a result of their work.

Equipment

You may wish to cover your equipment and supplies, even if you are working from home. There's still the chance of being burgled! Tell your home insurer if you have a home office: some insurers will let you cover business equipment as an extension of your home insurance. If it's just paperwork and a computer, there may be little change to your premiums. If, however, you propose to store stock at home, they might increase.

If you have a work space outside your home, there are special 'packages' to cover the contents of small offices.

Professional indemnity

Some professions, where expert advice is given – such as accountancy and investment, taxation and law, engineering, architecture, surveying and so on – are open to claims of negligence and misconduct. Some professions must have professional indemnity insurance in order to practise, but (as yet) not all. Since legal claims are increasingly fashionable, you may find this kind of insurance a wise investment.

Public liability

This is only necessary if members of the public visit your premises (in case they are injured or become ill) or if their property is damaged. If you run a catering establishment, healthcare practice or salon, you must seek appropriate cover. You should also ensure that you are familiar with the new legislation regarding disability access to your premises, and the required facilities for disabled people.

Pensions

It seems very hard, when you are barely making enough to survive, that you must also consider your pensioning requirements. In fact, in some instances, these are something you need to make decisions about before you even start your independent journey.

If you have worked previously for a company with a pension scheme, you must choose whether to transfer the benefits into a personal pension or leave them in situ. This is not an easy choice and it will depend on your personal circumstances. Once again, it is worth seeking guidance from a financial adviser.

As an independent, you will almost certainly be paying national insurance contributions automatically, and so you will qualify for a basic state pension.

There are many personal pension schemes available, and choosing between them can be a minefield without professional guidance. You may decide that a pension is only part of the financial arrangements you wish to make for your older age: some people have the kind of business that can be sold for a lump sum and will use that to provide a retirement income; others may decide to develop a portfolio of provision – perhaps a residential or commercial letting property, plus a range of investments, plus a personal pension.

Whatever you decide, do *something*. It's easy to think that there's endless time in which to start making these plans. Without jeopardising the present, be aware that the future sneaks up on us and there may come a day when you really don't want to work quite so hard.

Taking business from previous employers

When you are planning to go independent – perhaps you are in the research phase, but still working for someone else – it is very tempting to mention your plans to your current clients in the hope of taking them with you. Even if you don't actively solicit previous clients or customers, sometimes they will seek you out when you start up on your own.

Check your prior contract of employment to ensure that there are no clauses which relate to the 'poaching' of your former employer's business. You may find that when you signed your contract, you also agreed that you would not work for the company's clients for a particular period of time after leaving their employment. Some businesses, such as hair and beauty salons, may include a clause to prevent you from setting up a new salon within a certain radius. Be aware that companies can and do sue former employees for taking business away from them.

Jeremy Pemberton and Max Mlinaric run a small but fast-growing company in south west London that provides IT services to other small businesses. They supply, install and maintain complete computer systems and networks, with an ongoing service for maintenance such as the latest anti-virus protection. They started as a pair, but took on two employees and moved from an office in Max's home to a suite of offices, all within an year.

In the beginning, things were not easy. Jeremy had been employed for three years by someone in a similar business who implied he might eventually make him a partner. Max joined the same company at a later point. Neither were given contracts of employment or even agreement letters. The two felt that they could work together, improve the services they were offering, and make a business of their own. They believed there was a gentleman's agreement that, should they leave, they could take with them the clients they had brought in.

Max explains: 'We went to see our boss to explain that we wanted to set up on our own. He wasn't surprised, may even have been expecting it. We agreed a severance package, even to the extent of buying equipment we didn't really need and reimbursing the money for a training course Jeremy had taken several months before. We felt that we were leaving on good terms.

'The clients started following us, which he was a bit anxious about, but when he saw a draft quote that was dated about a week before we left him, he accused us of trading on his time. We hadn't actually sent it before we left him. We sent it on day one,' explains Max.

Jeremy takes up the story: 'We had wanted to make the break in a painless and ethical way, maybe even continuing to do some business together, so we were really worried when the angry phone calls came in. We consulted a solicitor who told us that we were within our rights to plan our new business while still employed, but if we had been approaching clients before leaving employment, that would constitute a breach of good faith. We hadn't done that but, inadvertently, we were sailing quite close to the wind.

'Our advice to anyone starting up is to speak to a solicitor before you do anything else, then to an accountant. Set a specific date for your launch. Ensure that there is no perceived movement before that date. Plan, by all means, but don't do any work or approach clients before your set date. Then tell your employer you are leaving. Only then tell your clients.'

Codes of practice

All professions and most trades have umbrella organisations, part of whose remit is to produce codes of good practice. There are statutory regulations in the professions which apply whether you are independent or not, and no doubt practitioners in these areas will already be fully conversant with them. However, in other areas of work, the codes are subscribed to entirely on a voluntary basis. You may wish to find out about the code of practice relating to your sphere of work and make a decision on whether you wish to adhere to it. If so, you can probably use the accolade in your promotional material.

Quotations, agreements and contracts

Your professional or trade organisation may be able to help you design the necessary documents for any quotations you need to give, and for your agreement letters or contracts. Where possible, have these in a standard format, so you can quickly and easily personalise them for each new client or customer.

Quotes

Be sure to date each one and show the name and address of the potential customer. Be precise about what the quote is for, where necessary adding in any relevant code numbers, quantity numbers and the exact names of the products being supplied. If you are offering to supply goods, the cost of which may rise after a given time, be sure to add a covering sentence to your quotation. Most quotations will have a line such as, 'This quotation is valid for 60 days [or whatever] after which we cannot guarantee to maintain these prices.'

Letters of agreement

For large-scale or ongoing projects, you should consider having a written agreement or contract with your client. This confirms legally what you have been commissioned to do and on what terms. If your customer or client does not offer a formal agreement, there's nothing to stop you from producing one which must be agreed and signed by you both. If this will be a regular requirement, you may find that it is worth consulting a solicitor who specialises in business law to help you design the letter or contract, and put together your terms and conditions.

Contracts

These will vary depending on the nature of your business and the kinds of projects you undertake.

To give you some idea of what a contract might contain, the following is a short version of the standard consultancy/client agreement, offered as guidance to members of the Institute of Public Relations:

Agreement between

_____(name of practitioner)

and

_____(name of client)

Date _____

Draft contract letter/memorandum of agreement

(a) Appointment and programme
This part of the agreement confirms the appointment of the practitioner to carry out an agreed programme, details to be attached.

(b) Commencement and duration
Dates are given for starting the programme and the period of duration.

(c) Fees
The practitioner's service fees, exclusive of VAT, based on management, executive travelling and administration time in the UK, are listed as an annual figure, a monthly amount or on another basis (such as a daily fee level). This section also points out that the practitioner reserves the right to negotiate a revised fee if the client changes their requirements.

(d) Disbursements/operating terms
This lists items which are subject to a specified handling charge.

(e) Payment terms
This outlines how the practitioner's fees, and separately, expenses will be paid: by a Banker's Standing Order and on which set date, or by other methods, to be detailed.

(f) Termination provisions
This covers how the contract might be terminated by either party, the length of notice and arrangements for final payment.

(g) Trade standard terms of agreement
These appear on an accompanying document but are listed here as an integral part of the contract.

(h) Signatures
These are required from both parties.

Standard terms of agreement
Again, every area of business will have its own requirements. To give you some idea what might be covered, this is taken from the Institute of Public Relations' version:

(a) Cooperation
The client agrees to assist the practitioner by offering all relevant information.

(b) Exclusivity
The practitioner will not represent conflicting interests.

(c) Disbursements and expenses
A list of those items which might apply to an agreed programme of work.

(d) Approvals and authority
Where written or oral agreement from the client is necessary.

(e) Copyright
Who owns what.

(f) Confidential information
Not disclosing client information without permission.

(g) Insurance
Covering professional indemnity and client's property.

(h) Disputes
A referral to the Institute in the instance of a dispute.

(i) Payment in foreign currency

(j) Employment poaching
See pp. 161–3 above.

(k) Force majeur
A release from contract in the event of national emergency or war.

(published with the kind permission of the Institute of Public Relations: info@ipr.org.uk)

Jury service

Just as you think that you have hit every trip wire, something else pops up. In my case it was a call to do jury service. I was working under contract, helping to organise the annual Women's Own Children of Courage Awards at Westminster Abbey just before Christmas, always a lively but labour-intensive affair. It took months of detailed arrangements, bringing the children and their families from all over the country to London; inviting all kinds of celebrities; filling the Abbey with local schoolchildren; making the security arrangements for a special royal guest; and organising a lunch at the House of Lords afterwards.

In addition, there was a press campaign to organise, which meant fitting interviews and photocalls for television, radio and newspapers into the children's very tight schedule. And there I was with a request to undertake jury service just four weeks before the event, for a trial which would take at least ten working days and possibly more. Panic came close to the surface at this point!

Thankfully, someone I knew had had a similar summons and he reassured me that the court would be sympathetic to my plight. In fact, it would be very difficult for the legal system to ask me to break a legal contract.

What you should know is that it is every UK citizen's civic duty to perform jury service if chosen. There is a daily fixed-rate financial loss allowance and a subsistence allowance.

If jury service is likely to cause you genuine hardship by way of lost revenue or damage to your normal business, you may write to the Jury Officer of the court to which you have been requested to attend. Explain fully why serving on a jury would create special difficulties for you. You may be asked to provide evidence of loss of earnings (such as an accountant's letter) but everyone I know has received sympathetic, prompt and courteous treatment.

If your request is accepted, your jury service will either be deferred until a later date, or you will simply be excused on this particular occasion.

Things to do

- Build a cushion of funds before starting out.
- If you need a set-up loan, consider the most cost-effective way of borrowing for your circumstances.
- If you are approaching a bank or grant-making organisation, create a business plan and obtain help if necessary in putting it together.
- Build up a fund which enables you to turn undesirable work away.
- Take a cool look at what insurances are really necessary to you and what pensioning you need.
- Check your previous contract before taking business from former employers.
- Design a form for quotations.
- Put together a letter of agreement or standard contract, seeking professional help if necessary.
- Don't panic if you are asked to do jury service!

Carol Spenser

'You have to be good at marketing yourself – that's what it comes down to in the end.'

Carol Spenser is one of the UK's top style consultants. Based just outside Norwich, she frequently travels throughout the world on commissions.

I took a degree in English at Lancaster University and followed it with postgraduate qualifications in business studies. In the 1980s I went into public relations, working on the media and marketing campaigns for leading international companies, including Gillette, Guinness, Roger & Gallet, Maybelline and Interflora.

When my first child was born at the end of the 1980s, I trained in image/style consulting so that I could work flexible hours and be self-employed.

I founded my own company in the early 1990s, initially called Public Persona. It was hard work but successful from the outset and soon I was under contract to train staff for the Saks hairdressing chain, Principle stores, and Monet jewellery. I also arranged staff seminars for Marks & Spencer. This training side has continued over the years, with companies such as Alexon, Anne Harvey, Windsmoor and Laura Ashley, culminating in a three-year contract to develop and implement a personal shopping programme for Debenhams.

But also from the beginning I was keen to establish a media presence, making time to put together make-over features for women's newspapers and magazines such the *Daily Express*, *Weight Watchers* magazine and *She*. I became a regular monthly columnist for *Women's Journal* and was thrilled when I was once nominated as Columnist of the Year. Later I was also asked to put together readers' events and workshops for some of these magazines.

I proposed the 'Style Counsel' concept to BBC Good Morning in 1991 and the following year it was launched with top hairdresser Nicky Clarke and me as co-presenters. It lasted for several years, but that didn't prevent me from becoming style presenter for Carlton TV's Capital Woman and for UK Living (part of Sky TV), as well as launching the 'Kiss 'n' Makeover' strand on GMTV with Gary Hooker.

My first *Style Counsel* book was launched in 1995, followed a year later by *Wedding Style Counsel*. There are now six books and I really do wonder if I shall write another. It's always possible!

Throughout I have offered a Makeover-by-Mail service, which in the last 12 years has offered individual advice to more than 20,000 women about their appearance. The same service, under the name Personal Style Directions, is now available via my website, for both women and men.

On a one-to-one consultative basis I have helped hundreds of men and women, some of them in very high-profile positions, to improve their appearance and with it, their confidence. This area of personal development is one which has become increasingly acceptable over the last decade, but not many style consultants manage to make a good living on this service alone. You have to be good at marketing yourself – that's what it comes down to in the end. If you want to last more than a year, you need lots of services and products aiming at different market sectors. For me, this has been the public, the media, retailers and corporate organisations.

I believe that I am the only person to have commissioned market research to find out what services people really require. One important thing I discovered was that there was a negative reaction to the word 'image'. In this country, many people see an 'image' either as something fake – imposed by a consultant – or as the kind of changes Madonna and David Bowie undergo every so often! In reality, we all have an image, even if we pretend we don't. Not caring about your appearance is just as much an image statement as any other. Even so, I decided to call myself a style consultant, based on my market research and this, I believe, has made me more approachable and successful than my competitors.

I have to take into account the British character, which is highly individualistic. In the US people like to be told what to do and they will often follow their colours and styles religiously. Here it is wise to give people more flexible advice, so they can interpret it with their own likes and dislikes and can adapt it to their own lifestyles.

Carol's advice:

Be sure to have a firm agreement or legally drawn-up contract. I was very naïve at the beginning and trusted people to pay me. One client would pay a deposit, with a balance to come three weeks before the work was due to start. When the balance did not arrive, I would do the work anyway and then have to fight for the outstanding amount.

Register your company name and any logos. I've had so many ideas stolen and I had a legal battle over the Style

Counsel name. It was hijacked by a well-known fashion designer and it cost thousands of pounds to prove that I owned it by prior usage! I also ensure that I own the rights to the photographs and illustrations in all my books.

Be careful how much you give away for free when you are making a 'pitch' for new work. By all means, demonstrate what you can do. Show case studies of past work, and show slides or illustrations, but don't give away a how-to guide. If you want to leave proposals with the potential client, I suggest you give them a bullet point outline.

John Mitchell

'I am not very good at taking orders – the RAF proved that to me – but I am always willing to take good advice and learn from someone who has knowledge that I need.'

John Mitchell is a tiler and mosaic-maker based in Cornwall.

Initially I wanted to be a civil engineer, in true Isambard Kingdom Brunel style. I went to Cornwall Technical College in Camborne but it proved very hard financially for my parents to keep me there. I therefore took an apprenticeship in the RAF – one of Lord Trenchard's Boys – and spent the following three years learning to be an aircraft engine fitter.

It was old-style military discipline in those days but there were good sports facilities. I also played rhythm guitar back then and earned on the side playing in local rock bands.

I had 18 months fitting Vulcans and a further two years based in Aden but I wasn't happy. I spent too much time doing things for silly reasons. Even after I qualified, I would still find myself painting stones white for an official inspection. In the end, I chose 'discharge by purchase'.

It was the 1960s so I free-wheeled for a while and grew my hair. I did a variety of temporary jobs: in hotels, on building sites and in bars. Then I got married and started a family. I ran a caravan site on the Cornish coast but it was a struggle; I took on decorating jobs and did the bookings for holiday flats. I had the chance to go back into aircraft fitting with Rolls Royce in Derby but I felt that the three children would have a better life in Cornwall.

I started to do some work for a local developer who was building a L-shaped complex of apartments. The rectangle was completed by a 10-metre long pool. Watching the company who built and tiled the pool, I thought: 'I could do that.' I have a strong interest in ancient history: this started with a book called *Warfare and the Ancient World* and, unlike school history which was just a series of dates, this made the Greek and Roman empires and the impact they had on our world come alive. It led to an interest in Greek and Roman mosaics – I have always thought they were spectacular – and these have lasted through 2,500 years of war, fire and floods. So when I saw the pool tilers throw away bits of tile, I collected them and decided to create a 1.3-metre panel of Caesar Augustus. There weren't enough colours but I found a supplier in Truro. I enjoyed doing it but also knew I could do some things better: the way I had cut the tiles, for instance.

Afterwards, someone who worked for a pool company, supplying chemicals and equipment, saw the panel and asked if I would like to do more. Soon he called with a tiling job for a pool and also for some panels. I created a lobster for one hotel and a butterfly – a Malaysian *Clarissa Terrinos* – as the logo for another.

Suddenly, after having been strapped for a number of years, business was booming. During the summer, with suit and clipboard, I was the estate manager for a number of developers across the Duchy. In the winter I built swimming pools and made mosaics.

Then my marriage ended and I moved to a complex close to a beach on the north coast. I became manager of the complex and I still am. And after 20 years, I'm still creating mosaics and building pools.

My interest in Roman history has continued. I have read the shortened version of Gibbons *Decline & Fall* but have only managed the first of the full nine volumes so far. But I've made several pilgrimages to Rome and intend to go again.

I've turned 60 now so there's a limit to the number of pools I want to tile. I am a member of the British Association for Modern Mosaics and recently I have bought some beautiful Italian marble. My ambition now is not just to take on commissions for mosaics but to do my own versions of some of the classical designs – not copies, but interpretations. I would also love to floor my lounge in marble but that would be a lifetime project.

I am not very good at taking orders – the RAF proved that to me – but I am always willing to take good advice and to learn from someone who has knowledge that I need.

John's advice:

Don't be afraid of failure. If the worst happens, you can work for someone else for a time and then, if you really want to be independent, try again.

You may not make a lot of money – it's never been a goal of mine – but you can find a real sense of satisfaction in completing a project by your own efforts. There is a measure of contentment to be gained in that. I could have worked for a major airline company and had a proper pension, but life is short. We work long hours in this country and you should have something more out of it than money.

10

The Accounts (& Tax) Department

The bliss of a healthy cash flow – invoicing – late payers and when the worst happens – tax-deductible items – national insurance – income tax & self-assessment – VAT – finding an accountant – DIY accounting – financial crisis management

One of the great advantages of the independent way of working is that your success does not depend on another person's whim. Sometimes you lose business or fail to gain a piece of work that you feel was naturally yours; but on the whole, you are the director of your own fate.

If you are to maintain that position, it is worth ensuring that your financial accounts are as well organised as possible. This not only keeps your nerves calm – because you know the bills are being met – but also enables you to plan properly for the future.

The bliss of a healthy cash flow

In order to achieve some kind of control over your income, you will want to establish a good cash flow. Unless you are on a retainer or a contract, maintaining a positive cash flow can sometimes be difficult.

Cash flow is not about profit. During any given year you may be showing a very pleasing profit overall, but you may still fall prey to cash-flow problems. It works like this: the 'flow' of money into your account must match, both in time and quantity, the 'flow' of money going out to pay your bills and expenses. If all your major bills fall in a one- or two-month period and your payments come in at totally different times, you may be in danger of a cash-flow deficit.

One way to check the peaks and troughs is to make a month-by-month outgoings chart (or spreadsheet). Make 13 columns: the first one on the left-hand side is for listing by name, all your bills and expenses for the year; the other 12 are for the months of the year. Simply fill in the figures, showing each expense as they fall in each and every month.

Some payments will be regular monthly ones: mortgage, rent, community charge, pension, national insurance contributions, permanent health cover, mortgage protection, mobile phones and any hire purchase. You may chose to pay fuel bills, insurances and cable television access monthly too.

Add in the quarterly, half-year and annual payments: car vehicle licence, car insurance, servicing and MOT, professional subscriptions and water rates. Estimate your variables: accountancy and bank charges, stationery, equipment repair and servicing, and your twice-yearly income tax.

You may choose to list business expenses separately from personal expenses. It is your chart, make it as useful as possible.

Lastly, put in a monthly payment for your living and travel expenses. Now be brave and add the columns up, month on month. You will soon be able to see which parts of the year are particularly expensive and which are lighter.

Match this chart with another one estimating where income is likely to come in. This will very quickly show you where there is a major discrepancy, and hopefully, will help you to identify where you must build a cushion of income to accommodate the various shortfalls.

These charts can also be used to form the basis of a cash-flow statement, which is useful if you have to put a business plan together. Such plans are required when you apply for a loan or grant from a bank or financial organisation, or grant-making trust, or even if you require an overdraft facility for the first time.

Invoicing

Sometimes, even though your income (and therefore a level of happiness) depends on it, invoicing can be a chore. This is particularly so if you have to recharge a lot of expenses. But you won't get paid until you do it, so light candles, put on soft music, get comfy and just get on with it.

Make your invoices clear and simple. They should include the date of issue, the name and address of the client, a banner saying INVOICE and an invoice number (make up a numbering system for yourself, but don't start with No. 1 – it might frighten the first client). Include any reference numbers your client or customer has used in their ordering of your services or products. Then state clearly what the invoice is for. Examples might be:

- to servicing and repair on [date of the actual work] of [whatever equipment it was]
- to a public relations service during the month of [whatever], the programme for which was agreed by you
- to the supply and delivery of [number] of [describe products]

List all servicing and work first, and expenses or delivery charges second. In some businesses, fees might be charged on one invoice and expenses on another.

Clearly list all amounts, draw a line and give a total. If you are VAT-rated, show the VAT as a separate figure under the sub-total and then make a grand total. Display your VAT number at the bottom of your invoice.

Finally, add in your terms. An example might be: Payment within 28 days of date of invoice.

Take two copies: one for your files and one for the accounts. Post the invoice using a first-class stamp. Ensure that it is addressed to the correct individual or your commissioner.

If you regularly incur lots of expenses on behalf of your clients, develop a standard format for your invoice so you just have to fill in the variations. Keep a running list of the expenses so you don't have to spend an hour sorting them out at the time you are doing your billing.

Late payers

One of the reasons that some of us run into cash-flow problems now and again is because our clients forget to pay us. It seems so unfair: in addition to worrying about finding new work, there's the anxiety about being paid for the projects you have completed or the goods you have supplied (and possibly have already paid out for). You have worked hard to set yourself up; you have given your customers or clients the best possible deal and a high standard of work; you have been attentive and committed to their best interests. How could they let you down?

Often the worst culprits are very large companies that can well afford to settle your relatively minor invoice promptly. The problem may not lie with whoever commissioned you, even though they sometimes fall behind with the paperwork and mislay your invoices, or fail to obtain the correct internal authorisation. Sometimes, the hold-ups are with the accounts department of the company you have supplied. People who work in accounts departments receive regular monthly pay cheques. They have *no* appreciation whatsoever of your predicament resulting from their late payment, and they frequently make it clear that they do not care very deeply. Some will treat your request as though you are asking for a donation, rather than accepting that they are the people at fault and that they are *in debt* to you. It's very galling and sometimes extremely stressful.

There are all kinds of measures you can take, up to and including taking your client to court. This – or even the threat of court action – should be the very last resort. The UK has been at the forefront of strengthening EU legislation to promote a culture of prompt payment, and the right of small companies (those with fewer than 50 employees) to charge interest on money owed by large companies. Since August 2002, we also have the right to claim compensation for debt recovery costs. There are excellent Internet sites – a brilliant one called www.payontime.co.uk – explaining your rights and how to enforce them.

In the end it is up to you, the supplier, to decide whether or not to use these new rights. Most of us wish to keep our clients and so don't want to be threatening if there is a personal and friendly way to redeem any late-payment situation.

Avoiding the problem in the first place

Depending on the nature of your business, late payment may be a hazard you have to live with. However, take a moment to see if any of the following are appropriate to negotiate under your terms of business:

- Ensure that any contract or letter of agreement between you and a client states quite clearly to whom payment should be made, the time period for payment (that is, by what date), and method of payment (cheque or electronic bank-to-bank payment).

- If you are investing in a lot of goods or materials on behalf of your client, ask for an amount up-front. Try to make it at least half, if not all, of what you have to pay out. If you have any concerns about a purchaser, ask for bank and trade references. You can also check out a limited company's creditworthiness via Companies House or agencies such as Dunn and Bradstreet or Experian.

- If you are a consultant or accepting a six- or 12-month assignment, ask for a monthly retainer paid in advance. Expenses, unless they are hefty, are normally invoiced and paid in arrears. If there are likely to be major expenses, try to arrange a 'float' or deposit.

- Include terms on your invoices. The normal term for a monthly invoice is 28 days but some people (including me) put 14 days. Any terms that you offer, such as 'payment with 28 days net of invoice date' is in fact a period of credit that you are extending to your client.

- You can also state that there will be a interest charge for late payment, although it is sometimes difficult to see practically how this might be claimed on smaller amounts.

- Consider offering a discount for instant or prompt payment. Some customers will be delighted to accept this.

- Ensure that, if you are VAT-rated, you are on a cash accounting system. In this way you won't be paying the VAT on invoices for which you have not yet received payment.

If your late payer is a new client, try telephoning to ensure that your invoice has been received and signed off. This can be very effective because you are getting to the nub of any problems straight away. Always send in a statement on the very day that the payment is due but fails to appear, and follow it up three days later with a telephone call, fax or email. Be polite but firm about knowing when they anticipate that you can expect your payment. If they come forward with something unrealistic, point out your terms and ask them to make the payment quicker.

If you don't get a response, continue to phone, fax and email until someone replies. Ensure that you keep copies of all correspondence and a note of all your costs in case the situation deteriorates.

Before the rest of this section becomes heavy and depressing, it might cheer you to hear about a debt collection agency in New York which proved particularly successful. It was called Smelly Tramps, and that's just what it provided. The agency employed some of New York's niffiest hobos to collect late payments: they would hang doggedly around the foyers of smart companies and agencies until they were given a cheque. It worked in no time!

When the worst happens

If you are dealing with a large company

When you are hitting a wall with the accounts department and you are beginning to lose either your temper or the shirt off your back, have a quiet word with whoever commissioned your work in the first place. Sound embarrassed to have to point out that the accounts department is sluggish and it is becoming a significant problem for you.

Point out that the contract or letter of agreement was very clear about terms and timing of payment because you are an independent practitioner and late-payment has a real impact on your working and personal life. Ask the commissioner to speak to the accounts department on your behalf. They will hate doing this but it sometimes results in better treatment in the future. (Some enlightened companies have a special fast-track payment system for small suppliers and independents. We bless them!)

Legally, you are entitled to interest from the day after the stated payment day. It is up to you whether, in light of future client relationships, you want to try and claim this interest. If you wish to do so, you should inform your client or customer in writing that you are claiming interest under the late-payment legislation and mention the current daily rate. The letter in itself may prompt a satisfactory response.

If there is still no positive outcome, the amount of interest you can currently claim is the basic interest rate plus 8% on the gross figure – including VAT. If the base rate is 4%, you would therefore claim 12% which, for example, on an outstanding debt of £1000 is £120 over a period of 30 days. Alternatively you may wish to ask for compensation, the amount of the figure in the example currently being £70.

Some enlightened companies have a special fast-track payment system for small suppliers and independents. We bless them!

If you are dealing with a small company or individual

You may feel that small concerns, even more than a large company, should understand the dilemma they are creating for you. Possibly they do. The first thing is to remain very calm and matter-of-fact: there could be a hitch that you do not know about. Try to establish if your client has a cash-flow problem of his or her own. Knowing about this will not necessarily help you get paid, but you may be able to establish whether payment is likely in a short time or a longer one, and make your own financial arrangements accordingly.

Ask for part-payment as a gesture of goodwill. If your client or customer is having financial difficulties, see if you can arrange a structured payment over a number of months. This may be inconvenient for you, but it is better than receiving nothing at all, and your client or customer may be grateful for your understanding and the practical solution you are offering.

If your client is still being unhelpful, ask if other suppliers are unpaid. If necessary, call other suppliers and see if they are experiencing the same problem. Then you will know if it's a localised problem (i.e. just you) or if there's a fundamental problem with the client's business. Then you can take the following actions:

- Send a statement, giving terms, payment date and method of payment.
- Follow up with phone calls, faxes and emails.
- Devise a strongly worded letter of your own, pointing out that you will be claiming for interest and reminding them of the daily interest rate.
- Send a solicitor's letter if the amount concerned is a large one.
- If you are paid a cheque and it bounces, you have a legal contract in the form of that cheque regarding the client's willingness but inability to pay. You can sue accordingly on this broken contract.

- If after several attempts at retrieving your money, you are still unsuccessful, you should consider action via the County Court.

Nowadays, County Court procedures are designed to be user-friendly. Local offices will provide you with information about procedures, copies of forms and help with filling them in. Remember to take several copies of all your invoices, statements and correspondence. There is even an online service, Money Claim Online, to claim debts of less than £100,000.

If you suspect that the company or individual is likely to go bankrupt or into liquidation, and you are owed a lot of money, you must move quickly to establish yourself as a creditor. When a company goes into liquidation, the tax man and the banks have the first call on any remaining assets. Other creditors then form a queue.

Tax-deductible items

Keep your receipts!
From the day you first decide to go solo, you should start keeping all your receipts for expenses. This includes every cost incurred while you are developing your new business. Legitimate expenses when you are researching and setting up your business – known in the tax game as pre-trading expenditure – can include:

- fees relating to consulting a professional adviser
- travelling for research purposes (sneaking a look at the competition, seeing estate agents, looking at office space and so on)
- subsistence (meals when researching away from your base)
- phone rental and call charges
- stationery – letterheading, etc.
- start-up equipment
- fees/costs for training courses
- reference books
- making prototypes of goods, obtaining samples, or making up your presentation folders ready to pitch for new work

As you progress, you can continue to claim the above expenses against tax when they occur, along with:

- costs relating to new business 'pitches' (hire of laptop or slide equipment, portfolios or work folders, photocopying and presentation folders, travel and so on)
- advertising and some sales promotion items
- bank charges
- bookkeeping and accountancy fees
- business insurance
- some legal costs – for instance, towards recovering a bad debt, preparing contracts, fees to register trademarks or patents, and some work relating to the setting-up of a lease on premises
- part of your car maintenance, petrol, insurance, 50% of your residents' parking permit, car park and meter charges
- taxis when out on business
- other business-linked travel: underground, buses and trains
- all computer purchases
- if you use your computer regularly as part of your work, the government now allows check-ups at the optician and the cost of close-work spectacles
- all your business stationery, including invoices
- meals out if you are working late or away from your office
- postage
- newspapers, magazines and trade journals relating to your work
- training courses
- professional fees
- even if you have a workspace outside your home, you can still claim a percentage of your home phone bill if you make business calls in the evening and at weekends
- if you have an office or studio, then general expenses – cleaning, cleaning materials, and supplies such as loo rolls, light bulbs and coffee
- part-time assistance

If you work at home, a percentage of your fuel bills can also be offset against tax.

Keep a petty cash book for tiny items, such as newspapers and parking meters, where receipts are not given but the costs none the less tot up over a year. For each entry, record the date, what it was for and how much it was for. Remember to fill in your cheque-book stubs, so they tie in with invoices you have paid and with receipts.

Then make a note of the cheque number, on the invoice or receipt. Your accountant or bookkeeper will thank you. (If you use your cheque book to obtain cash or for a private bill, make a note on the stub at the time. No-one remembers to do these things afterwards.)

Whatever you do, make a habit of collecting those receipts. After a while it becomes second nature to ask for a receipt in a taxi or petrol station or shop. Store all the receipts in a special container, be it an envelope, box file or drawer. Empty receipts from your wallet, handbag and briefcase regularly. Don't leave them blowing about or shoved into the glove compartment in the car: individually, they may be for quite small amounts but over the course of a year they will add up to a notable sum on which you do not have to pay tax.

Some receipts don't specify what the payment was for. As you go along, discipline yourself to scribble on the back of the receipt what the cost was for and maybe even the reason for purchase. Examples might be: 'new portfolios/pitch for new business', 'plants for office', 'reference books for such-and-such a project'. Your accountant will give you gold stars for this, and it will be invaluable should someone from the Inland Revenue ask you what the receipts were for.

Your accountant will also be able to advise you of any other tax-deductible expenses which apply to your individual business.

Your income and personal expenses are not eligible, of course. Some people are able to claim a clothing allowance, particularly when overalls are required or you are allied to the fashion industry, but others of us cannot, even though we buy certain kinds of clothes specifically for our working lives. Meals with potential new clients are not eligible.

There is tax relief when you buy capital equipment that is exclusively for your business, with a sliding allowance relating to depreciation. If, when you start your business, you use something that you previously used privately (your home computer for example), you can claim a capital allowance on the market price of the equipment estimated on the day you started up.

Always bear in mind that unless you make a profit, you won't have any tax to pay. So, make the profit first and worry about the tax as a distant (but not unimportant) second priority.

Other records

From now on you will have to keep every other kind of piece of paper relating to your business, including:

- business bank statements
- business paying-in slips
- cheque-book stubs
- copies of your invoices to clients
- copies of invoices you receive for goods or services
- your personal bank account books and paying-in slips
- building society books and annual interest statements
- annual mortgage statements
- annual statements relating to any pensions or savings plans

Again, establish a safe, well-organised space for these items. Have properly labelled files or box files – it can save hours of time later on if you have a system of popping papers into the right place as you go along.

If you use an accountant, all these records will have to be sent to him or her at least once a year, or quarterly if you are VAT-rated. I keep duplicates of most records (but not of receipts unless they are also a guarantee for the goods), both for my own reference and in case some are lost in the post or damaged along the line.

A sales ledger is a valuable tool. This is quite simply a list of all your sales, which may take the form of a list of invoices. In this you should record the date your invoice was issued, the name of the client and the amount it was for. If you are VAT-registered, you will need two extra columns – to show the total amount including VAT, and then the VAT as a separate item.

If you receive any cash payments you will need a cash payments book, and in this you will need to record the date of the transaction, your own reference number, the name of the customer and the amount paid.

At the time of writing, all records must be kept for six years. This requires quite a lot of space. Most people I know keep files for about the last two years in their office, easy to reach, and store the other four years' worth in a garage/attic/top of the wardrobe. But be warned: it is *very* important to keep these files. You can be inspected by the Inland Revenue at any time and you must be able to substantiate your tax claims, with the relevant documentation. If you fail to disclose income or you cannot produce your proofs, heavy fines can be imposed.

National insurance

There is a special schedule of contributions for self-employed people, with rates that become income-related over a certain level of earnings. Regard it as just another form of taxation.

If you fall behind with payments, understand that this might affect your state pension and benefits such as basic maternity allowance and incapacity benefit.

Your national insurance contributions will be collected automatically twice a year, along with your income tax.

Income tax and self-assessment

When you start up, you must inform your local tax office, either by letter or online (if you fail to do so within three months, there's a fine). The tax office will send you the appropriate forms and away you go. However, you cannot just announce that you are self-employed. The Inland Revenue has set rules to identify those who qualify for self-employment. To do so, you must:

• be working for more than one customer
• be in control of what you do, how, where and when you do it
• provide any major pieces of equipment you require for your job
• be free to hire staff, under your own auspices
• correct your own work in your own time and at your own expense, if it is unsatisfactory

If you do not fit into these criteria – for example, if you outsource for your former employer or only have major one client at a time – you may come under the IR35 net, which means that you will be taxed as if you were salaried. Your local tax inspector or your accountant will advise you. This is currently a very complex area, but the Inland Revenue has become more user-friendly these days. They have a dedicated phone line (*see* under 'Resources', page 235) for advice and registration, and it is well worth checking the website. There are special pages on starting up and there are Business Support Teams to help you in your first year of trading.

Part-time people have another challenge. They must show the Inland Revenue that they are not working on a casual basis (which falls into yet another tax category) but as a business or profession. If you are part-timing, you must inform the tax office and explain that your work is regular, and that you will be keeping business records. Some advisers suggest that you register for VAT even if you don't reach the limit.

Self-assessment means that we sole traders both calculate our own tax bill, and then pay it in advance. The level of tax is based on the previous year's earnings.

Those who fall into the self-employed category pay income tax in three stages. The first falls at the end of January; the second at the end of July. If you have done well and your profits are higher than you and the Inland Revenue expected, you will have a third 'balance' payment at the end of January the following year. This can hurt, particularly as the amount is added onto the tax for the coming year.

The self-assessment form is in fairly plain English but even so can be very confusing. It can be done online or in hard-copy form. To avoid yet more fines, ensure that your self-assessment form is in on time and you make your payments before the deadline. It is madness to pay more than you need to. If you find yourself in trouble, facing a tax bill you cannot meet, speak to the Inland Revenue in advance or ask your accountant to do so on your behalf, to see if there is a way to pay in instalments. Don't wait until the tax bill is all red and inflamed. Even so, you may have to pay interest, but you might just avoid receiving a fine.

VAT

Value Added Tax is a form of tax-gathering on behalf of the Government. You will only have to register for VAT when you reach a certain turnover; in this instance your profit is irrelevant. If you become VAT-registered and at any point your turnover drops below the current level, and is likely to remain so, you can ask to be de-registered.

Basically, the system is as follows. You pay VAT on goods and services you purchase. These sums, called inputs, can be reclaimed. You then charge people VAT on your goods and services and these are called outputs. The balance between the outputs (that is, the amount of tax you charge) and the inputs (that is, the amount that you reclaim) is the VAT you must pay quarterly to HM Customs & Excise. This is the simple bit. What is VAT-rated and what is exempt, or zero-rated, is a mystery to most of us and you may need professional guidance to establish the pattern for your business.

What is very necessary is that you keep your records scrupulously. You must:

- Put your VAT number on every invoice, along with your company name and address and a description of the goods or services supplied.
- Show the amount of VAT as a separate item on your invoices, as well as the net figure and the overall total.
- Show your VAT as a separate figure in your sales book.
- Keep all your VAT returns carefully filed.

Once registered, you can anticipate an inspection at some stage from HM Customs & Excise. The inspector will expect to see records for up to the previous three years.

Failure to pay VAT on time or to provide proper documentation can again lead to substantial fines. You may find it useful to keep a separate bank account for your VAT money. Simply transfer VAT across when you receive a large payment, or perhaps on a monthly basis, so you know the funds are there at the end of each quarter.

Note: There are all kinds of variations and pitfalls in all these areas of taxation, and I strongly recommend that you take professional advice. Accountants *like* all this stuff. They can do in a few minutes what would take the rest of us many hours to do. Unless you are fascinated by this kind of work, find an expert.

Finding an accountant

There is a professional body, of course, but possibly the best route to finding an accountant is a recommendation from people you trust. If none of your family or friends can suggest someone, ask well-run businesses you know of, your suppliers or customers perhaps, or even your bank manager. Try to find an accountant who specialises in small businesses. If he or she runs a small business themselves, even better.

When you have a name, go and see this person. You are selecting a professional adviser for your company and one who will make a lot of difference to its success or failure. This is therefore a very crucial appointment. You must be able to trust your accountant and his/her advice, so it is very important that you feel comfortable with them. You need to be able to ask what may well be 'silly' questions, without embarrassment, and there could be an instance when you have to admit that you have hit a difficult patch (hopefully temporary). If you find them intimidating or arrogant, you will not be able to build a worthwhile relationship. Of course, you are not marrying your accountant, so you can always change if you need to.

DIY accounting

Some people enjoy figures and the administration side of bookkeeping and therefore decide to do their own books. Nowadays there are some excellent software packages, with spreadsheets, that help you do to this correctly and effectively. However, you may find it wise to check with other independents or your computer supplier to discover which package is right for your business.

Financial crisis management

Even the most experienced independent can miss the first sign, but if there are second and third indications of change in a previously successful pattern of trading, immediate action is called for. The horns must be drawn in, and all outgoings examined, with a view to pruning down or cutting out completely. Emergency measures may mean taking any form of work that brings in funds, even though you normally would not consider it. Do not make the mistake of accepting extra loans, unless there is guaranteed income in the foreseeable future and your financial adviser can prove that this is the only solution.

If things start to go horribly wrong, radical action is better taken sooner rather than later. When there is little or nothing coming in, you cannot meet your expenses, and you are using up your emergency funds and starting on your savings, go for help. See your accountant, financial adviser, the bank, any organisation from whom you have a loan or grant. Be honest: tell them you have hit a wall and ask them what help is available. Take stock of all your outstanding bills. See where you can arrange special payments over a period of time, or a suspension, for example, of your mortgage or loan repayments.

It takes enormous courage to face all this, but the alternative is even more ghastly. If you let the bills accumulate, and your debts mount up without action, the problem just gets bigger and worse until ultimately, you cannot pay your creditors and they start to take action against you. A creditor can make you bankrupt; if you are a sole trader, you stand to lose everything. For the time being, jump off the tightrope, put your dreams in a safe place, and go for any job you can find.

Even the most experienced independent can miss the first sign, but if there are second and third indications of change in a previously successful pattern of trading, immediate action is called for.

Things to do

- Make a cash-flow chart so you know where the hiccups and bumps come.
- Design your own invoice.
- Take note of the processes for late payment.
- Set up a system for keeping your receipts and other paperwork.
- Inform the local tax office if you are starting up on your own. Seek advice from the tax inspectors if you are unsure of your tax status.
- If you are likely to hit the current limit of turnover, register for VAT.
- Look for a compatible accountant.
- If you hit problems, act sooner rather than later.

Trish Gittins

'I have never had a career path; everything has just happened to me. I find that exciting nowadays.'

Trish Gittins from nantwich in Cheshire is a freelance IT consultant.

Throughout childhood I wanted to be a nurse and I even once applied to the Manchester Royal Infirmary but in the end didn't want to leave home in my teens. I had already left school and was a trainee manager with Marks & Spencer, so for a while I stayed on. Then an opportunity arose to join the civil service at a manufacturing plant for the Ministry of Defence. I discovered that I enjoyed working in a predominantly male environment and I appreciated the logic of a production process. I was on the clerical side and, because there was good training and promotion, I became an executive officer, eventually running the department I had first joined.

I married and had a daughter, Kate. We had just bought a house and spent all our spare money decorating it when my husband, Pete, became ill and eventually died. It was a dreadful time but looking after him and then somehow managing on my own made me stronger. I felt that if I could cope with that, I could cope with anything.

The local doctors' surgery offered me part-time work which was good because I could spend time with Kate. Later I remarried and moved to Yorkshire where I played housewife until I became bored. There weren't many opportunities but a job came up with a steel company in Sheffield that made props and other equipment for the mining industry. Again I was in a factory setting and I was fascinated by the processes, and the costings and systems that go behind them. My manager was also financial director and he wanted the stock control computerised. I was 38 by then and had had nothing to do with computers but, to my amazement, I took to it instantly. The potential blew my brain – it still does!

Then came the miners' strike, a terrible period. I had to cross the picket lines: everyone I knew was affected in some way or another. Orders in my company disappeared, so did the cash flow. Finally, the doors closed and I was made redundant. I loved the new technology and I had valuable experience, but no qualifications. Then someone suggested that I retrain as a programmer. I applied to Manpower Services and at 42 became a full-time student. It was like being reborn. The learning situation was tough but I enjoyed every minute of it.

Afterwards I joined a small company that built its own PCs and software and I found myself writing software for integrating manufacturing. I would see the customer, take the brief, create the software, install it and train the staff to use it. It brought together all my experience from over the years. Sadly the company over-extended itself and once again I was made redundant.

I had had enough of that! Then, by accident, I found an advert for an IT consultant. I didn't know such a thing existed but I went to see the recruitment agency and knew that this was the right way for me. I have never had a career path; everything has just happened to me. I find that exciting nowadays.

The agency took me on and I was soon working for IBM on electronic point-of-sale for supermarkets. I went to a different store every two weeks to train the back office staff. This assignment lasted 15 months. Shortly afterwards my marriage broke up and I sank myself into work.

I had to set up my own limited company, Highcrest IT Ltd. I effectively became my own employee. It was daunting but I went to an accountant to ensure that everything was correct.

IBM gave me more work; there were a couple of contracts that lasted just a few months. I even had one with Marks & Spencer, which brought me full circle! Then I went to Glasgow for a time, working for an IT recruitment agency and one job that came in – with Scottish Power in East Kilbride – particularly appealed to me so I went for it myself. It was to be the first in a series of utility companies. I returned to England to work for East Midlands Electricity, and then went on to Powergen, now called E-on. I'm on a six-months renewable contract with them at the moment. I still work through an agency which is a big plus. It means that I'm paid regularly: I don't have to chase money.

Trish's advice:

Before going freelance, check the trade magazines to see what people are looking for and ensure that your skills are pertinent and up-to-date. Contracting is very strong in the IT field because it's a quickly changing market and companies have to adapt their workforce easily to meet it.

The best way to keep the work coming in is networking. Keep in touch with recruiters, former colleagues, and other contractors (they may have an overspill or hear about projects that are appropriate to you).

Have a fall-back. With my daughter and son-in-law, I'm the director of a company which builds houses. We started with just two, now we are looking at building five or six at a time. Hopefully, this will provide my pension!

Maureen Gallagher

'I find it difficult to say no when a lot of people are asking to work with me, but I have to do it. How can I talk to people about life balance, if I'm stressed out myself?'

Maureen Gallagher is an occupational psychologist and management consultant, based in Windsor.

I left school in Manchester to read geography at Liverpool University. I'm not really sure why, but maths was my other A-level subject and I wasn't attracted to the kind of jobs that would lead to. Afterwards I spent two years with the Voluntary Missionary Movement in Kenya teaching English and geography in a girls' secondary school. Most Kenyan teachers gravitated to the cities, so schools like this one, in the bush 30 miles from the Ugandan border, were short staffed.

I loved it and didn't want to come home, but the priests advised me to have a career and see more of the world. It took ages to readjust to the wealth back here. It was a shock to see so many goods in the supermarkets, all those shelves of toothpaste and flour!

ICL had offered me management training before I went abroad so I contacted them again when I got back. They directed me towards the training side of human resources, where I stayed for five years. By then, I had gone as far as I could and, ever ready for a challenge, I answered an advert for a post with DEC (Digital Equipment Corporation). They didn't give me the job I applied for; instead they created a job specially for me as European Organisational Development Consultant. I worked one day a month in the Reading head office but otherwise spent the time travelling. As a US company, the culture was very different: it was ahead of its time in human resources, very innovative.

Unfortunately DEC didn't anticipate the growth of the PC market and so were taken over by Compaq – which has since been taken over itself. In a strategic move, I joined what is now PricewaterhouseCoopers: my ambition then was to be a human resources director, and I therefore needed to deal with top people. I had a creative, hard-working team, and learned a lot, but the value set was not a good fit. I realised that there were many companies I wouldn't want to work for, and at this point an older friend asked me to set up a management consultancy with her. I love freedom and challenge and, through this offer, I realised that I would achieve neither through being a HR director.

We didn't take clients with us, we started from scratch. Neither of us were sales people but fortunately, friends recommended us and we had work in our first year. The partnership worked well for three years but then we hit difficulties. It wasn't a good time. We had just taken on premises and a full-time secretary; there was a shortage of work and suddenly money was haemorrhaging away. It was very scary. I talked to my father who pointed out that if I didn't try, I would never know if it could work – great advice. So I continued the business alone. I looked at ways to minimise the growing debt and considered returning to employment. I had several job offers but when it came to the crunch, I didn't take them, even though there was still no work coming in. I phoned the people I know well and eventually found more work.

Nowadays I work with leaders of global companies in the IT and telecoms field, and some in the financial sector, to help them create exemplary leadership behaviour in complex environments. I work from the premise that you cannot be a leader unless you can lead yourself. I firmly believe in the potential in people: we all have everything we need but then we limit ourselves. I help people identify what limits them and then develop who they really are. It's a great privilege. Top people can influence many others, so I feel that I am helping not only them but also their families and all their employees.

Recently I have gone into partnership. It's a big change after working by myself for a decade.

I find it difficult to say no when a lot of people are asking to work with me, but I have to do it. How can I talk to people about life balance, if I'm stressed out myself?

Maureen's advice:

To get the best out of working on your own, you must know what's important to you. What sustains me through the long hours is the belief that what I do is worthwhile. If you are going into business, find something you feel passionate about, that you really enjoy. You are in trouble if you feel it is a burden. What keeps you going is feeling that you have achieved something. What's the point otherwise?

I have also learned that everything is in the detail. Recently I walked the El Camino in Spain for six weeks. It was a wonderful spiritual journey, but I also realised the difference it makes when someone cares about what they do. We stayed in hostels along the way. Some were very basic. In others, someone had dusted under the beds and served us coffee when we arrived. One woman came to us with a bowl of cherries. Small things, these – but they really enhanced our enjoyment.

11

The Long-Term Planning Department

Making it grow: making the business more profitable – increasing business from your existing clients – seeking new clients or customers – offering a new service or product – taking over part or all of someone else's business – forming a partnership – taking on employees – working with associates – outsourcing – more planning – training

Businesses are not static but organic; they change, expand, sway, wobble, blossom forth or curl around the edges. It's very easy to become caught up exclusively in the day-to-day work, but a wise independent takes a regular step back to look at the pattern of growth, both current and potential, of their business. We are, after all, aiming for increasingly prosperous harvests.

For some people, keeping their little business ticking over is all they really require. Maybe their focus is on other goals in their lives: bringing up children, preparing to climb Everest, winning a Gold at the Chelsea Flower Show or taking a diploma or degree course. You may therefore assume that this chapter holds nothing for you. Wrong; it does. Trends, products and services date like any other commodity and most things have a shelf life, after which they become stale. Customers' needs change too. If you are to be successful – even if you only work one day a week – you need to be up-to-date, if not a trend-spotter.

For most independents, of course, the emphasis will be on making the whole business grow and become more successful – which usually means more profitable, less labour-intensive, and wildly interesting and varied – but with the minimum of hassle.

Making it grow

Making the business more profitable

As part of the process, examine the profitability of your enterprise on a regular basis. Is there any way to improve it *without* taking on more clients or customers? Consider the following:

- Becoming rich is *not* about spending your money, but rather keeping it or investing it. Better still, use it to generate income under its own steam (e.g. by investing it or purchasing property that will give you a rental income) while you are putting your energies elsewhere – although nothing runs entirely by itself, so constant vigilance in these matters is always wise.
- Reduce costs: keep a watch on the costs that leech away your profit. Ensure that you have the most cost-effective workspace, and that your phones, IT and insurances are the best value for your requirements. See if there are other ways in which you can economise without disturbing the quality of your enterprise.
- Increase your fees or profit margin; you will need to adjust your fees or prices to cope with inflation anyway. If you are continuing to give excellent service and you are keeping abreast of what else is happening in the market, you may be able to raise your income steadily without doing extra work (*see* Chapter 2, *The Research & Development Department* – 'The likely demand', 'Competition' and 'Your added value').

The other way of growing your profitability, of course, is to expand your business – and you can do this in a number of ways:

Increasing business from your existing clients

Research has shown that many independent practitioners look to their current clients when planning expansion. In a recent survey of independent public relations practitioners, conducted by the appointments agency, The Counsel House, more than half relied on their existing clients when they were looking for more work.

Look closely at all your favourite customers and see if there is any possibility of expansion within their companies. Are there other departments you could be contacting or other potential purchasers of your services that you can meet? It is certainly worth seeing where else your skills or products could fit into other parts of their businesses. Do they have other colleagues or departments, or subsidiary plants, branches, shops or offices? Do they have overseas connections? Can you think of ways in which you can bring new customers to them? Or can you find them new resources? Do you have skills in your personal toolbox which may be useful to them? If so, write a proposal or have a word with a key person, on the lines of 'I don't know if you realise this, but I can also offer . . .'.

You can even imply that, as they are an existing client, you will offer them an exceptionally good-value rate for your work or products.

Seeking out new clients or customers

It has been mentioned in this book before and I make no apology for repeating that marketing, promotion and networking are continuing strands in every independent's business. It's easy to be complacent when the work book is full but anyone can lose a client at any time. It may not be their fault, either, merely the way the world turns on its axis.

It is therefore very wise to check your mix of income. Are you too reliant on one customer?

Offering a new service or product

The art is to anticipate what your customers or clients will want in the future. You should know before they do! It's rather impressive to be the one to tell them what the latest trends are, or the likely challenges – whatever field you are in.

By all means, continue to supply whatever products and services are 'classical' in your line of business. If they are fulfilling a need and are the best of their kind, and if they offer value – and a good profit for you – there is no point in offloading them, no matter how long you have been providing them. Even so, beware of looking outdated. You cannot afford to be behind the times, and there's no excuse for being so: as an independent you have more flexibility than most, and more opportunities for getting out and about and seeking out what is new, exciting and different.

Successful marketeers keep abreast of trends by studying the media – both national TV and newspapers and their professional or trade press; attending exhibitions and workshops; keeping an eye on competitors; looking at the websites of practitioners in other parts of Europe or abroad; and identifying who is up and coming in the industry, then making an effort to meet them or hear them speak (whatever is appropriate to your business). By keeping an eye on the trends and how people in your area are spending money, you should be able to offer new services or products in advance of your competition.

Additionally, listen to your clients and customers. If you ask them what their problem areas are, or what is missing from their working lives, they will sometimes admit to a requirement that you may be able to address. You can quite literally 'go shopping' for them.

You might also consider whether extra training would enable you to offer a new kind of service. It's very easy, when you are fully stretched, to ignore training – so we deal with that issue later in this chapter!

Taking over part or all of someone else's business

Expansion by take-over is a well-established business ploy. You will obviously take all the necessary steps to research a prospective business, and verify its profitability, its creditworthiness and the commitment of its customers, as well as its prospects.

There are three main reasons why someone would want to sell a business:

- they wish to retire
- they want to do something completely different with their lives
- the business hasn't proved profitable

In respect of a potential take-over, the first two instances make attractive propositions – particularly where there is a good client or customer base and a solid track record of profitable business. This will no doubt be reflected in the purchase price. The third should not automatically be discounted, although it should be treated with extreme caution. It is possible that your way of managing affairs will turn a poorly run business into a success; you would be able to buy it for very little, and there might be tax advantages too. If the nature of the business is a 'fit' or can be absorbed into what you are already doing, it is worth investigating further.

Be sure that any additional business doesn't swamp you and your resources. Also, be certain that this is a marriage made in heaven, not just a financial match – in other words that you like it, are fascinated by it and truly want a long-term relationship. You may be together for some time. If you are not keen to start with, you should not be contemplating a liaison. It could end in tears.

It's easy to be complacent when the work book is full but anyone can lose a client at any time. It may not be their fault, either, merely the way the world turns on its axis.

Forming a partnership with someone else

Sometimes, even though a similar business may not be for sale, there is a synergy between you and the other practitioner – suggesting that together the two of you could more than double the business. Again, research the other business and be sure that you can form a good working relationship with the prospective partner. Ideally you both need to have the same work ethic, the same approach to obtaining clients, and the same attitudes to work-life balance. Many a partnership has come to grief because one partner believes in grabbing any business, no matter how shady the client, when the other has areas of business that morally they won't touch. Other partnerships have come apart because one partner takes regular breaks and holidays and the other is a workaholic. Many people say that a working partnership is closer than any marriage . . . and certainly you are likely to spend as many hours with your work partner as you do with your significant other.

If you do consider a partnership, it is wise to make a full partnership agreement from the beginning. This means taking decisions about what you would wish to happen in the following circumstances:

- a partner marries
- a partner divorces
- a partner dies
- a partner becomes disabled or chronically sick and can only work part-time or not at all

In the last three instances it is usual for one partner to have the opportunity to buy the other out; alternatively the business is dissolved or sold, and proceeds are split between the partners or their dependents or, in the case of a death, their estate. Such events are tragic in themselves and bring about more than enough emotional trauma, without having to worry about losing the business too. A partner could suddenly find themselves in the position of having to buy the other half of a business without sufficient funds, or trying to find another partner quickly, or needing to re-form as a sole trader. To avoid such problems it is well worth exploring the merits of having life insurance policies on the lives of each partner, written under trust to benefit the other partner.

There are other areas which you may wish to resolve more informally. For instance, what would happen if a partner wished to develop the business in a different way, or was found to be inefficient, or lost business through some failure of practice? Most good solicitors can guide you through the standard partnership agreement and suggest where it can be personalised to your business and circumstances, and an independent financial adviser can recommend suitable life insurance policies.

Taking on employees to allow you to accept new work

If there are ongoing parts of the work that don't stretch you or interest you, but instead block you from doing the thing you do best, consider how you might offload these. Naturally you will wish to oversee the work and check its quality before it goes to the client or customer, but it may not require your input throughout.

One way forward might be to consider employing someone else on either a part-time or full-time basis. This requires considerable planning and careful attention to budgets. The costs of employing other people are quite steep and, as employees, they will have rights and the kind of protection that you may not even accord to yourself – such as holiday and sickness entitlement, maternity leave and pension provision.

Sometimes a small business will undergo that uncomfortable phase when there is too much for one person to do but not quite enough for two. Many of us have had the experience of paying an employee but, for a time, taking home less ourselves than they do.

Working with associates

One alternative to taking on new employees is to collaborate with other independent practitioners. This can work extremely well, particularly if you are involved in project work. It means that you can put together a 'dream team' for each project, selecting those associates who have the right mixture of skills, strengths and contacts.

Sometimes these associates will be friends. This is still a business arrangement, however, and must remain on that footing. The plus point of friends as associates is that you can usually rely on them through the thick and thin of a project; the minus side is that you all tend to have parity. It may therefore be necessary to set guidelines and boundaries.

Where you have obtained the business in the first place, it is only sensible to establish that you will be taking the lead and that you are the main contact point with the client. This may mean setting up a chain of reporting from your associates, so that you can accurately update your client at any time. It is also wise to have the chain of command in place, in event of any dispute or confusion about roles and responsibilities. Arrange to have regular meetings and updates with your associates: it's all too easy for crucial details to be overlooked.

Just as you will arrange a letter of confirmation of the contract or commission from your client, so it is important to have a letter of agreement with each associate. This should cover an exact description of the duties you expect them to undertake; the timeframe for completion of the work; the means by which that work will be inspected, where appropriate; and the amount, method and timing of payment and of any expenses incurred. Specify the anticipated expenses too.

If someone brings you in as an associate, insist on knowing precisely what is expected of you. Ask for a comprehensive briefing and check how much interaction you are expected to have with the client. You don't want to appear to be poaching the business; at the same time you must know if you are required to keep the client up-to-date on progress.

Painter and decorator, Mark Davies, from Windsor, always wanted to be his own boss. After school he spent a short period working for someone else to learn his craft, but soon went solo. His work comes in mainly from recommendations and, now and again, a big project crops up.

'Either I allow more time and do it all myself, or if it is a very large job, such as a suite of offices, or there's a tight deadline, I'll pull in other people. There's my brother, who is fully employed but will help me on his days off, or there's another painter I know locally whose work is good. But I'm always the one to look after the client and it's up to me to make sure all the work is of the same high standard,' Mark says.

Outsourcing

Sometimes clients will ask you to provide, perhaps as part of a larger project, work that you do not have the skills for, or are unable to accomplish timewise. You may be able to accept this work if you know a supplier, or another practitioner, or a company that can undertake it to the standard you require. You can therefore delegate the work to them, perhaps arranging to take a mark-up. This is where you invoice and duly receive payment from the client; you then pay the supplier, minus a management fee. Alternatively you can agree a commission with the supplier, whereby the client pays the supplier or practitioner direct, who then pays you the management fee.

This is outsourcing, and it requires all the contractual arrangements we have covered previously, texturalised to your business. In short, you must be sure that the supplier or practitioner is in a position both financially and in terms of work capacity to complete the work within your client's time framework. If necessary, visit the supplier and check the facilities or staff, whatever is appropriate. Arrange a comprehensive briefing for the supplier, either directly with your client or through you. Ensure that letters of agreement are drawn up. Establish where responsibilities lie, should anything go wrong: you don't want to be paying for other people's mistakes. If the project is a large one, seek legal advice and establish a formal contract.

More planning

Some people find that a business plan helps keep them on track. They set themselves sales or profits targets, or a certain level of turnover, and make a game of trying to reach them. Such structures are much beloved of banks and loan- or grant-making organisations: they regularly ask for projections, usually over one, three and five years, and like to see progress towards fulfilment.

Your plans depend on the kind of business you have, of course, and on what your personal 'drivers' are. Targets can be something you aspire to, aiding your motivation and spurring you on, or they can become the bars of a cage – meaningless aims in themselves. Many of our public services are now so target-orientated that they have forgotten the real reasons for which the targets were set. Reaching them has become a target in itself. By all means sketch out your plans for the coming years. Have a rough diagram of how you would like your business to develop in a perfect world. But please do not make such a rigid framework that you are pressured or inhibited by it. Part of the joy of independence is that you can be spontaneous, follow unlikely paths and find new worlds to conquer. You are not restricted by heavyweight managements; you can respond to new opportunities in a way that larger organisations envy.

As long as you are covering all your expenses and commitments, you can wander off in whatever direction pleases you. Don't make yourself into a mini corporation, unless that's your specific aim. In your long-term planning, it's worth checking to see if you have the mix of work right. Just because you are good at one thing, doesn't mean that you personally cannot grow into something more. You can spend a certain number of days doing what you have always been known for, and you can also take off in a new directions on other days.

Training

If we are reasonably successful, we assume that all is well. Our clients are happy with us, and will probably stay that way. What more effort could we possibly be asked to put in? We start believing that we know it all, but there's a very good chance that we don't. To stay ahead, we must plan to *be* ahead.

Invest in the future of your business by investing in your own training. It is usually worth every effort to keep your core skills up-to-date. The world changes very quickly these days, in every sphere of activity, and you owe it to yourself to keep abreast of every improvement in practice. Learning new techniques may save you time or give you something extra to offer to your clients. By all means let those factors act as incentives.

It's often more than just your basic skills that need constantly brushing up. Scan the list below and see if your business might not be improved from your learning about:

- using the Internet
- e-business
- marketing
- direct mail sales
- writing skills
- making presentations
- media training
- financial planning for small businesses

Take every workshop you think might be useful and interesting. You may pick up good ideas that can be translated. You may also meet interesting new contacts.

Things to do

- Keep an eye on the costs and see where you can reduce them without losing quality.
- Look at ways to increase your income without increasing your workload. See if there is more work within your current client-base.
- Consider offering a new product or service, or expanding by taking over other, similar businesses.
- Judge whether you can expand your business by working with associates, taking a business partner or employing staff.
- Have a short- and longer-term plan, but stay flexible.
- Keep your skills up-to-date.

Pete Robbins

'It would have been impossible to stay on my own. The thinking in sales is towards expansion.'

Pete Robbins from Hampton in Arden in Warwickshire runs two companies, distributing and selling health and safety equipment. From the start, he intended to make his enterprise grow and, after six years, has eight employees.

I was always a salesman. Over the years, I was a representative for a number of companies, from Singer Sewing Machines to Associated Biscuits, and so in some ways used to working on my own. On occasions I would win top salesman awards because I was bringing in the business, but all too often I wasn't following the company 'script'; I wasn't really conforming.

I toyed for years with the idea of setting up on my own. I thought, if the bosses can do it, so can I. I had never had to look for jobs, I was constantly being 'poached' from one organisation to another. In the end, I was working for a company that had a franchise for Swedish products. It was the franchising company that approached me and asked me to start something up, selling disposable respirators. I had no set-up money, so put together a business plan with view to getting a loan, and I took it to an accountant. He laughed at my efforts but was impressed by the concept and helped me. Even then the bank didn't believe my sales projections. But within weeks I had a company of my own called Segré, and money to pay into the bank, even before they sent me a paying-in book!

Taking on a franchise, particularly from overseas, can be a minefield. Often foreign companies don't understand that the UK market will be different from their home market. Usually they will give you good credit but no contribution towards the marketing and promotion. That's down to you.

I was fortunate. I had back orders and some existing customers, and my daughter Julia soon joined me. She was just out of university and due to start teacher training, but I persuaded her in, and it's great because she has the same attitude to work as me. It would have been impossible to stay on my own. The thinking in sales is towards expansion. In the early days, I took on someone else who knew the industry but he had been around too long and was idle. Calling him down to sack him was awful, although it was his own fault. Even the customers approved when I let him go, though none had told us he wasn't up to the job. But it taught me not to give employees *carte blanche.* They will often work in the way they were first taught, but that might not the way you want them to operate.

It's developed into a very friendly company and I am really proud of that. There's a great atmosphere. That has a knock-on effect because our customers enjoy working with us. We all socialise. Often I hear more about what's going on over a drink than I do in a formal sales meeting. But while it is friendly and there's flexibility and compassionate leave if someone is going through a difficult time, I would not tolerate someone telling me they are in one place, when they are in fact elsewhere. The day I catch someone doing that, they're out.

At the same time I don't expect my employees to have the same dedication to the business as I do. Except of course for the family.

My wife, Sue, supported me from the beginning and began doing part-time work. Eighteen months ago we took on Factor Safe, the company that was distributing our products – and others as well – and she came in full-time. The second company is more labour-intensive and generates more paperwork because of the large range of products. But she's trying to pull back a bit.

What we had to learn with this company was not to be afraid to turn business down if it doesn't bring in profit. It's easy to get into the habit of doing anything and everything that comes your way, but the chances are that not all of it is cost-effective.

There's never enough time; that's why it is so essential to delegate. I still make a 'tick list' of all the things I've got to do, but now I make reasonable targets and I give myself a bit of leeway.

Pete's advice:

A sense of humour is essential. It's also very important to know where you want to go. I am always being told off by my accountant for taking risks, but it's usually about something that has to be done and I know will work. You must listen to your own inner voice. By all means take outside advice – accountants and banks – but they are traditionally very conservative and they won't make any decisions for you. You must make your own. And that's right because they don't know your business. You do.

The best thing I have done is to buy a bolt hole on the coast. It takes you away from it all, even though you continue to think about the business and even check in now and again. But if you holiday at home, you will almost certainly wind up going into the office.

Patricia Orr

'Yes, it was a worry, taking on staff, keeping the books, working out VAT, but it was worse, when working on one's own, knowing that if you were sick you could well lose a client.'

Patricia Orr is a public relations consultant. She runs an agency called Third Sector PR, which specialises in the voluntary sector and particularly in health and social care issues.

When I took A-levels, fewer people went to university. I was young for my age so, while I was wondering what to do, my parents persuaded me to take a secretarial course. After a boring diet of shorthand, typing and bookkeeping at St James's Secretarial College in London, the thought of having money in my pocket began to grow.

I started working at just 18 and enjoyed my newfound freedom. At 20 a friend introduced me to an influential family on the then unspoiled island of Santa Cruz in the Canary Islands. I spent an idyllic year in Tenerife with a family of six children, teaching English and learning Spanish.

On my return I was influenced by close friends who were having a ball in public relations. I joined Charles Barker and Sons, then one of the largest London agencies. This was the start of my PR career and I was soon taking the Institute of Public Relations exams.

Marriage followed. Alexander and Jonathan were born and I took on the role of a housebound housewife, bored and unfulfilled. A job abroad arose for my husband and we started a new life in the tropical beauty of Kenya with a 21-month child and a baby of three months.

Very sadly the marriage did not work out, and I had to swiftly fall back on my secretarial skills to make ends meet. The United Nations had just started up its Environment Programme in Nairobi and so I became an international civil servant. It was intensely interesting and broadened both my learning and horizons. I graduated to the Office of the Executive Director, preparing briefs for his missions abroad.

At this time I met Patrick, my second husband, and we had Toby, my third son. A wonderful time of sun and safaris followed. Then came serious decision time: whether to stay or to return to England for education and family reasons. We came home, which proved a serious culture shock.

After a spell with the family firm I returned to the UN, firstly at London's UN Information Centre, then as Assistant Representative (Information) at the UN High Commissioner for Refugees. It was the 1970s and the world watched in horror at the plight of the 'boat people' fleeing in rickety boats across the South China Seas.

Juggling my lifestyle with the demands of three boys was challenging. Getting further in the UN could have meant an unconditional posting abroad (you had to be prepared to move to another country; you took an oath to do this), but I didn't want to lose the UN connection and joined and eventually chaired the Westminster Branch of the UN Association.

I then moved to the forestry sector, to put the case for

private woodland owners with Timber Growers UK. But the guilt factor became stronger: I wanted to see more of my children, so I took a part-time job with (now) CancerBACUP to set up a PR and media facility.

This set me on the track I've followed since, the voluntary sector. I spent five years with the Royal National Institute for the Blind, heading up their public relations team before deciding that, with my children through much of their schooling, I could risk the salary cheque.

At 50, I set up in a small London flat with one client. I lacked confidence and had all the frustrations of a one-man-band: rushing to the nearest photocopy shop and post by 5.30 p.m. Pitching for new business was nerve-wracking, with the constant guesswork of what to charge. I took desk space in a charming office in Battersea and was then persuaded by my husband to share offices in Victoria with his rather larger PR company which concentrated on Africa and world development issues.

I then took on an assistant. I enjoyed sharing the day and having a companion, even if I did take home less pay than than at the start. Now I've had a partner for five years, as well as a junior and several associates. The clients have increased, but I wouldn't wish to grow much larger. I like the day-to-day variety of running a hands-on operation and achieving tangible successes.

Yes, it was a worry, taking on staff, keeping the books, working out VAT, but it was worse, when working on one's own, knowing that if you were sick you could well lose a client.

Pat's advice:

Independents need good health, organisational skills, attention to detail and plenty of drive. The rest is down to confidence and building a rapport with your clients. In the media sector it means a 24/7 job – not only to be there for the client, but to create opportunities.

Taking on employees is a responsibility. The more you invest in your staff, the higher the return in terms of dedication and commitment. It can be hard to let go, but you must let them have their heads and take their own decisions. It may not be quite the way you would have done it, but if the client is happy and the standard is maintained, that's what you are after. And, hey, you have to remember that you're getting older and that's how they do things these days.

The Human Resources Department

negative stress – coping mechanisms – making boundaries – isolation – mentoring – time management – dealing with rejection – hobbies and other interests – holidays – everyday maintenance – personal award scheme

So how are *you* doing?

If you have made the great step into solo working, are you whizzing along, are you flying, or are you scraping along on your bottom? Is your journey as you planned it or is it a very different experience?

It's probably been a bit of everything, but almost certainly not what you anticipated. Hopefully you are feeling empowered, proud of your achievements, excited by new prospects and wholly optimistic. It's also extremely likely that, as with any skill, you haven't quite mastered the timing first time around. It takes practice, guidance from people who have been doing it for a while, readjustment to the mindset now and again, and sometimes a total rethink.

In the early stages, it's very easy to undermine yourself, all in the best interests of your budding business. The three major minefields are:

(1) *Workaholism.* The business has taken off well; you are finding it tough but totally engrossing. You feel you must take advantage of absolutely every opportunity that arises and if that means working all the time, so be it. It might be just beginner's luck, you tell yourself, and it might not last.

This kind of working is fine in short bursts, but it can get out of hand. Your life then becomes a kind of bizarre race between how long you can keep the pace going before you fall over, versus the time when the work suffers and finally does run out. The trouble is, if the work were to peter out first, you would then be anxious and desperate to replace it and would put in the hours to find more, and soon you would be back to working at the same manic level.

This kind of working pattern becomes obsessive/compulsive and therefore very unhealthy. It has an impact on you and your health but it can also take a toll on family relationships and friendships too.

(2) *Poor time management.* This is sometimes akin to workaholism but is usually more about spending too much time on unproductive work. Hours spent on work that actually brings you money is therefore reduced; alternatively you start to put in unnecessarily long hours. There is a cross-over with workaholism in that you are afraid to turn work away, even when you know you are unable to accomplish it properly. Like workaholism, poor time management leads to a panicky, stressed, out-of-control working life which can result in personal burn-out.

There are all kinds of defence mechanisms that kick in when it is suggested to someone that they are overworking. There's the 'I am doing this for my future/my family's future/for you/ for the good of the world' defence; the 'It will settle down, it's bound to be difficult in the first few weeks/months/years' one; the 'I'll calm it all down just as soon as I've paid off the mortgage/repaid the start-up loan/bought the computers I really need' response; and last but not least, the 'I'm the boss now, so what I say goes' argument. Yes indeed, but perhaps you should ask yourself this: 'Is this the ideal life I set out to make for myself?'

(3) *Trouble.* It's going wrong, it's not working and possibly you hate the whole thing. Some people become ostriches and pretend that everything is fine. They have launched themselves publicly in an independent practice and don't want to admit that their grand plan is a sad little thing or that they are simply not enjoying the journey all by themselves.

There's a variation on the ostrich approach, and it is surprisingly common: this happens when the work or the orders are not coming in and, rather than face the problem immediately, you start to convince yourself – as the pile of bills grows ever higher – that just one big order will pull everything around. It may well be true; just one order might do the trick, but is it *really* likely to happen? Are you being unrealistic and waiting too long? How long before you run into trouble? If you haven't a hot prospect on the horizon, other action is called for, however humiliating or otherwise uncomfortable.

It's like putting off going to the dentist when you feel a twinge. Do it quickly and you may only need a filling; delay it, and the tooth may have to be pulled.

negative stress

All the above scenarios engender stress. Of course, we all need some level of stress in order to be motivated. Some people enjoy a certain level of risk in their lives, and are at their best when the deadlines are close or there's a hint of danger in the air. Others prefer a calmer working atmosphere in order to be creative. But there comes a certain point, individual to each one of us, when the stress is not positive – it is very destructive.

There are two manifestations of harmful stress:

- *Physical*: the lesser symptoms include restlessness, impatience or irritability, tiredness, insomnia, an increase in smoking or drinking, a lack of or increased appetite, indigestion, headaches, feeling faint and increased sweating. In turn these lesser symptoms can lead to high blood pressure, high cholesterol, heart disease, skin rashes, weight gain or loss, exhaustion and recurring migraines.
- *Psychological*: the physical symptoms of stress will be accompanied by other effects, such as poor concentration, constant anxiety, an inability to switch off and relax, poor work performance, silly mistakes, a tendency to be accident-prone, loss of sex drive, irrational worries, oversensitivity to criticism and depression.

If you have more than two of the physical symptoms, please consider reporting to your GP. There are also many excellent alternative therapies and relaxation techniques that would also be of great value. Physical exercise often helps balance adrenalin levels: match this with a yoga class that includes deep-breathing exercises, meditation sessions and an osteopathic or deep-tissue massage. At the same time, you owe it to yourself to look hard at the causes of the negative stress, and take control of the problem.

Change is always difficult. A major change, such as setting up on your own, is stressful all by itself. Then add in any extra pressures, such as overwork, bad debts, or a lack of or too much business – and up those stress levels go.

Coping mechanisms

You are the central character in this particular play. If something is amiss with the main player in this one-man show, the whole thing fails to work. If you are reliant on one piece of machinery, it is fairly certain that you will look after it very carefully. You will ensure that it has regular services, and that any small creaks or high-pitched whines are attended to immediately. You will check its fuel, its temperature and its revs, and you will probably polish it now and again too. Now that you are an independent practitioner, you are the main piece of equipment in your business, so you must accord yourself the same five-star treatment – so start oiling and polishing and checking those revs!

Making boundaries

If you were an employee, or if you have ever engaged an employee, one of the major conditions of the contract relates to hours working, and time off. Part of the interview is inevitably about the expectations relating to flexi-time, overtime and holidays.

Few independent practitioners expect to work a neat and tidy set of hours. It is fairly certain that, like all managing directors, you will work longer than your directly employed friends and relations – unless they are at director level too, of course.

Naturally, your new enterprise is worthy of your full attention – at least, that is, while you are working. But if you are working exceptionally long hours, are getting too tired and very fractious, and your family or friends are moaning that they never see you, you have to ask yourself about your contract (the one you should be making with yourself). Ask yourself what the real value of your business is. It is worth sacrifice? If so, what will those sacrifices be?

- One or two extra working hours per day?
- One to two evenings a week of additional time?
- The occasional half-day at weekends?
- Working every weekend?
- Working on some public holidays (unless those are your business peak times)?
- All public holidays?
- Giving up other holiday breaks? For one year? More? How many more?
- Giving up hobbies?
- Cutting down on seeing friends?
- Cutting down on treats you enjoy? For one year? More?
- Reducing the amount of exercise or sport you enjoy? For one year? More?
- Reducing the time with your partner/spouse?
- Cutting down the time you spend with your children/parents?

It's your choice: you are on your own now so you have to decide. I urge you to make a definite choice in the matter and write your own contract of employment. Select from the above list what is acceptable and appropriate to you and your new business, and make every attempt to stick to it. Talk to your partner or spouse; see what they would find acceptable too. If necessary, negotiate. Too many relationships are diminished by the demands of work and business. You need support from your family, not the occasional company of resentful strangers.

Too many relationships are diminished by the demands of work and business. You need support from your family, not the occasional company of resentful strangers.

For example, you may decide that you will work one or two extra hours per day, plus (when necessary) one half-day at the weekends. You will take all your public holidays but might do a limited amount of paperwork on, say, Boxing Day or Easter Sunday afternoon.

You will have one or two long weekend breaks in the first year but not a major holiday until you have successfully made it into year two. Then you will ensure that the whole family has two weeks away.

You might decide that you will cut down treat trips for the first six months, then review the situation; but you will not give up your yoga class/Sunday football/weekend round of golf. You might not be able see all your friends individually, but you will throw the occasional party/picnic/barbecue and catch up then. Time with your family: no change! Now, that would be a reasonable and healthy choice, but only if you stick to that contract.

Being independent means that you make the decisions in every aspect of your life. Hopefully your ambition will not be driven only by the revenue you can generate, but by the quality of life you are able to attain. The starting point therefore is putting boundaries around your work. Review your working pattern regularly. Change it not only to suit the circumstances of your work, but to suit you, the main player.

I had one friend, a graphic designer, who believed that if he couldn't make a decent living within 40 hours a week, he was getting something very wrong. It took him some years to achieve this ambition but eventually he did it. Very sadly, he died young, and all his friends were glad that he hadn't 'lived to work', but had had a lot of good-quality time with the people he cared about.

Isolation

Humans are social animals. One of the stresses many independent practitioners face is coping with working alone. Whether your office space, studio or workshop is at home or 'outside', you are likely to be there for many hours by yourself. Some people relish the peace, and work better because of it; others find it intimidating. If this is your experience, you may need to develop strategies to overcome these feelings of isolation. I know independents who have adopted one or more of the following:

- *A pet.* It may sound corny but a dog, cat or parrot could be the company you seek. Dogs also need exercise and so will drag you off to the park several times a day to see other dogs and humans and give your mind and body a break. Whatever kind of pet is it, they will be on your side and you can chat away to them without the neighbours becoming spooked. Be sure that your pet is happy to stay at base or in the car when you go to business meetings, however. It's just not professional to walk in with a briefcase and a poodle.

- *Music.* Play classical music or hard rock, or whatever fills up the silences best for you – but ensure it does not interfere with your work or can be heard during phone calls. You may be able to work well to music, but if your clients hear it, they may assume that you are partying – or at least not concentrating.
- *Work out.* Make a point of going to the gym/swimming pool/a class at lunchtimes, rather than in the evening. You can talk to people there, grab a healthy soup or sandwich and network at the same time.
- *Meetings.* Rather than having a full day out, then working alone for several days afterwards, spread your business meetings across the week. Make some of them at lunchtimes to break up your working day.
- *Networking.* After reading Chapter 6 on networking, hopefully you will be joining various organisations and looking for opportunities to meet new people anyway.
- *Other independents.* Link up with a group of people who are also working on their own. You may not be doing exactly the same thing but the chances are that now and again other independents in your area may welcome a coffee break, lunchtime sandwich or drink after work when you can all share your experiences. This can form the basis of a network which may prove invaluable in times of crisis or low energy. It is interesting to note how many of the 'case studies' in this book have automatically formed this kind of support group around them.

Mentoring

One of the latest developments in working practice, alongside life coaching, is the role of mentors. By and large, these are people who are senior in their field and are willing to give part of their time to become a personal adviser to someone at the beginning of or partway along their career path. The advantage is that your mentor, unlike a bank or professional adviser, has no commercial motivation. They are completely objective, with only your best interests at heart. A good mentor is someone for you to bounce ideas off, moan to, test solutions against. With them, you can redefine your thinking and defuse your frustrations.

Mentors are not restricted to your current career situation but can take a wider view, taking your personality, set of talents and expectations into account. They should be able to suggest avenues of consideration, areas of research or training, and even be able to arrange meetings with useful or influential contacts.

Many medium-sized as well as major companies and organisations now run mentoring schemes for their executives. The Prince's Trust, which makes grants to young people starting up their own businesses, automatically assigns a mentor to each grantee for their first three years of business. With more than 7500 volunteer mentors, helping 5000 people starting up each year, the Trust is one of the largest mentoring networks in the country. As a result they have been closely involved with setting standards for business mentoring via the government agency, SFEDI.

Stefan Warhaftig, the Trust's training and support manager, explains: 'The people who approach the Trust aren't coming for a mentor but rather for a grant. Even so our research among grantees shows that mentoring proves to be the thing of highest value to them.

'Our volunteer mentors are not business advisers. They are certainly not there to help someone with their tax forms. Their remit is to mentor the people, not the businesses. We train the mentors in soft skills, so they can relate to these young people, understand the value of listening, help them through the process of decision-making, discuss the problems of motivation and help boost confidence. Help the person, and the business will thrive.

'We try to match backgrounds and interests but often the best relationships grow when the mentor and grantee are complete opposites.

'The mentors are standing back from the grantee's situation; there's no vested interest. As a result, the grantees know that they can trust their mentor's guidance.'

And it's not just organisations that seek mentoring: some high-profile individuals clearly benefit from an even more prestigious mentor, and they pay them for their time and experienced input. You too can adopt the system. If you know of someone more senior than you, maybe recently retired, whose perspective and advice you would value, why not approach them about being your mentor? Make it clear what you are asking for. There are no set rules.

If you are experiencing particular problems, such as how to pitch for a business grant, or with working in isolation, tell them so. Explain that you believe these to be the challenges that are currently holding you back. Be sure to tell them how much you would appreciate their input.

You may wish to suggest an occasional but regular meeting where you could talk to them about the progress of your business, and seek their advice and ideas. Such meetings might be once a month or even once a quarter. Alternatively, you might wish for the option of weekly or monthly phone calls.

Make a firm arrangement on time so your mentor will know that you will not become a pest. Confirm with a letter.

If they are in a consultancy capacity, be prepared to pay some kind of fee, if only a very good lunch or a present. Their advice might help you build a successful life: that has a very real value. Give them regular feedback on your progress, successful as well as negative, if you think they will welcome it.

Time management

Often we are panicked by our clients or customers into subscribing to their agendas, which may be driven by many elements – such as office politics – rather than by genuine need. As a result their deadlines may be totally unrealistic.

Stephen Covey, who wrote the brilliant *Seven Habits of Highly Effective People* points out that '"time management" is really a misnomer – the challenge is not to manage time but to manage ourselves'. He believes that rather than focusing on *things* and *time*, we should be focusing on *relationships* and on achieving *results*.

In business terms, working time is a resource to be allocated. It is tempting, but a cop-out, to simply recommend that everyone lives by lists, prioritising their activities and matching them against their diaries. If only it were so easy! Certainly it is true that no-one can manage their time efficiently unless they are organised. A large diary is often the key tool in being organised, both for keeping your appointments and also for recording how much time you are spending on any one project. Whether it is an electronic diary or a book, you can see how and where you are spending your time so that, if necessary, you can aim for a better balance between (for instance) hours spent earning, time on administration and hours dedicated to business growth.

Lists, with priorities, are also very sensible. Most of us could not function without them. Even so, this still does not tell you how to do three days' work in two days. The art of time management for an independent is to find ways of reducing the chores, and streamlining the administration and record-keeping in order to have the maximum time for paid work and networking. This is difficult when, on the face of it, you have no-one to delegate to.

It is not just a question of prioritising. Often we are panicked by our clients or customers into subscribing to their agendas, which may be driven by many elements – such as office politics – rather than by genuine need. As a result their deadlines may be totally unrealistic. If you can identify such situations, you may be able to find a way to defuse the tensions and therefore buy yourself more time to do the work properly.

If you are overstretched, and find yourself cutting down time on the important aspects of running your enterprise, you might like to check the section on time-wasters in Chapter 7, *The Production Department*, and in addition consider the following:

- Go back to your objectives now and again to remind yourself of your original mission. Skim through your marketing plan, your Unique Selling Points and so on, just to refocus on who and what you are.
- In terms of time, your first priority is the work that only you can do. The chances are that the client is buying your talent, your flair, your experience, your expertise, your clout. This is the work that you should not offload.

- If you bring in associates or extra hands to cope with some of the activities which don't require your particular input, be aware that you will still have to spend time overseeing every part of the work or project to ensure that it is up to your standards. The chances are that the more junior the person you bring in, the more of your guidance they will need. Sometimes, it is better value to bring in someone of a fairly senior level who will quickly understand what is required of them and will work under their own steam.
- There will be parts of your business – and personal – activities which can be delegated fairly easily. It may be that some aspects of accounting, record-keeping or administration can be done by someone else. Unless you are very good and very quick at keeping your books, consider outsourcing to a professional bookkeeper. It's quite possible that a good bookkeeper can do in a few hours what has been taking you a day or more to accomplish. If you can earn more in that day than you pay the bookkeeper, it is a false economy to continue doing your own books.
- The same might be true for office/studio/shop cleaning, or general administration. Some years ago I had work which took me all over the country. It was exciting but very tiring, and there was always a pile of administration to do when I reached my office base. I advertised in *The Times* and found a part-time treasure, a lady who was just starting to return to work after bringing up her young children. She came for a few hours a week and tore into the paperwork, whizzed through the invoicing, chased payments, ordered stationery, made divine coffee and watered my plants. Bliss. What is more important, it freed me up to do more income-generating work.
- You might also take a good look at your home chores too. If you are racing home, only to start doing the housework or DIY or waxing the car, check the cost-effectiveness of this. Now that you are an independent, it might be more valuable to you to pay someone else to do these chores for you, while you are bringing in more by way of networking or staying for a few more hours on paid work.
- Most independent practitioners become adept at juggling timetables and workloads, but if you are truly overstretched, you face several options:

- you do the work all by yourself and take the stressful consequences;
- you collaborate – that is, you share the work with either one associate or a group of associates, whose standard of work you find acceptable and whom you trust;
- you turn the work down because you are unable to do it professionally and to your preferred standard. You may be able to recommend someone else for the work and ask that person for an introduction fee or commission on sales.

This is where you must make a decision quickly, action the consequences and move on. If you make what you consider later to be a mistake, don't beat yourself up: this is a learning curve and you make the best judgements you can with the knowledge you have at the time. As in all other spheres in life, it's easy to be wise after the event.

- Keep tight schedules on non-productive but essential aspects of your work. When you are pushed timewise, ensure that meetings are kept on course. If you have made an appointment to see a client, double-check their availability on the day. Take an agenda and only be diverted if there is further work being offered.
- If someone you are seeing is renowned for being long-winded, make the appointment late in the day (they usually want to go home on time). Announce courteously at the start of any meeting that you will have to leave by a certain (but reasonable) time. Unless something very urgent arises, when the deadline approaches, start gathering up your papers (but resist openly checking your watch).
- Check your email/answer phone/faxes at certain points of the day but don't make a fetish of checking every hour on the hour unless you are waiting for something urgent.
- The great habit of handling paper only once is still a classic. It takes discipline to bin, file or action immediately but it still saves constantly shuffling the papers around.
- Don't skip lunch or your coffee breaks. These are more than refuelling stops; they give you time to reflect on your progress and create space for good ideas and solutions to surface through your intense concentration.

Remember that periods of working time are also periods of your life, yours to give to others if you wish. Don't forget, in your drive and anxiety, to spare a little time to help someone else, even if it's just a phone call. Have a laugh, send yourself up a little (or better, a lot), learn something, experiment, enjoy what you are doing and be proud of your achievements.

Dealing with rejection

Some independents – particularly those who have not been responsible for their own marketing in their previous lives – may have a problem with rejection. This is mixed with the natural disappointment you feel when you fail to win a piece of work, or when a contract is not renewed. It may happen for other reasons too, but the bottom line is you are *out*; you have not won or kept the business and that's that!

Even when you work in the smallest company, you are unlikely to take such rejection personally; the incident is dismissed with a shrug. This is probably because gaining new business has been a team effort. When you are an independent practitioner it is very easy to feel that your failure is down to some deep personal flaw.

Rejection is a frequently occurring element in some lines of work, particularly modelling, acting, public relations, advertising and some kinds of journalism. In these fields, it is not just the work or ideas being rejected, but the personality and sometimes even the appearance of the practitioner as well.

If rejection is an issue for you, coping mechanisms will have to be developed. You could start by looking at the more obvious reasons that you didn't win the work or have your contract renewed. These might include:

- The organisation already had someone in mind but was adhering to company policy in putting the work out to tender.
- Your fees were too high – or not high enough.
- Your experience, while excellent, was not a perfect fit. Many companies are surprisingly unimaginative and cannot see that experience often translates very easily from one field to another. If they want you to draw a kettle and you only have illustrations of teapots and ironing boards, you may not get the work.

- The team leader didn't like you. You happen to look a little like someone who was nasty to him in the school playground or you remind him of a frightful aunt.
- You have worked for them for too long and they have forgotten how good you are. They think that change automatically is progress.
- Someone new has come into the client's management structure. Often a newcomer will try to make their mark by changing the look of things. One way they can do this is by letting go the previous job holder's suppliers and bringing in new ones.

Not one of the above means that you are a bad person! Not one of these has anything to do with your talent or your lovely inner self. So, go and bang dustbin lids for a while because you are disappointed; be irritated because you have wasted time on an unproductive pitch; but as regards you and your personality, get those shoulders shrugging. Be philosophical: maybe you wouldn't have enjoyed the work anyway, or it would have prevented you from finding a totally new path. Either way, don't burn even one more brain cell on it: move onwards and upwards.

Rupert Hanbury Tenison specialises in photographing architecture, lifestyle and travel. He says: 'The rejection thing is interesting. I often wonder how good I am. I've just come back from a trip to Bali; I was one of eight photographers worldwide chosen by Ibal Designs to reflect Bali after the terrorism there. They had obviously seen my work and been impressed. I'm honoured to be have been selected. Despite this, I recently submitted some images for a geographical society calendar – they have used my pictures in the past – but this time none was accepted. Each time this happens I worry that I've lost it, but the next assignment always manages to quash those insecurities. I expect that most creative people go on this rollercoaster.

'I understand why the majority of young people who start up on their own give up in the first year. It seems on the face of it a lot easier to work from nine to five and have a salary. But I don't particularly like being told what to do.

'I don't think of myself as dogged but I suppose I must be. I always trust that work will come in – and it always does.'

If you are constantly failing to win business, you will need to check that there is not due reason. Look again at your 'product' or service, and at your prices. Is there any way in which you are being unrealistic? If necessary, take professional advice. Check through the list of professional advisers in Chapter 2, *The Research & Development Department.* Most will be experienced in helping people set up and may be able to identify the problem for you. It may be something quite simple or you may have to resort to a major rethink. Whichever it is, it is better to tackle the problem early rather than when you have committed too much time or money to it.

Hobbies and other interests

Tempting though it is to become the complete 'work machine' when you first start out, it is essential that you sustain some interests outside your business. For a time, it might be appropriate to focus on the business, but in the longer term do try to resume other interests. As my friend Peter Fox, a very clever car mechanic, points out: 'You don't drive a car in top gear all the time.' Find an hour here and there to do something entirely different: it will recharge you, and can also save you from becoming so concentrated on your work that you cannot see the wood for the trees – and, frankly, from becoming an immense *bore!*

Holidays

Take them. It's true that holidays are expensive: they cost the price of the travel and accommodation, and they cost the time you are not working. In other words you pay twice what the employed will pay for their holidays.

When you are first getting established, you probably feel unsafe about being absent for very long, but you can always take your holidays as short breaks. Make it a long weekend or add a day onto a public holiday. I did not take a proper holiday for the first five or six years of independence. Now I realise that I could quite easily have done so. The person who talked me out of my holidays was not a client, it was me! Finally, I became desperate for a change. I announced with defiance in the air that I would be away for a whole week. I put my fingers in my ears. Nothing exploded. My clients nodded abstractedly and asked me to remind them of the dates again nearer the time. They assumed I would have holidays just as they themselves did.

As long as it doesn't coincide with one of their deadlines, your clients are unlikely to mind you having holidays. You will benefit from the change of pace and the different perspective. It doesn't matter what you do, just be totally unavailable and removed from your everyday life. Take the obvious precautions: let everyone know when you leave and when you will be back.

Leave a message on the answering machine. If you really must, if you are feeling particularly insecure or you are genuinely likely to lose existing or new business, invite people to leave a message because 'you will be checking in during the week'.

Try not to pick the messages up more than once or twice during your holiday. Even then, respond only to the very, *very* urgent ones. And don't take work with you. Partners and holiday friends will not approve and it is self-defeating anyway.

If it is appropriate, have a 'locum'. This is someone who will hold the fort or be available for client crises. They might collect your messages and post for you, or you might arrange to give their phone number 'for emergencies' either on your message tape or just to chosen clients. Be sure that you wholly trust this person not to walk off with chunks of your precious business. I doubt this happens very often. Usually, friendly independents are grateful to swap these services, knowing they can call on you when they have a holiday, flu or a family upheaval.

Everyday maintenance

If you are sick, you cannot work. If you don't work, you won't have an income. This is the nasty-tasting bullet that independents have to bite. Having flu is a luxury. Anything more serious is an appalling thought.

You therefore need to take proper measures to look after *you* – your major asset. Your personal maintenance is not a matter of vanity or pride, but a necessity. Gone is the time when you could cruise through the day with a hangover or snooze quietly in corners because you partied all night.

You can still do those things if they appeal to you, but now they will probably have to be reserved for weekends. As an independent you are as good as your last job, and I know of not one client who wants someone who looks as though they died last week working on their business.

So, from now on, go for all your dental check-ups, and attend the 'well woman' or 'well man' clinics at your GP practice. If you use a computer all day, see a optician once every two years when young, and annually later on, and take those stiff shoulders to a masseur at least once or twice a month. If you believe in integrated health, as I do, see your acupuncturist, TCM practitioner, osteopath, chiropractor, herbalist or naturopath on a regular basis to maintain peak condition. You take the car for a regular service; now it's your turn. Find ways you enjoy of keeping physically fit. Eat regularly and properly; don't be tempted to live on coffee and take-aways. Sleep well.

Personal award scheme

Please don't forget to be the kind of boss who rewards the staff. When you next have a planning session, build in some rewards for yourself.

Your journey of independence will be very personal to you. Hopefully it will bring not only an interesting worklife and a series of challenges, but also lots of rewards. These may or may not be financial. There is a enormous satisfaction in knowing that, all on your own, you have won a chunk of new work, or created something rather special for a particular client, or that you have successfully negotiated a sticky period when the business was not doing quite so well.

All these achievements deserve recognition of some kind. Please don't forget to be the kind of boss who rewards the staff. When you next have a planning session, build in some rewards for yourself. Only you know what is the treat that you will relish: it might be time off, an evening out, a weekend away or a new car. It could be a day at a gym or a spa, or it may even just be just switching off the phones and curling up in a chair with a good book. It doesn't matter, really; it's just that you should reward yourself now and again, as part of the quality of your new lifestyle.

If you have a family or partner supporting you emotionally and maybe even financially during this time, don't forget to reward them too. The chances are that they have lived and breathed your new venture alongside you. While you are treating yourself, take extra time out to say a resounding 'thank you'.

Later on, you may wish to create bigger and better rewards, and some of these might be business-linked. They might include buying a letting property or holiday flat to supplement your income. You may wish to start a portfolio of investments or collect first edition books or vintage port – things which should gain in value, be a hedge against a very rainy day but bring you pleasure in the meantime. You might give yourself the latest in laptops or an expensive but worthwhile training course. You are the chairman of the board, you decide!

Things to do

- Take an objective look at the hours you are putting in. Are you coping or are you too stressed? Does the working pattern need adjustment? If so, adjust!
- Make a contract with yourself regarding your working hours, overtime and flexi-time.
- Decide if isolation is an issue and if so, develop strategies to deal with the solitary times.
- Consider having a mentor.
- Look at what other help and support you might need, not only to run your business but the rest of your life too.
- Keep your hobbies and take holidays.
- Have a personal reward scheme – enjoy!

Steven Black

'Sometimes I don't speak to anyone from the time the boys go to school until they come home, particularly now that people use email rather than phoning you. After a few days, you can go stir-crazy. So it's important to have people you can call and chat to, or groan with because no-one has sent you a cheque!'

Steven Black from Edinburgh is a writer and editor, specialising in nursing.

I wanted to be a journalist when I was 15. I was brought up in Edinburgh and read English literature at Aberdeen University. The timing was wrong and I dropped out after two years. Looking back, I was too young to cope with the experience and it took me a long time to make up for what felt like failure.

Both my parents were nurses, so after a short spell as a hotel porter I decided to go into the 'family business'. I trained at the North Lothian College of Nursing and Midwifery and, until 1989, worked at Edinburgh's Western General Hospital.

I enjoyed Accident & Emergency nursing but still harboured ambitions to get a degree. I chose a course in book and magazine publishing, a complete departure. I was married by then and my wife, Fiona, also a nurse, kept us both because I only received a grant in my final year. It was a fantastic course; I thoroughly enjoyed it.

It seemed obvious to go into publishing. I had spent one summer working at the Edinburgh Book Festival, and loved it. So after college I worked for a London academic publisher, selling in Scotland, Ireland and Denmark. This worked well until Fiona became pregnant with our twins. This meant re-evaluating how we structured our lives. We decided that she should return to nursing and I would become a house-husband. It was the hardest thing I have ever done! It would have been tough even with one baby, but with two . . .

I did various agency nursing jobs and later worked in the office of the nursing 'bank' which supplied nurses for shift work, but I wanted more. Then a friend left his post at *Nursing*

Standard, which is a Royal College of Nursing publication, and I applied. It meant working one week in London and the next in Edinburgh, and I did this for three and a half years. By then the boys started going to school and I finally decided to go freelance. It wasn't an easy choice. I spent a weekend with two friends, both writers working in the medical area, discussing how we could each make a living, whether we should link up and form a company or a cooperative, or work individually but come together for bigger projects. It was a valuable exercise.

Before I started I made sure that I had the most up-to-date computer and equipment, and I took a week-long course with Local Enterprise in Scotland. It was good to meet other people just starting up. We learned bookkeeping and marketing, and we all came away having compiled a business plan for ourselves. There was also a very small grant for the first six months.

One of the biggest challenges was deciding fee levels. For some projects, you're on National Union of Journalists' rates, but for more complex work you must decide what is reasonable and fair. In time, you develop an intuition for what the market can stand.

I continued to work for Royal College of Nursing publications, either in London or up here. I've been managing editor for *Nursing Management* and editor of *Nurse Researcher*. I have also worked for what is now NHS Education for Scotland (now part of NHS Health Scotland) and for Churchill Livingstone, the Edinburgh medical publishers.

I stay in close touch with the two friends who do similar work. That contact has been essential. Sometimes I don't speak to anyone from the time the boys go to school until they come home, particularly now that people use email rather than phoning you. After a few days, you can go stir-crazy. So it's important to have people you can call and chat to, or groan with because no-one has sent you a cheque! We get together for a Christmas lunch and one in mid-summer. We're now planning lunches around the equinoxes.

Steven's advice:

Know the way that you work, establish your own rhythm. I used to switch on the computer at 8.30 in the morning and try to get going. I couldn't do it; I just sat there feeling guilty. I have realised that what shapes my work is having the pressure of a deadline. Sometimes that means I will work until the early hours of the morning to meet it, but it's how I work best and the standard of my work is higher if I accept it.

Be prepared to travel around. We decided that, with a family, we didn't want to live in London even though it is the hub of the publishing world. We could have a better life in Edinburgh. Having made that choice we had to make it work. I can do a lot on email, but it's essential to do your networking by going to conferences and events wherever they are. You should also see what is local to you.

Richard Morton

'When I started out, I had to make an impact, be distinctive. Most people wore jeans and T-shirts then, so I wore a suit and kept my hair, which went grey early, very short and stylish. People remembered me.'

Richard Morton is a Geordie stand-up comedian who now lives in Kent.

No-one else in my family was funny, but I was a funny kid. It was a real gift; it just came naturally to amuse my family and friends. It didn't occur to me that I could make a career out of it. I passed three A levels and should have gone to university; instead I left Newcastle and, at 18, moved to London to become a punk rock musician.

At first I did anything – at that time you practically paid to get a gig. I worked in all sorts of day jobs and did session work to pay for my demo tapes. Then in the mid 1980s I formed a duo called 'The Panic Brothers' with another musician, Reg

Meuross, and we started singing around the pubs and clubs. Suddenly we took off and began to make a real living from it. We appeared on Channel 4's *Friday Night Live* and once supported Chuck Berry at the Hammersmith Odeon.

I always used to chat to the audiences and make them laugh, and our musical duo suddenly became a comedy double act. That's the biggest turn-on, people laughing. It's so addictive. I began to work up an act and, at the age of 30, I become a professional comedian.

Starting out, I had to make an impact, be distinctive. Most people wore jeans and T-shirts then, so I wore a suit and kept my hair, which went grey early, very short and stylish. People remembered me – for maybe the wrong reasons! You have to be disciplined as a professional because people pay to see you. So you must continue to write new material and keep the act fresh. I've no idea where my inspiration comes from. I've always found life absurd and I've always taken the mickey. The thing about comedy is that you can send yourself up too.

Since going solo I've been very busy, mainly doing gigs. The first big one was at the Comedy Store in London and I still perform there now as it's by far my favourite club in the world. My first big break came as a support act and I did several UK tours through the early 1990s with the likes of Jack Dee, Lee Evans and Jo Brand.

I had some successful shows at the Edinburgh Festival and numerous TV and radio appearances, presenting a couple of series on Channel 5 and Radio 2. My favourite TV work was Channel 5's *Comedy Store*, which I've performed on regularly since 1997. This is where they film your live performance, and that's why I like it the most: nothing beats the thrill of being in front of a real live audience when you are 'storming it' and they love you.

My gigs take me all over the world: Hong Kong, Singapore, Bangkok, Dubai and Montreal are recent trips. It doesn't matter where you are really as long as you are on stage somewhere and everybody's laughing.

I'm married now with a small daughter and my perspectives have changed. I'm not so tunnel-visioned, more balanced, not as self-absorbed. I also concentrate more on the financial side. Unlike the early days when I did everything myself, I have an agent now who books the gigs and collects the fees. Sometimes it takes months to get paid, but I keep track and chase the agent, making sure that a cheque has come in from some club or other.

It's good if you know other people who do the same as you: comedy is a small world and it helps to talk to other comedians. We all have stories about being passed over for a television show or the jobs that didn't come off. You share experiences of rejection. Oddly enough, I'm not really a confident person but I'm in charge when I'm on stage. Not everyone, no matter how talented, can do stand-up. It's physically demanding and, when you start out, hard financially. It takes about three years to create a good act and learn your stagecraft.

It also sounds more glamorous than it is. The bright lights are all on the stage. When I finish a show, I go home. There's no rock and roll and you can't have a drink if you're driving, and sometimes it's a four-hour drive.

Richard's advice:

Keep motivated by giving yourself treats. There's no boss to give you pay rises or bonuses, so give them to yourself. If I've worked long hours – I did 200 shows last year – I buy myself designer suits, something by Paul Smith or Ozwald Boateng, because you never know when you'll be back down the charity shops.

Comedy is like any other business, it's a rollercoaster. The high spots are not always stepping stones. So appreciate your successes, enjoy them, don't just rush on to the next thing. Comedy is a cracking way to make a living but it might not have worked; I never forget that it was my choice and nothing feels better than being independent and being your own boss. Oh yeah, and make sure you get yourself a good accountant, and never lose sight of the fact that it's better than doing a proper job!

Resources: More Information

Useful books

James Chan: *Spare Room Tycoon*, Nicholas Brealey, 2000
Steven Covey: *The Seven Habits of Highly Effective People*, Simon & Shuster Ltd., 1992 (and editions)
Laura Berman Fortgang: *Take Yourself to the Top*, Thorsons, 1999
Fiona Harrold: *Be Your Own Life Coach*, Hodder & Stoughton, 2000
Carol Spencer: *Style Directions for Men*, Judy Piatkus, 1999; *Style Directions for Women*, Judy Piatkus, 1999
Carole Stone: *Networking – the Art of Making Friends*, Vermilion, 2001
Sara Williams: *Lloyds TSB Small Business Guide*, Vitesse Media, 2003

Patents, copyright & trademarks

The Patent Office, Concept House, Cardiff Road, Newport, South Wales NP10 8QQ
Telephone: 01633 814000 or for enquiries, 08459 500505
Web: www.patent.gov.uk

Copyright Licensing Agency, 90 Tottenham Court Road, London W1T 4LP
Telephone: 020 7631 5555
Web: www. cla.co.uk

Institute of Trade Mark Attorneys, Canterbury house, 2–6 Sydenham Road, Croyden, Surrey CR0 9XE
Telephone: 020 8686 2052
Web: www.itma.org.uk

Institute of Patentees & Inventors, PO Box 1301, Kingston-on-Thames KT2 7WT
Telephone: 020 8541 4197
Web: wwwinvent.org.uk

Grant-making trusts

The Prince's Trust, 18 Park Square East, London NW1 4LM
Telephone: 0800 842842
Web: www.princes-trust.org.uk

The Prince's Trust – Scotland, 1st Floor, The Guildhall, 57 Queen Street, Glasgow G1 3EH
Telephone: 0141 204 4409

Shell Livewire, Hawthorn House, Forth Banks, Newcastle upon Tyne NE1 3SG
Hotline: 0845 757 3252
Telephone: 0191 261 5584/0191 261 1910
Web: www.shell-livewire.org

Late payment support

Money Claim Online (MCOL)
Northampton County Court, 21–27 St Katherine's Street, Northampton NN1 2LH
Help Desk: 0845 601 5935
Web: www.moneyclaim.gov.uk also www.payontime.co.uk

Taxation

Inland Revenue
Helpline for the newly self-employed: 08459 154515
Web: www.inlandrevenue.gov.uk/startingup

HM Customs & Excise
Helpline: 0845 010 9000
Web: www.hmce.gov.uk

Pensions

Guide to Pensions, Pensions Guide, Freepost, Bristol BS28 7WA
Telephone: pensions information order line, 0845 731 32 33
Web: www.pensionguide.gov.uk

Checking credit/information on individual businesses

Dunn and Bradstreet International, Holmers Farm Way, High Wycombe, Buckinghamshire HP12 4UL
Telephone: 01494 422000
Web: www.uk.dnb.com

Experian, Talbot House, Talbot Street, Nottingham NG1 5HF
Telephone: 0870 241 6212 or 0115 941 0888
Web: www.experian.co.uk

Professional services

Institute of Chartered Accountants in Endland & Wales, PO Box 433, Chartered Accountants Hall, Moorgate Place, London EC2P 2BJ
Telephone: 020 7920 8100
Web: www.icaew.co.uk

Institute of Chartered Accountants of Scotland, CA House, 21 Haymarkets Yard, Edinburgh EH12 5BH
Telephone: 0131 347 0100
Web: www.icas.org.uk

Small business resources

British Chambers of Commerce, 65 Petty France, London SW1 9EU
Tel: 020 7654 5800
Web: www.britishchambers.org.uk

Business Link
Telephone for local representation: 0845 600 9006
Web: www.businesslink.org

Business Connect (for Wales)
Telephone: 08457 969 798
Web: www.businessconnect.org.uk

Department of Trade & Industry
Web: www.dti.com

DTI Publications Orderline, Admail 528, London SW1W 8YT
Telephone: 0870 1502500
Web: www.publications@dti.gsi.gov.uk

Federation of Small Businesses, Sir Frank Whittle Way, Blackpool
Business Park, Blackpool FY4 2FE
Telephone: 08707 870329
Web: www.fsb.org.uk

Home Business Alliance, Freepost ANG3155, March,
Cambridgeshire PE15 9BR
Tel: 0870 749 6321
Web: www.homebusiness.org.uk

Invest Northern Ireland
Telephone: 028 9023 9090
Web: www.investni.com

Jobcentre or Jobcentre Plus
(*look in your phone book for the nearest office*)
Web: www.jobcentreplus.gov.uk

National Business Angels Network (NBAN)
Web: www.bestmatch.co.uk

National Federation of Enterprise Agencies, Trinity Gardens, 9–11
Bromham Road, Bedford MK40 2UQ
Telephone: 01234 354055
Web: www.nfea.org

Scottish Enterprise
Telephone for local representation: 0845 607 8787
Web: www.scottish-enterprise.com

Supplies
Yellow Pages
Web: www.yell.com

Thomson Directories
Web: www.thomweb.co.uk

Viking Direct (biggest UK wholesale stationers)
Freephone: 0800 424444
Web: www.viking-direct.co.uk

The Cast of Performers

Andie Airfix
Graphic Designer
Satori Graphics, Top Floor, Chelsea Reach, 79–89 Lots Road,
London SW10 0RN
Tel: 020 7352 6744
Email: airfix@satorigraphic.co.uk

Miti Ampoma
Journalist & PR Consultant
Email: miti@miticom.co.uk

Michael Austin
Chartered Accountant
Blue Dot Consulting Ltd., Riverbank House Business Centre,
1 Putney Bridge Approach, London SW6 3JD
Tel: 020 7371 0714
Email: michael.austin@bluedotconsulting.co.uk
Web: www.bluedotconsulting.co.uk

Richard Bailey
Photographer
Richard Bailey Photography, 36 Olive Road, London NW2 6UD
Tel: 020 8450 4148
Email: richard@richardbaileyphotography.co.uk
Web: www.richardbaileyphotography.co.uk

Steven Black
Nursing Editor/Writer
Titus Editorial Services, 25 Kingsknowe Gardens,
Edinburgh EH14 2JH
Tel: 0131 477 3930
Email: steven.black@blueyonder.co.uk

Richard Brassey
Book Illustrator
Email: richard@richardbrassey.com

Robert Carslaw
Interior Designer
Chelsea Reach, 79–89 Lots Road, London SW10 0RN
Tel: 020 7376 4440
Email: robert@robertcarslaw.com

Jem Davis
Legal Consulting
Tel: 020 7689 4854
Email: jem@legalconsulting.co.uk
Web: www.legalconsulting.co.uk

Mark Davies
Painter & Decorator
3 Maynard Court, Clarence Road, Old Windsor, Berkshire SL4 5BG
Tel: 01753 851063
Mobile: 07860 500 055

Richard Clark-Monks
Fashion Designer
Top Floor, Chelsea Reach, 79–89 Lots Road, London SW10 0RN
Tel: 0771 4247609
Email: rcm@uverdale.com
Web: www.uverdale.com

Peter Fox
Motor Mechanic
PEC Mobile
Tel: 0121 353 4174

Maureen Gallagher
Occupational Psychologist
Prisma, Castle House, 12 Castle Hill, Windsor, Berkshire SL4 1PD
Tel: 01753 839389
Email: prisma@gallagherm.demon.co.uk

Trish Gittins
IT Consultant
Blacksmith's Cottages, 3/5 St Johns Road, Laughton en le Morthen,
Sheffield S25 1YL
Mobile: 07703 173469
Email: trish.gittins@pgen.com

Nick Gundry BSc Hons, Dip. Couns. Psych., BACP Accredited
Counselling Psychologist
Estray Park, Budock, Falmouth, Cornwall TR11 5EE

Richard Harry
Blacksmith & Farrier
The Forge, St Nicholas, near Cardiff CF5 6SH
Tel: 01446 760303

Jack Jewers
Film Director
c/o Kate Staddon, Curtis Brown, Haymarket House,
28–29 Haymarket, London SW1Y 4SP
Tel: 020 7393 4400
Email: jack@september.co.uk

Monica Jönsson
Practitioner of Traditional Chinese Medicine
82 Nightingale Lane, London SW12 8NR

Jill Lee
Framer/poster shop
Artbeat, 703 Fulham Road, London SW6 5UL
Tel: 020 7736 0337
Email: jillarty@aol.com

John Mitchell
Mosiacs
4 Europa Court, Mawgan Porth, Cornwall TR8 4BB
Tel: 01637 860504

Richard Morton
Stand-up Comedian
c/o Off the Kerb Productions, 22 Thornhill Crescent,
London N1 1BJ
Tel: 020 7700 4477

Pete Robbins
Sales
Segre UK Ltd., Holly Farm Business Park, Honiley, Kenilworth,
Warwickshire CV8 1NP
Tel: 01926 484464
Email: peterobbins@segre.co.uk
Web: www.segre.co.uk

Patricia Orr
Public Relations Consultant
Third Sector PR, 16–18 Strutton Ground, London SW1P 2HP
Tel: 020 7222 5510
Email: pat@thirdsectorpr.co.uk
Web: www.thordsectorpr.co.uk

Julia Smith
Charitable Trust Fundraiser
Email: godricjulia@onetel.net

Carol Spenser
Style Consultant
Style Directions, Mendham Watermill, Mill Lane, Mendham,
Harleston, Norfolk IP20 0NN
Tel: 01379 855410
Email: styledirections@dial.pipex.com
Web: www.styledirections.com

Carole Stone
Author: Networking – the Art of Making Friends
Email: carole@carolestone.com

Rupert Hanbury Tenison
Photographer
Roscarrek Farm, St Neot, Liskeard, Cornwall PL14 6RY
Tel: 01579 321263
Email: rupert@rupert-tenison.com
Web: www.rupert-tenison.com

Althea Wilson
Artist
Althea Wilson Gallery, 43 Burnaby Street, London SW10
Web: www.altheawilson.com

Kristian Wood BSc (Hons) Ost GOsC Registered
Osteopath
KJW Osteopathy, 11 Poplar Mews, Uxbridge Road, Shepherds
Bush, London W12 7JS
Tel: 020 8749 7449
Email: Kristian@kjw-osteopathy.co.uk
Web: www.kjw-osteopathy.co.uk

Index